LEARN CHESS

A Complete Course

Cadogan Chess Series

Chief Advisor: Garry Kasparov
Editor: Andrew Kinsman
Russian Series Editor: Ken Neat

Other popular titles from CADOGAN CHESS include:

AGUR
Bobby Fischer: His Approach to Chess

AVERBAKH
Chess Endings: Essential Knowledge

CAPABLANCA
Chess Fundamentals

HODGSON
Chess Travellers Quiz Book

KING
How Good is Your Chess?

LIVSHITZ
Test Your Chess IQ (Books 1–3)

MEDNIS
How to be a Complete Tournament Player

REUBEN
Chess Openings — Your Choice

SUBA
Dynamic Chess Strategy

WEBB
Chess for Tigers

WOOD
Easy Guide to Chess

For a complete catalogue of CADOGAN CHESS books (which includes the former Pergamon Chess and Maxwell Macmillan Chess lists), please write to:

**Cadogan Books, London House,
Parkgate Road, London SW11 4NQ.
Tel: (071) 738 1961   Fax: (071) 924 5491**

LEARN CHESS
A Complete Course

C. H. O'D. ALEXANDER

and

T. J. BEACH

CADOGAN CHESS

LONDON, NEW YORK

Cadogan Books Distribution

UK/EUROPE/AUSTRALASIA/ASIA/AFRICA
Distribution: Grantham Book Services Ltd, Isaac Newton Way, Alma Park
Industrial Estate, Grantham, Lincs NG31 9SD.
Tel: (0476) 67421; Fax: (0476) 590223.

USA/CANADA/LATIN AMERICA/JAPAN
Distribution: Paramount Distribution Center, Front & Brown Streets,
Riverside, New Jersey 08075, USA.
Tel: (609) 461 6500; Fax: (609) 764 9122.

Published by Cadogan Books plc, London House, Parkgate Road,
London SW11 4NQ

Copyright ©1994 Cadogan Books plc

First published 1963 by Pergamon Press (in two volumes)
First Cadogan Books edition 1994

British Library Cataloguing in Publication Data
A CIP catalogue record for this book is available from the British Library.

ISBN 1 85744 115 X

Cover design by Brian Robins
Printed in Great Britain by BPC Wheatons Ltd, Exeter

INTRODUCTION

Chess is far more popular with schoolboys and schoolgirls than ever before and the number of young players increases steadily each year: while this book should be of value to anyone learning chess it is aimed primarily at helping these young players. We have in various ways, outlined below, adopted a rather different approach from that in most beginners' books and we hope it will justify the title.

First, we have given about 400 graded examples, ranging from the very simple to some which would tax a strong player (and including one or two on which the authors had some difficulty in agreeing the correct solution). From these, readers can learn in the best and most interesting way – by doing something themselves.

Amongst these examples we have included some 'group exercises'. The book is intended to be useful not only for individuals but for a number of players learning together, such as a school chess club or a chess class: the group exercises are particularly suitable for such sets of players to study or discuss together. The harder individual exercises can also be treated as group exercises – and equally the latter can of course be done by individuals on their own.

Next we have tried to meet a difficulty that arises in writing any chess book of this kind. It is easy to explain the very elementary points – the moves of the pieces, the standard mates and so on. It is also not too difficult to explain fairly advanced points, e.g. to give an explanation of the Ruy Lopez or to analyse a master game for the reader. What is hard to fill in is what comes between and it is on this that we have concentrated our main effort; we have tried by meeting the practical problems of the weak player to bring readers from the novice stage to that of being a reasonable school or club player.

Our presentation is on 'spiral' lines. In the early chapters we give the basic principles of the opening, middle games and ending, later chapters deal with each phase of the game in a more advanced and systematic way and much of the last four chapters points the way to a third stage of development, beyond the scope of this book. Because of this method of approach, the book falls naturally into two parts and we decided therefore to issue in two volumes although it was written as a whole. Each volume can be read as a self-contained unit, though naturally maximum value will be got by reading both.

Volume 1 gives the reader an understanding of the fundamentals of each part of the game. After working through this he should be able to play a sensible game — developing his pieces correctly, having some idea of the kind of thing to try for in the middle game and able to win endings in which he has a decisive material advantage. What he will not have is any systematic knowledge of the openings or of methods of attack in the middle game. Volume 2 introduces him to these. It gives a thorough analysis of the standard methods of winning material and of the techniques for attacking different types of defensive positions in front of the enemy king. It also gives a discussion of the main ideas underlying a number of openings and it extends the reader's knowledge of the end game. We believe that any reader who has mastered Volume 1 and wants to go further is bound to benefit substantially from the second volume.

Finally, in writing the book we have had in mind the common situation of a teacher, not a strong player himself (or herself), who is running — or would like to run — a chess section in school. We hope that the solutions will provide the material needed.

We should like to thank Leonard Barden and Peter Clarke for a number of constructive suggestions which have greatly improved our original manuscript — though these two writers are in no way responsible for any deficiencies in the final text. We shall feel well repaid for the pleasant labour of writing this book if it helps to increase the number of chess players and to bring them enjoyment from the best of all games.

Particular thanks are due to Sir Robert Robinson, O.M., F.R.S., the founder of the Pergamon Chess Series, without whose interest the Series would never have been realized and whose guidance and advice have been invaluable throughout.

LEARN CHESS

A Complete Course

Volume 1

First Principles

CONTENTS

CHAPTER ONE

The Moves

1.1. The Board

Figure 1 shows a chess-board.

Fig. 1

The board is placed so that there is a white square at the nearest right-hand corner. Before starting play, always make certain that 'white is right'.

1.2. The Pieces and Pawns

A set of chessmen consists of a number of pieces made in two colours. We always call the darker ones the black pieces and the lighter ones the white pieces.

At the start of a game the players usually 'toss for the colour'; in a match or tournament, however, it is decided in advance who shall be White and who shall be Black.

Pieces are represented on diagrams by figurines.

	white	*black*		*white*	*black*
King	♔	♚	Queen	♕	♛
Rook	♖	♜	Bishop	♗	♝
Knight	♘	♞	Pawn	♙	♟

Each player has one king, one queen, two rooks, two bishops, two knights, and eight pawns. Strictly speaking, the pawns are not called 'pieces', and we usually refer to kings, queens, rooks, bishops, and knights only as 'pieces', so that each player starts the game with eight pieces and eight pawns. Sometimes we do use 'piece' to cover pawn as well and it should be obvious when this is the case.

1.3. Chess compared with Draughts

You may have played Draughts already; if you have, it may help you if we compare the two games.

In Draughts there are only 'kings' and 'men' and all the moves are along diagonals, or squares of one colour. In Chess, each piece has its own special move and the black and white squares are all used.

In Draughts pieces are captured by jumping over them. This is never the case in Chess, a white or black piece or pawn being captured by an opposing piece or pawn moving *on to the occupied square* and removing the enemy. A chessman must not jump over a piece of either colour (the knight-move being only an apparent exception). If a square is occupied by a piece of the same colour, the piece may move up to the adjacent square, but may not go any further than this. If an enemy piece is involved, it may be captured by occupying the square, but it cannot be jumped.

Unlike Draughts, capturing in Chess is optional — you can take it or leave it!

Chess pieces may move forwards or backwards within the limits of their moves; pawns, however, may not move backwards.

1.4. The Rook and the Bishop

The piece represented by ♖ should always be called a rook, and not, as is commonly the case, a castle. We shall see later that there is a particular move involving both the king and a rook which is called 'castles', and this move must not be confused with the piece. The name 'rook' comes from a Persian word meaning 'fortress', and it is easy to see the resemblance between this piece and the turrets often seen on the battlements of ancient fortresses.

The rook always moves parallel to the sides of the board, and may move any number of squares forwards, sideways, or backwards in one move.

The bishop always moves diagonally, and may move any number of squares forwards or backwards along a diagonal in one move.

Rook and bishop can each stop at any intermediate square, but whereas the rook can occupy any square on the board, the bishop must always stay on squares of one colour. Thus the bishop in Fig. 2 can never get to a white-coloured square.

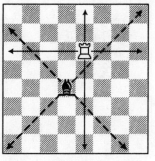

Fig. 2

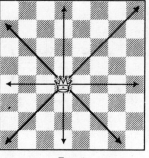

Fig. 3

1.5. The Queen

The queen is the most powerful piece of all. It can move like a rook, or like a bishop. In Fig. 3 we see that it has a choice of no less than twenty-seven squares to which it may move if placed near the centre of the board, and it can reach any square on the board in two moves by a number of routes.

1.6. The Knight

The knight (represented by the horse on which he is mounted) has a curious move. It may be described as 'two-and-one', the piece moving two squares forward, or sideways, or backwards, and then one square at right angles, this double manœuvre counting as one move.

Alternatively, think of the knight as standing at one corner of a two by three box of squares, when it may move to the opposite corner of the box.

Starting on a black square, the knight must land on a white square, and vice versa. It is not obstructed by pieces of either colour, since moving across the two by three box it passes between them. This is shown in Fig. 5 where the knight may capture either the black rook or bishop.

· Until you are quite familiar with the moves, take special care over knight moves for both sides; it is easy to overlook possible captures.

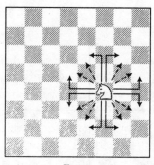

Fig. 4   Fig. 5

1.7. The King

The king is strictly limited in its movements. *It can move one square only* at a time in any direction (see Fig. 6).

1.8. Captures

Before we come to the pawn moves, here is an exercise in captures to help you to get used to moves of the various pieces.

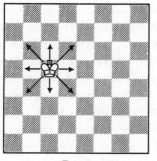

Fig. 6

Fig. 7

Exercise 1

In Fig. 7, state what captures may be made by

1. The white rook	2. The black rook	3. The white bishop
4. The black bishop	5. The white queen	6. The black queen
7. The white king	8. The black king	9. The white knight
10. The black knight		

1.9. The Pawn

The pawn gets its name from an old French word meaning foot-soldier, and like the infantry it must advance against the foe. Unlike any other piece *it is not allowed to retreat.* Its normal move is one square directly forward towards the enemy forces, but it is allowed to move two squares forward on its first move only. Each and every pawn may start with a single-square or double-square move at choice, but the double move may not be saved up, and having once moved a particular pawn one square forward, the option of the double move has been forfeited.

We shall see that at the start of a game the pieces occupy the back row (or rank) of each player, and that the pawns are lined up in front of them on the second rank. Any pawn may therefore advance either to the third or fourth rank on its first move, but only one rank further with each successive move. Later, in Chapter 4, we shall see what happens if a pawn succeeds in reaching the enemy back rank.

The pawn has a special capturing move. It does not capture by moving directly forward, but by moving one square diagonally forward to the left or right. It may not exercise its option of an initial double-square move to make a capture.

A pawn is often blocked by a piece or pawn (of either colour) directly in front of it; if it cannot make a capture, it is stuck where it is – and this state may go on for a long time. This rarely happens to pieces which nearly always have some move they can make.

In tackling the next exercise, note that diagrams are always printed to show the white forces moving up the page, and the black forces down the page towards the reader – this is usual practice, both in this and other books and for diagrams printed in chess columns published in newspapers and chess magazines. Until you have had a good deal of practice in working direct from chess diagrams, you will find it best to set out the pieces on a proper chess board and to look at the positon from both White's and Black's side of the board.

Exercise 2

Go back to Fig. 7, and say what possible captures and other moves can be made by each white and black pawn.

This concludes Chapter 1. Read it through again, and make sure you clearly understand all the basic moves.

CHAPTER TWO

Recording

2.1. Learning to Read

In the solutions to Exercise 2, we used such phrases as the black pawn on the right of the diagram. This is a clumsy and long-winded method and we obviously need some short cut. Several simple systems have been devised of which the English Descriptive and the Algebraic notations are in most general use in this country. We shall use Algebraic in this book.

You may find this rather a dull chapter, but it is well worthwhile mastering it. In doing so you are learning to read and write in the chess-world.

2.2. ... and to Write

Chess notation has another advantage besides its use in chess books and magazines. You can use it to keep a record of the games you play; then you can show your games to other people or look at them again yourself, either for interest or to try to improve your play by seeing where you could have done better. Moreover, when you begin to play in matches or in tournaments and use a chess clock, you will have to keep a record; so get used to it from the very beginning – then you will not find it worrying when you have to keep a score.

This is an important point and we strongly advise you to prac-tise making an accurate and clear record of your games as soon as possible.

2.3. The Starting Position

At the start of a game, the pieces and pawns are set up as in the diagram, and White has first move.

The pieces of each colour fill the back ranks, with the pawns lined up in front of them.

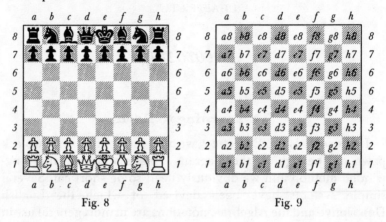

Fig. 8   Fig. 9

Make sure that the kings and queens stand on the correct squares. The lady has first choice and chooses her own colour. Thus, the white queen stands on a white square, and the black queen on a black square, with the kings then taking their places beside them. Note that the enemy kings are directly opposite each other.

Instead of writing these names out in full, we can abbreviate by using initial letters. The queen is denoted by 'Q', the king by 'K', the bishop by 'B', the rook by 'R'. The pawn is not mentioned. The knight is denoted by 'N' to prevent confusion with the king.

2.4. Naming the Squares

We need to be able to name the squares as well as the pieces; we do this as shown in Fig. 9.

2.5. Writing down the Moves

This is how to record a move:
(a) Work out the name of the square to be occupied, remembering whether it is White's or Black's move.

(*b*) State which piece or pawn is to occupy the square.

(*c*) Make the description of the move as concise as possible.

(*d*) A check is denoted by '+' − e.g. Rh7+.

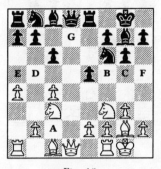

Fig. 10

In Fig. 10, some of the squares have been lettered for easy reference. Square 'A' is c2. If White wishes to move the queen to this square on his tenth move, he would write 10 Qc2.

Square 'B' is f5. If Black moves his queen's bishop to this square in reply, he writes 10...Bf5. The dots after the number 10 show that we are recording Black's move.

If White moves a knight to square 'C', he writes Ng5, whilst if his other knight goes to square 'D' he writes Nb5.

Similarly, if Black advances a pawn to square 'E', he must write ...a5, whereas a similar pawn move to square 'F' on the other side of the board is written ...h5. On the other hand, if White occupies 'E' with a pawn, the move is a5 (with no dots).

Square 'G' is d7. If Black's queen's bishop moves to this square, ...Bd7 is a sufficient description; but if the square is occupied by a knight, ...Nd7 is insufficient, since either black knight can make such a move. Black must write ...Nbd7 or ...Nfd7 to describe the move fully.

Captures are indicated by '×'. White could play Q×d8 and Black would reply ...R×d8. Or if, for example, White captures Black's king's pawn with his king's knight, he writes N×e5.

Exercise 3

The following questions on the Algebraic notation refer to Fig. 11. Set up the position on a board.

Fig. 11

White has just played 6 e5. Now record the next few moves described in the following statements.

Example: Black captures a white knight at his sixth move.
Answer: 6 . . . B×c3

1. White recaptures on the same square with a pawn.
2. Black now moves a knight to square 'A'.
3. White moves the queen to square 'B'.
4. Black advances a pawn to square 'C'.
5. White plays a knight to square 'D'.
6. Black advances a pawn to square 'E'.
7. White captures this pawn with his queen's pawn.
8. Black moves a knight to square 'F'.
9. White moves a bishop to square 'G'.
10. Black captures the queen's bishop with his knight.
11. White recaptures the knight with his king.
12. Black captures the pawn on square 'E'.
13. White plays his right-hand rook to the king's original square.
14. Black plays his bishop to square 'F'.
15. White advances the rook he has just moved two squares.
16. Black moves his queen to the square originally occupied by the queen's bishop's pawn.

(Don't worry about why these moves were played. They are part of a well-known opening but are given here just for practising chess notation.)

2.6. Recording Game-Positions

Apart from recording the actual moves of a game, it is often useful to keep a record of a position reached during the course of play. The obvious way to do this is to fill in details on blank diagrams such as that shown at Fig. 1; you can buy these or make them yourself, but such blank forms are not always available, and if many examples are to be given in a book they tend to occupy too much space. Once more there is a short cut — the Forsyth Notation. It is worth learning this as you will find it useful for recording positions, e.g. of unfinished games which you mean to complete at a later date.

2.7. The Forsyth Notation

We use the usual shorthand for white pieces and pawns, viz. Q, K, R, B, N and P. Black pieces are given by the corresponding *small letters* q, k, r, b, n and p.

The position is now recorded rank by rank, starting at Black's back rank at a8, giving the number of squares unoccupied by pieces or pawns as they occur, and separating the ranks with semi-colons.

By way of illustration, consider Fig. 11 in Forsyth Notation. It would be recorded:

> rnbqk2r; ppp2ppl; 4pnlp; 3pP3; 1b1P4; 2N5;
> PPPB1PPP; R2QKBNR. Black to move.

Compare this recorded position carefully with the printed diagram. Now compare Fig. 18 and its Forsyth equivalent:

> 4k3; 7N; 4K3; 8; 7Q; 8; P2n4; 8. Black to move.

Notice the 8's; you get these when a rank is unoccupied and it is important not to leave them out of the record.

Exercise 4

Use the Forsyth Notation to record the positions of Figs. 10, 7, 12.

2.8. Recording on Diagrams

If positions are to be recorded on Diagram Blanks, it is unnecessary to have rubber stamps of the figurines, or to attempt to draw in the pieces and pawns concerned. Use letters for the pieces and pawns, ringing the black ones. Thus 'Q' for the white queen, but for the black bishop, 'Ⓑ' etc. It is essential to state which colour is to move next.

This method will not be used in this book, but is useful for unfinished games in match and tournament play.

CHAPTER THREE

Check and Checkmate

3.1. The Object of the Game

Unlike Draughts, where the object of the game is to capture every piece of the opposing colour, the aim in Chess is to capture one man — the opposing king.

If White has captured nearly all his opponent's pieces and pawns whilst retaining most of his own material, yet has his king trapped, he has lost, and Black is the winner.

Having stated that the aim is to capture the king, we now come to a paradox — *the king can never be captured!*

3.2. Check

Whenever the king is attacked by an enemy piece or pawn, it is said to be 'in check'. It is usual for the player attacking the king to say 'Check' as he makes his move, but this is not essential, and the king is in check as soon as it is attacked, whether or not the opponent says 'Check'.

3.3. Getting out of Check

When the king is in check he *must* get out of check on the next move. There are three ways in which this may be achieved:

(*a*) He may move to a square where he is no longer attacked.

(*b*) A piece or pawn may be placed between the attacking piece and the king to shield him.

(*c*) The checking piece may be captured.

In Fig. 12 White can check the black king by Rd1 or Rg5. In the first case Black has eight possible moves to get out of check, and

Fig. 12. White to move

seven ways of escaping from the second check. See if you can find them all, and try to decide which is White's better check.

When your king is checked, don't panic but think of all the possibilities. First ask yourself, 'Can I capture the checking piece?' If it can be captured, that is frequently the best move to make, especially if the piece can be taken without loss to yourself.

Besides capturing, you may also be able to put a piece or pawn in the way or to move the king to a safe square. There is no general rule to tell you which is best; however, we shall see later that if the king is checked early in the game it is usually bad to move him except to make a capture.

What you should *not* do is to grab the king as soon as your opponent says 'Check', and then wonder what to do. Look at the position carefully, examine all the possibilities especially captures; then, when you have made your mind up, pick up the piece and move it.

This applies to all moves, whether you are in check or not. The great master Tarrasch used to sit on his hands between moves; a similar way of avoiding hasty moves is seen in the rule for learners at one school. 'When your opponent moves, the first thing to do is to put your hands in your pockets!' A rule like this helps one to play – as one always should – 'Touch and Move'.

3.4. Touch and Move

Once you have intentionally touched a piece you must move it if you can. This rule of 'Touch and Move' should be applied to all games, 'friendly' or match. However, if you touch a piece by mistake (for example by brushing it with a sleeve) you need not move it, and it would be quite wrong to try to make a player move a piece accidentally touched in this way.

If you wish to place a piece or pawn more centrally on its square, and it is your turn to move you should say 'J'adoube', or its English equivalent 'I adjust', *before* touching the piece, when the adjustment may be made without penalty. This should not often be necessary.

Certainly a player should not pick up a piece to move it, and then, on finding that the intended move would prove disastrous, announce that he only intended to polish it, and after replacing it on its original square, move some other piece!

A move is complete when you take your hand off the piece; until then, you may change your mind about where you will put the piece, but once you have let it go the move is finished and cannot be changed.

Finally, if you touch an opponent's piece or pawn, meaning to capture it, then you must do so if you can. In short, if you have touched a piece of either side, you must move or capture it if you can. If you are not allowed to do so by the rules — if, for example, to do so would leave you in check — then there is no penalty and you must move something else instead.

Exercise 5

Position 5.1   Position 5.2

1. White to move.

    (*a*) White has three checks. What are they?

    (*b*) What should Black reply to the bishop check?

    (*c*) One of the checks by the white queen is clearly a weak move. Why?

(*d*) Name all possible Black replies to the alternative queen check. State which reply is Black's best move, and give reasons for rejecting the others.

2. White to move.

    (*a*) White has three checks. What are they?

    (*b*) Two of the checks are weak moves. Why?

    (*c*) Can a piece or pawn ever be interposed between a knight and a king when the knight is checking?

    (*d*) After White has played the best check, state all possible Black replies.

    (*e*) After the king has moved out of check in 2(*d*), suggest a White move which wins a piece by a safe capture.

Position 5.3

Position 5.4

3. White to move.

    (*a*) White can play 1 Rc1+. What are Black's possible replies, and which would you choose? Give reasons.

    (*b*) Find another check by a white rook, and give Black's best reply.

    (*c*) Find a check by the white knight, and give Black's reply.

    (*d*) There is one more White check. What is it? Give Black's reply and state why this check is a good move for White.

4. Black to move.

    (*a*) In how many ways can Black check the white king?

    (N.B. In giving check, Black must not leave his own king in check.)

    (*b*) Why is check by Black's queen a good move, and how would he follow it up on the next move?

3.5. Checkmate

Set up the position in Fig. 13. Black has lost all his pieces and pawns apart from his king, and now White must aim to finish off the game by trapping the black king.

White can check with four different rook moves. If he plays 1 Re7+, Black simply replies 1 ... K×e7. The move 1 Ra8+ is safe for White, but drives the king on to its second rank at d7, e7 or f7. This is not a good idea for White, since the king is more readily

Fig. 13

trapped on the edge of the board. It is far better to leave the rook on a7 where it prevents the king moving away from the back rank.

There remain two checks by the rook on b1. If White plays 1 Re1+, Black's king cannot move on to the second rank, but he can play to d8 or f8. If, on the other hand, White plays 1 Rb8+, Black cannot move on to the second rank because of the rook at a7 and moves on his back rank would leave him in check, so that he has no move.

When the king has been trapped in this way, the king is said to have been checkmated, and White has won the game.

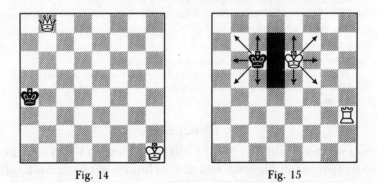

Fig. 14   Fig. 15

In Fig. 14, White has no less than seven possible checks with the queen. See if you can find them. Four of these are safe moves, since the queen is safe from capture, but those at b3, b4 and b5 are not safe, since the queen could then be captured by the king.

Now add a white bishop on e1 — this makes all the difference. White has the same seven checks available, and those at b3 and b5 are still unsafe, but 1 Qb4+ is now a very good move, since the black king cannot capture the queen, as he would then be in check by the bishop. Examination of the position shows that he has no square to which he can move without being in check, and since no other piece can capture the queen, and clearly nothing can be interposed between queen and king, Black is checkmated, and White has won.

Note the very important point that, in general, the nearer the queen can get to the opposing king without being captured, the more dangerous is the attack, since the king has little freedom of movement. In this example, Black has a choice of escape squares for all long-distance checks of the queen.

Figure 15 shows that two kings must never occupy adjacent squares, for if either moves towards the other it will be moving into check. Here we see that neither the white nor black king can move on to the three squares on the queen's file. This fact can be used when trying to trap the opposing king.

In these two examples checkmate was forced by two pieces working together against the black king. In Fig. 13, two rooks were used, and in the second example mate was achieved by queen and bishop. Now, at least two pieces are always needed to checkmate a king on the open board, and if one side has only a queen or a rook, these pieces alone cannot effect checkmate, so you must bring up the king to help win the game. In Fig. 15, the white king has advanced towards the enemy king, and White can now play 1 Rc3+, after which the black king must retreat to the knight's file, since all squares on the bishop's file are controlled by the rook, and the white king prevents its advance towards the safety of the centre of the board.

We shall see in Chapter 7 that this method can be used by king and queen or king and rook against lone king to force the mate. The final mating position is similar to that arising from Fig. 15, but with the black king trapped at the side of the board. Put the black king on a6 and the white king opposite it on c6 with white rook at h3. White can play 1 Ra3 mate, as the white king prevents the black king's escape. Again, put the black king on c3 and the black queen at h2, with the white king at d1. Black can play 1...Qd2 mate, the queen being safe from capture because it is supported by the black king. This is a typical case of the advantage of placing the queen as close as possible to the opposing king, provided it is safe from capture. All other checks would have allowed the king escape squares.

Exercise 6

In this exercise, ideas already explained in this chapter are used to force mate. In questions 1 – 10 there is a mate next move. Find it. If you think you have found two or more mates, study the position carefully, as there is only one correct solution in each position.

1. Black to move.
2. White to move.
3. White to move.
4. Black to move.
5. Black to move.
6. White to move.

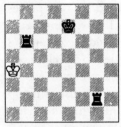

Position 6.1

Position 6.2

Position 6.3

Position 6.4

Position 6.5

Position 6.6

Position 6.7

Position 6.8

Position 6.9

Position 6.10

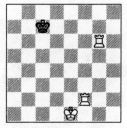
Position 6.11

7. Black to move
8. White to move.
9. (a) White to move. (b) Black to move
10. White to move.
11. White to move. Show how he can force mate in two moves, whatever Black replies.

3.6. Various Checkmates

There are innumerable mating positions with the chess pieces, and no one would ever dream of trying to memorize them. The essential thing is to look out for such opportunities in your games, and try and create positions where an opposing king has been exposed to attack, and hence checkmates are more likely to occur.

In Exercise 7, examples are given showing how all the pieces and pawns can be used to checkmate in different situations. The one factor common to them all is that the winning side is looking out for the chance of trapping the opposing king by moving his forces towards it.

Exercise 7

In each position there is a mate next move. Find it.

1. Black to move.
2. White to move.
3. White to move.
4. White to move.
5. White to move.
6. Black to move.
7. Black to move.
8. White to move.
9. Black to move.
10. White to move.

Position 7.1

Position 7.2

Position 7.3

Position 7.4

Position 7.5

Position 7.6

Position 7.7

Position 7.8

Position 7.9

Position 7.10

3.7. Mating Material

We have seen that a queen or rook needs help from the king or another piece to mate the lone king; rook and king is in fact the minimum material needed for such a mate. Bishop and king or knight and king are not enough and if you are left with no other material than this at the end of the game, the game is drawn.

3.8. Drawn Games

The game is drawn if:
(a) there is not enough material on either side for mate to be possible;
(b) one side is unable to avoid check by the opposition, but cannot be checkmated (this is called perpetual check);
(c) no capture or pawn move is made by either side for fifty successive moves of each player;
(d) the exact position is repeated 3 times with the same player to move;
(e) both players agree to call the game drawn;
(f) one side has no possible move but is not in check — this is called 'Stalemate'.

3.9. Stalemate

In Fig. 16, White has nearly mated Black. Realizing he needs the king to help the queen, it is very tempting to move 1 Kc4 or 1 Kc5 threatening to mate Black at once by 2 Qb4. Unfortunately for White, however, after, say, 1 Kc4 Black must move and he has no legal move, since all five squares round his king are attacked by White.

Fig. 16. White to move   Fig. 17. Black to move

Now, White is not actually checking, so that it cannot be checkmate. It is, in fact, 'stalemate', and the game is drawn.

When the opposition has little left, you must be on your guard against this possibility. More easily winning games are spoilt by beginners in this than in any other way.

The best way to win from Fig. 16 is to keep Black's king to the side of the board by playing the queen on to the queen's knight's file and then to bring up your king. Play proceeds 1 Qb2 (the only safe move to this file) Ka5 2 Kc5 (choose the square opposite the king), and White mates with the queen at b4 or b6 next move according to Black's second move.

In Fig. 17, Black takes advantage of the stalemate possibility of Fig. 16 to force a draw. He plays 1...Re6+, and after 2 Qxe6 the game is drawn by stalemate. If White avoids this by moving his king when checked, Black captures the queen and should himself win.

Fig. 18. Black to move

Figure 18 shows White threatening 1 Qe7 mate, and if it is Black's move, he must move his knight, since his king has no move. Unable to prevent the mate, he deliberately plays 1...Nb3. If White snatches the piece with 2 a×b3, it is stalemate. He should ignore the Grecian gift and refuse to be diverted from his immediate mate by 2 Qe7.

CHAPTER FOUR

Starting to Play: the Importance of Extra Material

4.1. Playing a Game

At this stage you should play as many games as you can. Get another beginner as an opponent and, if possible, a more experienced player to stand by. He should not tell you what to do during play, but he can help you by seeing that you do not forget any of the rules and, after the game, can tell you some of the ways you went wrong.

Try to form a plan of action when you play. Your object is to give mate and it is easiest to do this when the enemy king has few pieces or pawns to protect it; so try to take the opponent's men while keeping your own until his king is sufficiently exposed for you to trap it. Also watch for any chances either way of giving mate when there are still a lot of pieces on the board. You will find that besides trying to carry out your plans, you will have to watch your opponent's; in doing this you will begin to find out what chess is about and to enjoy the struggle which makes chess worth playing.

4.2. You Must Attack

If you want to be good, you must attack. Because so many games between beginners are won by blunders which lose pieces, some players are afraid to use their pieces actively in case they lose them, so they just move pawns and wait for their opponent to make mistakes. You will never learn like this: the pieces are there to be used and it is only by trying to attack, i.e. to do something

24

active with them, that you will learn how to use them.

4.3. The Triumphant Pawn

A pawn can only move forwards; so what happens if you get right across the board to the enemy back rank? In that case you exchange it for any other piece of the same colour that you like, except the king. This is called 'promoting' the pawn. Generally speaking, you would promote your pawn to a queen as this is the most powerful piece. You may do this even if you have a queen already, so that it is possible to have nine queens of the same colour on the board at once; in practice, one extra queen will almost always win, and if you do manage to promote a pawn your aim should be to exchange as much material as possible and mate with the extra queen.

Fig. 19. White to move   Fig. 20. Black to move

Figures 19 and 20 show exceptional circumstances. In Fig. 19, it is White's move. If he plays 1 f8(Q), we have a stalemate position, similar to that arising from Fig. 16, and the game is drawn. A draw also results if White promotes the pawn to a bishop or knight, since there is insufficient material left to force mate, but he can and should play 1 f8(R), when Black's only reply is 1...Kh6; after which White plays 2 Rh8 mate.

In Fig. 20, White threatens mate by 1 Qb5. If it is Black's move, and he plays 1...g1(Q), White simply carries out his threat, but Black has a better move. He plays 1...g1(N)+, taking advantage of the position of the white king, and after the king has moved out of check, Black continues 2...N×e2 and the game is drawn, since neither side has sufficient material for mate.

However, positions like these are very rare; look out for them, but you will find that promotion to a queen is nearly always best. The only questions you really need to ask yourself are, 'If I make a queen, will it be a stalemate?' (e.g. Fig. 19) and, 'If I make a knight, will it give a winning check?' (e.g. Fig. 20).

4.4. Winning Material: General Advice

If our general plan is (a) to win material; (b) to exchange off material until our opponent cannot defend his king; (c) to mate with the extra material; we must consider how material can, in fact, be won, and also what exchanges are worthwhile.

The simplest form of winning material is to capture any unprotected piece. This suggests that at every move we should look carefully at the move just made by our opponent and see if we can take advantage of it. We may plan to capture material next move, or within a few moves; we may have decided to bring more pieces into the attack; or, best of all, we may have an idea how to mate our opponent. Don't make the mistake of going ahead the moment the opponent moves, without looking to see why he made his move, and whether it makes any difference. Remember that your opponent will have had some idea behind his move, and you must find out if you can what this was, and whether it is dangerous to you.

If you are threatening mate, see if his move prevents it, or threatens to win the piece with which you intended to mate if you go ahead with your plan. If not, mate him. Even if he puts his queen where it may be taken, don't waste time taking it, for the mate is more important. If you have other plans, his move may cause you to change them, either because it prevents them, or because it sets up a more serious threat of its own. It is no good taking his queen as planned, if he promptly mates you in reply!

After each opposing move, ask yourself, 'Does it alter my plans?' Next, see if his move was safe. Perhaps he has offered you free material. You must then decide whether (a) you must attend to his threats; (b) take advantage of his move (if weak); or (c) carry on with your own plan. Whichever you decide, before making your move, ask yourself in turn, 'Is it safe?' and if you see no reason to the contrary, go boldly ahead and make your move.

4.5. The Value of the Pieces

A second and very common way of winning material is to exchange pieces and/or pawns to leave some material advantage, for even one extra pawn may prove decisive in a long game, since it may be possible to promote it to a queen.

If you are to know whether an exchange is worthwhile, then you must know what the pieces are worth. Here is a rough table, taking the pawn as the unit.

$$Q = 9; R = 5; B = 3\frac{1}{2}; N = 3\frac{1}{2}; P = 1.$$

We do not evaluate the king, as it cannot be exchanged.

We cannot, of course, exchange the queen for nine pawns, since there are only eight opposing pawns on the board at any one time, but we can see that the queen (worth 9) should not be exchanged for a rook (worth 5) and two pawns — total 7 — unless it leads to some more important advantage, such as a mating threat that cannot be stopped.

These values vary a good deal according to the position, and you should therefore use the figures as a general guide when exchanging, not as a set of rules that always hold good.

Exercise 8

Say whether the following exchanges lead to material advantage, material disadvantage, or approximate material equality:

1. Enemy rook for your knight and pawn.
2. Queen for two bishops and a pawn.
3. Queen for two rooks.
4. Knight and bishop for rook and two pawns.
5. Rook for four pawns.
6. Bishop for rook.
7. Bishop for two pawns.
8. Bishop and two knights for queen.
9. Rook and bishop for queen.
10. Queen for rook and three pawns.
11. Bishop, knight and rook for queen and pawn.
12. Two rooks for two bishops and knight.

4.6. Exchanges for Gain: Working Out the Profit

In Fig. 21, White is able to capture Black's king's pawn or knight.

Fig. 21. White to move

1 N×e5 would be bad, since 1...f×e5 wins 2½ units. Is there any advantage in capturing the knight? The knight is attacked four times — by the white knight, bishop, queen, and, indirectly, rook — and only defended three times — by the black pawn, bishop and queen. It may therefore be possible to win material. White can play 1 N×d5 c×d5 2 B×d5 B×d5 3 Q×d5 Q×d5 4 R×d5 and gains 1 unit. If Black recaptures in a slightly different order, by 1...B×d5 2 B×d5 c×d5 we reach the same result, as is the case if White starts with 1 B×d5, since Black can only equalize the material at each move until finally left with one pawn less. However, White must not start with 1 Q×d5, since Black would reply 1...c×d5 2 N×d5 B×d5 3B×d5, and then move his queen out of danger — e.g. 3...Qc7 — instead of capturing the rook, and so remain 4½ units ahead. In general, you should capture first with the piece of smallest value when you have a choice; this common-sense rule does not always work, but you will find it a good guide.

Note the method of *counting* the number of pieces and pawns attacking or defending a given square. This is much less complicated than, 'If I do this, he replies this, and I then reply that ...', etc. The general rule is that when you attack a piece with *more* pieces than defend it, you are likely to be able to gain something by taking it; when you attack with *the same or a lesser number* of pieces you will not gain. Of course you must remember the value of the pieces involved: to 'gain' two pawns for one rook is about as useful as to gain two pennies for one fivepenny piece. It is this that makes the pawn such a valuable defender.

You can use the same counting rule to help you find out whether it is safe to play a piece to an empty square. Usually, it will be safe if you defend the square at least as often as the other man attacks it; but remember that the piece itself does not count as a defender.

In Fig. 21, b5 is attacked and defended by one piece or pawn of each side, and 1 b5 is therefore playable without loss. In Fig. 22, d5 is attacked by three white pieces and only defended by two black pieces, so 1...d5 would lose material. White, on the other hand, can play 1 c5 since c5 is attacked by only one black pawn and is defended by two white pieces. Similarly, White can play 1 Ne4 where one unit of each side attacks or defends the square (note that the QN in moving to e4 *is not* counted as defending the square).

Finally, would Qd5 be sensible? It would be defended twice and only once attacked — all the same it would be a stupid move, because the queen is so much more valuable than the knight, and Black would just play N×d5. So, as well as counting, you must remember the values of the pieces.

4.7. More Complicated Examples

In Fig. 22, Black threatens to play 1...Bg4 and White could not reply 2 Q×g4 because of 2 N×g4, gaining 5½ units. If, on the other

Fig. 22. White to move

hand, White moved 2 Qg3 or 2 Qf4 Black would reply 2...B×d1, winning material (1½ units). White, however, is an aggressive player, and doesn't wish to spend time taking such defensive measures as 1 h3 to prevent 1...Bg4, if he can find a more attacking move. After consideration he plays 1 Nd5 and if Black plays 1...Bg4 replies 2 N×f6+. After Black has recaptured with queen or pawn, White continues 3 Q×g4, winning a piece. We see here how important it is to examine all checks where exchanges are involved; the king must get out of check at move 2 and Black does not get the chance to take the queen.

Fig. 23. White to move

In Fig. 23 it looks as if the black knight dare not move, since White would then play 2 B×d8. White again tries the aggressive move 1 Nd5, but this time it is White who has not looked deeply enough. Black plays 1...N×d5 and after 2 B×d8 himself continues 2...N×f4. White can now regain two pawns by 3 B×c7 and 4 B×d6, but Black emerges with an extra knight for two pawns — a gain of 1½ units.

Exercise 9

In this exercise, use the 'counting' method whenever you can, and when it doesn't work, see why.

1. If a game begins 1 a4 e5 2 Ra3 what should Black reply, and why?
2. White to move. How does he win a piece?
3. White to move. Is 1 N×e5 a safe capture?
4. Black to move. How does he win material?

5. Add WR on e3 and BR on f7 in Position 9.4. Can Black still win material? Give reasons.
6. White to move. Can he play 1 R×f7 safely? If Black replies 1...R×f7 give White's next two moves.
7. White to move. Can he win a pawn? Give reasons.
8. In 9.7, move BN to e8 and add BP on e6. Now can White win a pawn? Give reasons.
9. Black to move. Can he play 1...N×e4 safely? Give a reason.
10. White to move. Is 1 Bb5 a good move? Give reasons. Would it make any difference if White's b-pawn was on b3? Is so, say why.
11. White to move. How does he win material?
12. White to move. How does he win a pawn?

Position 9.2

Position 9.3

Position 9.4

Position 9.6

Position 9.7

Position 9.9

Position 9.10

Position 9.11

Position 9.12

13. Can White win material by 1 R×e5? Give reasons.

The remaining examples are more difficult, and provide a challenge to the player.

14. Black to move. Black, already a pawn ahead, can win a second pawn. Give the next two moves for Black, with White's reply to the first.

15. Black to move. Black has already sacrificed a rook and a pawn for a bishop, and is now 2½ units down. How does he play to regain his material with interest? Give the next three moves for Black with White's best replies to the first two.

Position 9.13

Position 9.14

Position 9.15

4.8. When to Exchange

The general rules for making exchanges are:

(a) Make exchanges when they lead to material gain.

(b) Exchange *pieces not pawns* when you have material *advantage*.

(c) Exchange *pawns but not pieces* when you have material *disadvantage*.

(d) Exchange when you are under severe attack.

The reasons for (b) and (c) are as follows. The fewer the pieces on the board, the more difference an extra one makes. You may hardly notice an extra knight with many pieces on the board, but if you have knight and pawns and your opponent just pawns, you can easily capture his pawns, promote your own, and win (see Chapter 7). However, if you have a knight only and no pawns, you cannot win, as this is insufficient material to mate. The player with the advantage should therefore try to exchange pieces, whilst his opponent should aim to exchange pawns.

When you are on the defensive, especially when you have little room for manœuvring, exchanges will often reduce the force of the attack and give you room to breathe. Hence (d).

In addition there may be special circumstances — e.g. getting

rid of an important defender when you are yourself attacking –
where exchanges pay. What you must not do is to exchange
because you are afraid of a complicated position. Practice in such
positions will improve your play more than anything else.
Anyway, you will find that a stronger player will beat you even if
you do try to make things easier by exchange; so you might as well
play a game with some interest in it!

CHAPTER FIVE

The Opening: Development and the Centre

5.1. Development

In the last chapter we talked about winning material and attacking the king. To be able to do this successfully usually depends on attacking some point more often than the enemy can defend it. This in turn depends on getting your pieces out quickly and moving them to squares where they have plenty of mobility so that you can shft them easily to any part of the board where you want them.

Moving the pieces out in this way is called 'Development' and the early part of the game in which you do this is called 'The Opening'.

5.2. Order of Developing Pieces

First we will consider the order in which pieces should be developed, and then the squares to which they should be played.

The queen is the most powerful piece, and it is therefore natural for a player to wish to bring the queen into the attack at the earlist possible moment. Let us take an example of what might happen if such a plan was carried out.

The game could start 1 e4 d6 2 Qh5 (developing the queen to a square which is at present safe, but not making any important threat, since 3 Q×f7+, or 3 Q×h7, would each lose the queen for a pawn — a serious loss of material) 2. . .Nf6 3 Qf3 (the e4 pawn must be protected, and the queen cannot remain at h5 without loss.

Even protection by 3 Be2 is insufficient, as Black would gain 5½ units by exchanging his knight for the queen) 3...Bg4. The bishop is protected by the knight, and cannot be exchanged by White without loss, so the queen must move again. Perhaps White might play 4 Qd3, and Black could reply 4...Nc6 developing a third piece. We find that after only four moves each, Black has developed two more pieces than White. Clearly White's early development of the queen has not worked out well. (See Fig. 24.)

The trouble about the queen is that it is so valuable that if any other piece attacks it, it has to move away. So we see that, as a rule, it is better to prepare the way before bringing the queen on to the open board: we shall see an important example of this principle in the next chapter.

Similarly, the rooks must avoid exchange by bishop, knight or pawn, and an attempt to develop a rook early by a4 or h4, followed by Ra3 or Rh3, is rarely good − also, as we shall see later, the pawns on the wings are frequently needed on their original squares to provide good protection for the king.

Generally speaking, you should bring out the less important pieces, *the knights and bishops, before the rooks and queen.* There are exceptions to this rule (there are to most rules in chess) and you will learn to spot these as you get experience − meanwhile you will find 'knights and bishops first' is usually sound.

Finally, the pawns. The main objects of moving pawns in the

Fig. 24. The queen came out too soon: not a sensible way for White to develop.

Fig. 25. A sensible development by both players.

opening are (*a*) to let the pieces out (only the knights can be developed without pawn moves), and (*b*) to hamper the opponent. Since, as we shall see, the right development is towards the centre, you will find that both for getting your pieces out and for hampering your opponent the central pawns — i.e. e-pawn, d-pawn and perhaps c-pawn and f-pawn — are the best ones to move, always provided they can move safely. *Do not make unnecessary pawn moves* — they waste valuable time, and, because of the nature of the pawn's move, can never be retracted. Fig. 25 shows a sensible development by both players: it might have come from 1 e4 e5 2 Nf3 Nc6 3 Bc4 Bc5 4 d3 d6 5 Nc3 Nf6 6 Bg5 Be6.

5.3. Centralization

A piece placed near the centre of the board generally has a greater choice of moves than one at the board's edge. Fig. 4 showed that a knight on one of the sixteen central squares had eight possible moves. Place it on b4 and there are only six possible moves, whilst on a4 there are only four moves. See what happens when the knight stands on b1 and then a1.

Similarly, Fig. 3 shows how many moves (count them!) a queen has when it is in the middle of the board; here again it has many fewer when in a corner. When near the centre of the board, pieces usually attack more squares in the enemy camp and defend more squares on their own.

Another big advantage of having your pieces near the centre is that they can easily get to any part of the board where they are wanted: this is especially important for the short-stepping knight — see how long it takes a knight on a3, for example, to get across to the king's side.

If you want to be able to move your pieces near the centre of the board and to stop the enemy doing so, you will find that you must get as much control as you can of the central squares, i.e. e4, d4, e5 and d5 and squares near them.

In Fig. 26 (opposite), White has managed this well and so he has more room for his pieces than Black. The process of playing in the centre and trying to get control of it is called 'Centralization'.

5.4. Opening Principles

You will find the following list of points a good guide on how to develop: there are exceptions, but you do not need to bother about these yet.

(a) Develop the less important pieces (bishops and knights) before the more important (queen and rooks).

(b) In general, develop a new piece rather than move one already developed.

(c) Moves by the central pawns are usually better than moves by the flank pawns.

(d) Don't make unnecessary pawn moves.

(e) Moves which help to control the centre are usually good.

You will find that the White development shown in Fig. 26 is a good one if your opponent allows you to get it; e4 and d4 are good squares for the pawns, f3 and c3 are the best squares for the knights and f4 and c4 good for the bishops. Of course you must always watch your opponent's play, and he will probably stop you from doing this: but if you remember 'quick development' and 'play in the centre' you should get a satisfactory position.

5.5. Castling

Assume that we have developed both knights and bishops. How are we to bring our rooks into play without advancing the outside pawns?

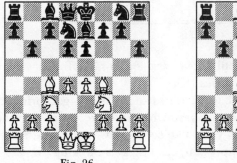

Fig. 26   Fig. 27

Fortunately there is a special move to help us to do this, called 'castling'.

We have already seen Fig. 26 as an example of good development by White: he has got two more pieces out than Black has and his pieces are all on strong squares for attack or defence. Now he must develop his rooks, and castling will help to do this.

To castle, you move the king *two* places along the back rank towards the rook, and then move the rook over the king to the next square on the other side of it. This manœuvre counts as one move, and is the only move in chess where you are allowed to move two pieces at once. Figure 27 shows the position after White has castled on the king's side, and the move can be recorded 7 Castles, or 7 0–0, where the two zeros stand for the two empty squares between king and rook when the player is about to castle.

If in Fig. 26 play had continued 7 Qd2 Bb7, White could have castled on the queen's side (recorded 8 Castles (Q) or 8 0–0–0, where the three zeros stand for the three empty squares between king and queen's rook), to reach the position of Fig. 28.

Fig. 28

In this case the king still moves *two* squares, but finishes nearer the centre than after Castles (K).

Castling is useful both to the rooks and to the king. It brings the rooks into the centre of the board when they work well together; they will help to support your own centre pawns and to attack the enemy's. Even more important, castling gets the king away from the open centre to find safety behind a barrier of friendly pawns: the king is the one piece you don't want to develop by advancing it early on in the game.

When castling, *always move the king first*, and then complete the move by placing the rook on the correct square. If you move the rook first to its square and release it before picking up the king, some unscrupulous player may claim that, according to the 'Touch and Move' rule, you have completed your move and cannot move the king. This is most unsporting play, and you should never try to take advantage in this way, but it is your own fault if you lay yourself open to such a claim. 'Touch and Move' cannot be claimed after you have moved the king two squares, since such a move by itself is illegal, and you can safely complete castling by moving the rook.

Here are a few important rules which will tell you when you are allowed to castle:

(*a*) Each player may castle once in the game, provided neither the king nor the rook concerned has previously moved.

(*b*) Castling may only be carried out when the squares between king and rook are vacant.

(*c*) You may not castle out of check.

(*d*) You may not castle into check, nor may the king move across a square which is attacked (i.e. it must not move 'through check').

Fig. 29

Figure 29 shows a number of these possibilities. Black has just made his twelfth move, and no king or rook moves have yet been made, though the white king escaped an earlier check by a bishop at Bb4 by interposing his own bishop at d2.

White cannot play 13 0–0, since that would leave him in check, but he may play 13 0–0–0, which places his king on c1 and his rook on d1 since the king does not move 'through check', even though the queen's rook crosses the square which is controlled by the black queen. In reply, Black may play 13. . .0–0–0 but must not play 13. . .0–0 when his king would have passed through check on f8 on its way to g8.

Beginners often get in a muddle over rule (c) and think that you are not allowed to castle if you have ever been in check. This is quite wrong; as long as you have not moved your king, it does not matter how many times you have been in check earlier in the game.

Exercise 10

In the following positions it may be assumed that kings and rooks standing on their original squares have not previously moved.

1. White to move.
   (a) If White plays 9 0–0–0, on which squares will the king and rook be placed?
   (b) State Black's possible replies to 9 Bb5+. Which would you choose, and why?
   (c) Apart from 8 Bb5+, how can White prevent 9. . .0–0 with his next move?
2. White to move.
   White plays 8 Re1+. Give all Black's possible replies, and state which of these moves loses material immediately. Which move would you choose, and why?
3. Black to move.
   (a) Is 1. . .R×b2 a good move? Give a reason for your answer.
   (b) How can Black win a pawn safely?

Position 10.1

Position 10.2

Position 10.3

5.6. Extending the Plan

In this chapter, we have tried to tell you how to bring out your pieces, but what are you to do next? This is where the Opening ends and the Middle Game begins; in this the players use their pieces and pawns to try to win material or give mate. There is no easy answer to this question, which is the heart of chess. Experience, backed by ability, will gradually teach you part of the answer — if you learn it all, you will be World Champion! What we shall try to do in this book is to help you understand why some plans are better than others, and to learn why some moves must be wrong.

Exercise 11 shows a complete game. You are asked to comment on moves at various stages.

Exercise 11

The game began:	*White*	*Black*
1	e4	e5
2	Nf3	Bd6
3	Bc4	Nh6
4	0-0	Na6

1. Comment on Black's opening moves. If you would have played differently at any point, say what you would have done, and why.

| 5 | c3 | Qe7 |
| 6 | d4 | |

2. Does this move allow Black to win a pawn?

6	...	c6
7	Kh1	Bc7
8	d×e5	Nc5

3. If Black had played 8...B×e5 White intended 9 N×e5 Q×e5 10 f4. Could Black have replied 10...Q×e4?

| 9 | Bg5 | |

4. What is Black's *only* reply that does not lose further material?

| 9 | ... | f6 |
| 10 | e×f6 | |

5. Show how White can win material if Black replies (*a*) 10...Q×e4; (*b*) 10...Qd6; (*c*) 10...Qd8.

6. What is Black's best move?

10	...	g×f6
11	B×h6	N×e4
12	Nbd2	

7. Why can this be called a good move on general principles?

| 12 | ... | d5 |
| 13 | N×e4 | d×e4 |

8. Is 13...Q×e4 a better move?

| 14 | Nd4 | Qe5 |

9. What is the point of this move?

| 15 | f4 | Qd6 |

10. How can White prevent Black from seeking safety in castling?

| 16 | Qh5+ | Ke7 |
| 17 | Qf7+ | Kd8 |

11. How can White combine development of another piece with indirect threats to Black's queen and king?

	18	**Rad1**

12. Give another very good move for White.

	18	**...**	**Bd7**

13. What should White play to follow up his last move and force gain of material?

	19	**Ne6+**	**B×e6**
	20	**B×e6**	**Re8**

14. Show how White can force mate in two more moves.

5.7. Group Exercises

We think that some of the exercises in this book are best looked at by a group of learners together with a better player to help them. You will still find them valuable if you have to do them on your own, but may find it hard to see the answers to all the questions that are in your mind. Brief answers are given in the solutions at the end of this book.

Group Exercise 'A'

This first Group Exercise consists of a number of short games, all won easily by one or other player. What you are asked to discover, is why the loser was so easily beaten. You may not agree with all our comments — that's excellent, for it shows that you are beginning to have ideas of your own — but you should make sure you understand the comments that are made. You may consider the games are very one-sided. They are! Just because of this they highlight errors constantly made in less one-sided games.

Criticize the following games, pointing out where either side could do better. There are some obvious errors, and others which are rather more hidden.

Game 'A': 1 e4 e5 2 Nf3 d6 3 Bc4 a6 4 d4 b5 5 Bb3 f6 6 d×e5 f×e5 7 Qd5 Ra7 8 Qf7 mate.

Game 'B': 1 e4 e5 2 Nf3 Qf6 3 Nc3 Bb4 4 Nd5 Qd6 5 c3 Bc5 6 d4 e×d4 7 Bf4 Qc6 8 Bb5 Q×b5 9 N×c7+ Kd8 10 N×b5 with a winning advantage.

Game 'C': 1 e4 e5 2 Nf3 Bd6 3 Bc4 Nh6 4 d4 e×d4 5 N×d4 0–0 6 B×h6 g×h6 7 Nf5 Bc5 8 Qg4+ Kh8 9 Qg7 mate.

Game 'D': 1 e4 e5 2 Bc4 Nf6 3 d3 d5 4 Bb5+ c6 5 Ba4 d×e4 6 d×e4 Q×d1+ 7 K×d1 N×e4 8 Be3 Na6 9 Nf3 Bc5 10 B×c5 Na×c5 11 Bb3 N×f2+ 12 Ke2 N×h1 with a big advantage.

Game 'E': 1 e4 e5 2 Nf3 Nc6 3 d4 d6 4 Bc4 Nge7 5 d×e5 N×e5 6 N×e5 d×e5 7 B×f7+ K×f7 8 Q×d8 with a winning advantage.

Game 'F': 1 d4 f5 2 Bg5 h6 3 Bh4 g5 4 Bg3 f4 5 e3 h5 6 Bd3 Rh6 7 Q×h5+ R×h5 8 Bg6 mate.

Game 'G': 1 e4 e5 2 Nf3 Nc6 3 Bc4 Nf6 4 d4 N×e4 5 d×e5 Bc5 6 Qd5 B×f2+ 7 Kf1 0–0 8 Q×e4 Bb6 9 Bd3 g6 10 Bg5 Qe8 11 Bf6 h6 12 Qf4 Kh7 13 Ng5+ Kg8 14 Qh4 h5 15 Q×h5 g×h5 16 Bh7 mate.

Game 'H': 1 e4 e5 2 Nc3 Nf6 3 f4 e×f4 4 e5 Qe7 5 Qe2 Ng8 6 Nf3 d6 7 Nd5 Qd7 8 d×e5 discovered check (i.e. by the queen which was hidden behind the pawn) Kd8 9 d×c7+ Q×c7 10 N×c7 with winning advantage.

CHAPTER SIX

Learning to Attack

6.1. The Weakest Point

In the starting position the pawn on f7 is only protected by the king. This makes it a natural target for attack and many openings and middle game plans are aimed at this weak point. In fact it is tempting to start an attack on it as soon as you have one or two

Fig. 30. Scholar's mate

pieces (e.g. a queen and a bishop) in play and not to bother developing the others. Such an attack can be dangerous – as we shall see it may result in mate – but it is wrong. As a rule *attacks only succeed when you have better development or better central position or both:* attacks made in a hurry without having built up such an advantage first get beaten back, and then the attacker finds he has lost a lot of time for nothing. We shall see how all this applies to attacks on f7; in studying attacks we shall also learn something about how to use (and how not to use!) the queen.

43

6.2. The Beginner's Way – Scholar's Mate

The quickest way of all to attack f7 is to bring the queen and bishop to bear on it. Consequently we see beginners' games like this: 1 e4 e5 2 Qh5 Nc6 (or d6) 3 Bc4 Nf6 4 Q×f7 mate (see Fig. 30). This is Scholar's Mate, which has won more games between beginners than any other manœuvre in chess. Indeed, some near-beginners, having lost to this manœuvre, meet 1 e4 with 1...e6 since now 2 Qh5 Nc6 3 Bc4, does not threaten anything. However, 1...e6, though not a bad move, is not a line of play to be attempted until a player has considerable knowledge of the game, and against it White will not continue 2 Qh5, but 2 d4, controlling the central squares, and opening lines for his bishops. More important, we should not be frightened of the natural 1...e5; we should learn to repel the attack. We saw in Chapter 5 how an early queen advance could be turned to advantage by the opponent, who gained time for development by attacking the queen. Let us apply our basic principles to meet Scholar's Mate – i.e. find out the immediate threat, and try to meet it with moves which develop our pieces and attack the centre.

Suppose, then, that you are Black, and your opponent opens 1 e4 e5 2 Qh5. The pawn on e5 is attacked and must be defended. Here are five ways – by Nc6, d6, Qf6, Qe7, and Bd6. You must not play 2...g6 attacking the queen, since White would reply 3 Q×e5+ followed by 4 Q×h8. You should be able to see that 2...Nc6 is the best move – a developing move which centralizes the knight. The only other sensible move is 2...d6. This is not bad, but it has two disadvantages in that it shuts in the king's bishop, and loses time in some variations where it can be played advantageously to d5 in one move (cf. section 6.3). The moves of the knights to c6 and f6 early in the game are nearly always good, because c6 is usually the best square for a knight, and it is always good to play moves you know you will want to play sooner or later. So 2 Qh5 Nc6 and now 3 Bc4 threatening 4 Q×f7 mate. Black could defend by 3...Qe7 or 3...Qf6 but these obstruct his own pieces, so better is 3...g6 and if White wants to continue his attack on the pawn on f7 he must play 4 Qf3, again threatening 5 Q×f7 mate. Black replies 4...Nf6 and White must find a new way of mounting his attack. If he plays 5 d3, hoping to attack the black N on f6 with his queen's bishop, there is no immediate threat, and Black moves over to the attack himself with 5...Nd4. If White then plays 6 Qg3 Black replies 6...N×c2+ and 7...N×a1. If White plays 6 Qe3, Black has 6...N×c2+ and 7...N×e3. White is compelled to play 6 Qd1, and after 6...Bg7 we see that Black has three pieces developed and White only one.

In place of 5 d3, White might continue his attack on the f7 with 5 Qb3, threatening 6 B×f7+. Black replies 5...Qe7 — his bishop has an outlet on g7 — and White might play 6 Nc3, protecting his e5 and hoping to attack with 7 Nd5. Black has the upper hand now, however, and attacks with 6...Nd4. White replies 7 Qa4, since 7 Qa3 QN×c2+ would lose the queen. Black moves 7...c6 stopping White's Nd5, and threatening to win a piece by 8...b5. White is now in terrible trouble and has nothing better than 8 Bb3, to which Black replies 8...a5 actually threatening to win the queen for a bishop by 9...b5 10 Qa3 Qd8.

The force of the threat justifies the pawn advance instead of a normal developing move — you should be warned, however, that it takes a very strong player to spot the right occasion for such a manœuvre, and it is only White's previous bad play that has made it possible here. 9 Qc4 (the only way to escape!) b5 10 Qd3 (10 Qf1 is an inglorious end to White's hopes!) a4 11 B×a4 (trying to get something for his lost piece) b×a4 12 Nf3 (White realizes that he must develop something!) Ba6 13 Qe3 N×c2+ and the queen is lost (see Fig. 31). White, of course, need not have come to grief as badly as this, but you will find that if Black plays properly he will always beat back the attack and at least get ahead in development.

Fig. 31. It didn't work this time!

6.3. Variations on the Theme

Instead of playing 4 Qf3 after 3...g6 White might try 4 Qg4 or 4 Qh3. These moves carry no immediate threats, and Black is free to carry out his own plans. 4...Nf6 is a reasonable move, developing and centralizing a piece, but Black has an even stronger reply. The queen is now on the same diagonal as the black queen's bishop, and Black can play 4...d5 attacking both queen and bishop with one move. If White now plays 5 exd5, or 5 Bxd5, Black replies 5...Bxg4, or 5...Bxh3; if White moves the queen out of danger, Black replies 5...dxc4 winning a piece.

If instead of 3 Bc4 White tries 3 Nf3, intending to follow up either with 4 Nxe5 or 4 Ng5, Black ignores the threat to his e5 pawn and plays 4...Nf6 continuing to harry the queen.

An attempt to alter the order of moves by playing 2 Bc4, or 2 Qf3, in place of 2 Qh5, is simply met by 2...Nf6 since the e5 pawn is no longer under fire.

Play a number of games with a player of equal experience taking White and Black alternately, and you will soon find that there is nothing to fear in the Scholar's Mate attack, and that, in this form, the early attack by queen and bishop is not good.

6.4. A More Successful Attack

Suppose the game begins 1 e4 e5 2 Nf3 d6 3 Bc4 Bg4. This is rather inferior play by Black, though not positively bad. 2...d6 is weaker than 2...Nc6 and 3...Nf6 is better than 3...Bg4 since it is usually better to develop the kingside pieces quickly and get castled. White now plays 4 h3. This is often a good move when it attacks a piece on g4, since that piece is normally compelled to move again, and no time has been lost by the pawn move. As a rule, you should not play it just to stop a piece going there, as this does lose time. If Black plays 4...Bxf3 White can safely play 5 Qxf3. This time the queen has come out without loss of time — it is Black who has lost two moves developing and exchanging his bishop, and is now behind in development. Further, the queen is not subject to attack by the dangerous white-squared bishop which has just been exchanged. Finally, White has an immediate threat of 6 Qxf7 mate. Black can no longer play 5...Nf6 safely, since 6 Qb3 threatens both 7 Bxf7+ Ke7 8Qe6 mate, and 7 Qxb7 (a frequent disadvantage of the too early development of the queen's bishop which should be remembered). If Black replies to 6 Qb3 with 6...Qd7 7 Qxb7 Qc6 (to prevent loss of the queen's rook) 8 Bb5 wins the queen. Black must play 5...Qd7 but after 6 d3 Nc6 7 Be3 White is ahead in development, and the queen is well placed on f3.

Try to see why the queen sortie is better here than in the Scholar's Mate attack. The queen is developed without loss of time; it cannot be so easily harried after the exchange of the black bishop; and the old threat of Nd4 is readily met by 7 Be3, followed, if necessary, by the exchange of this piece for the black knight. Even Black's stock developing move ...Nf6 proves unsound in this case, since White's lead in development enables him to play 6 Qb3 effectively − a move which had proved unsound in the Scholar's Mate variation. This underlines the fact that sensible-looking moves cannot always be regarded as good without examination to ensure that there are no special snags in the particular position concerned.

6.5. Another Way to Attack the Pawn on f7

We can also attack the pawn on f7 with knight and bishop by playing our bishop to c4 and king's knight to g5. An early attack like this usually turns out badly because it gets beaten back with loss of time; this is especially true when Black can meet it without bother by castling. Look at this example of what can happen.

1 e4 e5 2 Nf3 Nc6 3 Bc4 Bc5 4 d3 Nf6 5 Ng5? 0–0. Now 6 Bxf7+ Rxf7 7 Nxf7 Kxf7 hoping to expose Black's king is not good. White would lose 1 unit and leave Black with a clear lead in development. Also he would have exchanged his king's bishop − the very piece which is best fitted to attack the black king along the empty white-coloured squares. So the game might go 6 Nc3 d6 7 0–0 Bg4 and now White is in trouble due to being behind in development. If he replies 8 Qd2 (8 Qe1 is worse, leaving the pawn on c2 unprotected, and inviting a threat to queen and rook by Nd4 and Nxc2) h6 9 Nf3 (9 Nh3 Bxh3 10 gxh3 Nd4 is no better) Bxf3 10 gxf3

Nd4 (threatening N×f3+ and N×d2) 11 Kg2 Nh5 12 Rg1 Nf4+ 13 Kf1 N×f3 14 Qd1 N×g1 15 K×g1 Qg5+ 16 Kf1 Qg2+ 17 Ke1 Q×f2 mate (Fig. 32). If, on the other hand, he replies 8 Nf3 Nd4 9 Bg5 B×f3 10 g×f3 Qd7! (a useful manœuvre to attack the exposed king when the opposing bishop prevents the queen operating along its original diagonal as in the previous variation) 11 B×f6 Qh3! 12 Bg5 N×f3+ 13 Kh1 (White can only avoid mate by 13 Q×f3 Q×f3) Q×h2 mate.

When we looked at attacks on the pawn at f7 by queen and bishop we saw that there were cases when they were justified; this is also true of these knight and bishop attacks. Consider the game 1 e4 e5 2 Nf3 Nc6 3 Bc4 Nf6 4 Nc3 d6. Black's fourth move is weak; he should have played 4...Bc5 or, better still, 4...N×e4 (5 N×e4 d5). White replies 5 Ng5 attacking the weak f7, and Black can only defend it with 5...d5 — now it is apparent why his fourth move was unsatisfactory. White plays 6 e×d5 and emerges from the opening with an extra pawn and the better game.

A second example is 1 e4 e5 2 Nf3 Nc6 3 Bc4 Bc5 4 Nc3 Ne7 (another thoroughly bad move) 5 Ng5 0–0 6 Qh5. Suddenly the game is almost over! Black must stop 7 Q×h7 mate and plays 6...h6 but after 7 N×f7 Black has nothing better than 7...R×f7 8 Q×f7+ leaving White with a winning advantage in material. Still worse would be 7...Qe8 8 N×h6+ (double check by knight and bishop, which is even better than 8 Nd6, winning the queen) Kh7 or Kh8 9 Nf7+ (by the queen) Kg8 10 Qh8 mate (Fig. 33).

Fig. 32. A white 'attack' that didn't come off . . .

Fig. 33. . . . and one that did!

In these cases, weak play by the opponent allowed the early attack to be made without loss of time: without such weak play, an attack like this should not succeed.

A very interesting example of the N and B attack comes in the well-known 'Two Knights' Defence' in the following way. 1 e4 e5 2 Nf3 Nc6 3 Bc4 Nf6 4 Ng5. Here Black cannot castle and it is not obvious how he should defend. His best move is 4...d5! (we use an exclamation mark ! for a good move, and a query ? for a bad move). If you are Black, then the central advance of d5 is nearly always good if you can play it safely (often you are not able to do so): so watch for a chance to get in when you can. Here White has gone against basic opening principles by attacking from an undeveloped position, without Black having made a weak move to justify it: so it is not surprising that Black should have a powerful reply. Chess makes sense! This position is too complicated to examine further here but is discussed in Volume Two, Chapter 7: Black has a satisfactory game.

Many openings are based on the idea of attack, sooner or later, on f7 as we shall see in Volume Two. In some of these White gives up pawns (or even pieces) to get a rapid development; these are the gambit openings and have led to some of the most beautiful attacking games on record.

6.6. Sometimes the Queen is Deadly

We saw in section 6.4 that it is not always bad to bring the queen out early. Here is another situation in which it pays to use the queen early on.

Remove White's f2 and g2 pawns and Black's e7 pawn. Black to move could play 1...Qh4 mate. This is due to the uncastled king having no protection along the diagonal. You should always watch for a chance of a sudden raid by the queen when this diagonal is open. Look at these examples to see what can happen.

A game starts 1 f4 e5 (Black sacrificing a pawn for speedy development – 'From's Gambit') 2 fxe5 d6 (2...Qh4+ would be met simply by 3 g3) 3 exd6 Bxd6 4 Nc3 (Nf3 is much better) Qh4+ 5 g3 Bxg3+ 6 hxg3 Qxg3 mate. Black can even sacrifice his queen at the fifth move by 5...Qxg3+ 6 hxg3 Bxg3 mate.

Our next example often occurs in play. 1 e4 e5 2 Nf3 f6. This is a poor move — it fails to develop a black piece; it takes away the square f6 from the knight; and it opens up the diagonal that leads to the black king. 2...f6 is, in fact, so weak that White can afford to give up a piece to mount a winning attack. He plays 3 Ne5 fxe5 (better is 3...Qe7 4 Nf3 Qxe4+ 5 Be2, but White is better placed with two pieces developed, and Black's queen is in possible danger on the e-file, as in Exercise 11) 4 Qh5+ Ke7 (if 4...g6 5 Qxe5+ and 6 Qxh8) 5 Qxe5+ Kf7 6 Bc4+ Kg6 7 Qf5+ Kh6 8 d4+ (this check by the queen's bishop, previously masked behind d4, is called a discovered check — see Vol. Two, Chap. 1) g5 9 h4. At last Black is not in check, but it is a short-lived respite. If Black plays 9...Bb4+ 10 c3, and Black must move his bishop. He might play 10...Be7 to prevent 11 Bxg5+ and 12 Bxd8. White would then finish the game with 11 hxg5+ (this is a double check by pawn and rook and the king must move) Kg7 12 Qf7 mate.

But remember that it is usually bad to bring the queen out early. The two situations when it is good are these: (*a*) When it can find a safe square from which it can't be chased away (6.4 showed a case of this); (*b*) where you can see that it leads to an immediate advantage.

6.7. Mating Attacks

In this section we give some examples of mating attacks. You will see that in each case the attacker can bring more pieces against the king than the defender can bring to rescue it. This is true for

Fig. 34. White to play

Fig. 35. White to play

most successful attacks; big armies beat small ones as a rule.

In Fig. 34, won by Greco, the seventeenth-century player, White has sacrificed a knight to open up the king position, and Black's pieces, being undeveloped, are not available for immediate defence. White breaks down the final barrier by 1 R×h7+ K×h7 2 Qh5 mate. You will find that this idea of sacrificing to open the rook file on the enemy king, and then mating because he cannot escape to the knight file, often occurs in play. This point about the rook file is that there is nowhere to go on the other side of it, so you only have to block escape to the knight file. You will see the same idea in some of the examples of Exercise 12.

In Fig. 35, Black's king is caught in the middle of the board, and White's pieces are massed in attack. Black has just played . . .b5 hoping to drive the queen away, and White would reply 1 Qe6+, if the black knight did not stand on d8. An 'if' like this should always make you think − play 1 R×d8+ and the 'if' disappears! So 1 R×d8+ R×d8 2 Qe6+ Kf8. Now what? 3 R×d8+ Be8 gives you an advantage − but when you have seen a good move always have a look round for a better one and here there is one: 3 Nd7 double check and mate.

Figure 36 gives a position won by Dr. Max Euwe (world champion 1935-37) against Loman at Rotterdam in 1933. Dr. Euwe (White) has already sacrificed a knight to open the rook's file for attack against the king: can you see how he now forces mate? 1 Qh7+ Kf1 is no good − but he finds the clever sacrifice 1 Qh8+ B×h8 2 R×h8 mate.

Fig. 36. White to play

Fig. 37. Black to play

In Fig. 37, Black has no immediate check, but he can play 1...Bf3 threatening 2...Q×g2 mate. The bishop cannot be taken by the pawn, since that would leave the king in check by the queen. White must either give up queen for bishop, or play 2 g3. Black plays 2...Qg4 3 Nd2 Qh3 threatening mate at g2. After 4 N×f3 e×f3 the mating threat can only be parried by giving up his queen, and Black has an easy win with his extra material.

It is worth comparing the mates from Figs. 36 and 37, as they have something in common. In each case, all the defender's pawns round his king are on squares of one colour — in Fig. 36, Black's two pawns are on white squares, whilst in Fig. 37, White's three pawns are all on black squares after 1...Bf3 2 g3. When this happens, *you attack on squares of the other colour.* Then your opponent's pawns don't help the defence — they just get in his own way: they block squares to which the king could escape and they stop other pieces coming to help him. Look out for positions like this in Exercise 12.

There are many standard mating patterns, based on the position of the pawns in front of a castled king, and we shall consider these systematically in Vol. 2, Chap. 5; in the meantime, don't be frightened of castling because so many mates seem to be directed at the castled king — this is because castling occurs in a very high percentage of games. An attacking player is usually delighted when he can persuade his opponent to leave his king in the middle of the back rank, where it is even more exposed to attack (cf. Fig. 35).

Exercise 12

This exercise gives a number of positions in which sufficient pieces are massed against the king to force early mate. A number illustrate the ideas already illustrated in this chapter, others introduce new ideas for forcing mate. The mates may not all begin with checks or sacrifices of material.

1. White can force mate in two moves.
2. White can force mate in two moves.
3. White can force mate in three moves.
4. White plays a move after which Black cannot avoid mate.
5. Black has just played ...Rae8. White can now mate quickly.
6. White's king has no move because of the black bishop on f5. Black finds a surprising way of opening up the white king-position and mating quickly.

7. White can force mate in a few moves.
8. White has a move which threatens a mate that can only be stopped in one way, when White is able to threaten a second mate which cannot be parried. (N.B. Do not look for a sacrifice this time.)
9. Both kings are open to attack, but it is Black's move, and he gets there first. Black mates in three moves, and the second one is a sacrifice.
10. Black is well behind in development, and his king is open to attack. White threatens mate, and Black can only stave it off for a few moves.
11. Both kings are a little exposed, though White's looks more vulnerable. White must act quickly. He can mate in four moves.

Position 12.1

Position 12.2

Position 12.3

Position 12.4

Position 12.5

Position 12.6

Position 12.7

Position 12.8

Position 12.9

12. White has sacrificed a knight, but opened up Black's king-position. Black has just played . . .Rf8 but White ignores the threat to his queen, and forces mate in three moves in brilliant fashion.

Position 12.10

Position 12.11

Position 12.12

6.8. Don't Miss Your Chances!

Most of us can find a winning line when we know one is there — as, for example, in the exercises in this book; but can you find a win when the same position comes up in play? Your opponent certainly is not going to tell you that there is one.

This is much harder; to succeed you must learn to recognize the signs which make a position say to a good player, 'You ought to be able to win something here.' This will help you in two ways: to see when you have a chance to win something and to learn what kind of positions you should try to get. Here are some of the 'signs'.

(*a*) *Badly Placed Enemy Pieces*

If you see an enemy piece that is not well enough protected or has got itself trapped in an awkward position, see if you can win it. Always look carefully at your opponent's last move with this in mind.

(*b*) *Better Development*

This may take several forms.

(i) You may have more pieces in play than your opponent.

(ii) You may have more room for manœuvre.

(iii) You may have got your pieces working together better and directed better against the really important points in the position.

(You will often get (ii) and (iii) if your pieces have more control of the centre.)

The effect of better development is that you can bring more pieces to bear on a target than your opponent can. If the target is the king, you may be able to give mate; if it is another piece or a pawn, to win it.

(c) Better Pawn Position

We can only say a little about this here — it is too difficult a subject to try to do more at this stage, but it is too important to miss out altogether.

As you know, pawns cannot retreat; therefore if you move your pawns to bad positions you cannot get them back again, so there is something permanent about a bad (or good) pawn position. Also, pawns form a very good defence barrier because no one wants to have to give a piece to take a pawn. So if the enemy has a bad pawn position in front of his king this is usually a good sign for the attack.

Later on (Vol. 2, Chap. 5) we shall study closely good and bad pawn positions in front of the king: we have seen a few examples already. Generally speaking, if the pawn position has been broken up — by exchange of some of the pawns or by their having been advanced away from the king — this is a sign that a useful attack may be possible. We have also seen that to have all the pawns on squares of one colour is bad.

Broken-up or ragged pawn positions elsewhere on the board are also bad; but it is too early to study these yet.

In the following revision exercise, there is always some clear-cut method of gaining an advantage. Try to find out how to do it, and see why it was possible. In each case the opponent's previous move is given. When you have solved the problem, see if you can find a better move for the losing player. Sometimes you will find that all his troubles arose from one careless move — the one given — and all would have been well for him had he not made that move. In other examples his position is difficult, but he could have found a saving move, or at least one that postponed disaster for many more moves. In others, the position is so hopeless, with king exposed to attack, or pieces ill-developed or congested, that there is no saving clause. Trying to find out which of these is true will help to develop both your powers of analysis and your chess judgement.

Revision Exercises

In each position, find the play that leads to greatest advantage. Also, suggest improved play for the opponent on his last move — e.g., in position 1 you must decide what would be the best move, if any, in place of 1 Kh1. Sometimes no improvement is possible.

R1.   White's last move was 1 Kh1 out of check. Black to move.
R2.   White's last move was 1 N(c3)d5. Black to move.
R3.   Black's last move was 1...N(b8)a6. White to move.
R4.   Black's last move was 1...N(f6)d5. White to move.
R5.   Black's last move was 1...R8d4. White to move.
R6.   White's last move was 1 R1d2. Black to move.
R7.   White has exchanged twice on e5, Black's last move being 1...dxe5. White to move.
R8.   White's last move was 1 B(e2)b5. Black to move.
R9.   Black's last move was 1...N(f6)xg4. White to move.
R10.   Black's last move was 1...N(c6)e7. White to move.
R11.   White's last move was 1 R2c7. Black to move.
R12.   Black's last move was 1...(f7)f5. White to move.
R13.   Black's last move was 1...K(h8)h7. White to move.
R.14. White's last move was 1 K(g1)h1 out of check. Black to move.
R15.   Black's last move was 1...a6. White to move.
R16.   White's last move was 1 B(b3)xd5. Black to move.
R17.   White's last move was 1 b5. Black to move.
R18.   Black's last move was 1...Ka8. White to move.

Position R1

Position R2

Position R3

Position R4

Position R5

Position R6

Position R7

Position R8

Position R9

Position R10

Position R11

Position R12

Position R13

Position R14

Position R15

Position R16

Position R17

Position R18

R19. Black's last move was 1...K(b8)c8. White to move.

Position R19

CHAPTER SEVEN

Finishing the Game

7.1. Important Mates

Many games come down in the end to king and queen against lone king or king and rook against king; you must therefore know how to win these endings from any position on the board.

7.2. Mate with King and Queen

Your plan here is quite straightforward; you use your king and queen to drive the enemy to the edge of the board. Your opponent will try to keep his king in the centre but he cannot succeed if you play properly.

Fig 38

How should White play in the position of Fig. 38? A series of checks is useless, e.g. 1 Qa5+ Kd4 2 Qd2+ Ke5 3 Qg5+ Kd4 4 Qg4+ Kd5 and White is getting nowhere. Instead you must use the queen to confine the black king and then bring your own king up to help. Here is one way. 1 Qc3 (as near as we dare to go: if the queen went to d4 or e5, Black would take it) Ke4 (keeping in the centre) 2 Kg2 Kd5 3 Kf3 Kd6 (now he must leave the centre) 4 Ke4 (better than 4 Qc4 when Black returns to the centre by Ke5) Ke6 5 Qc6+ Ke7 6 Kf5 Kd8 (he could stay off the back rank for one more move by 6...Kf7 7 Qd7+ Kf8 8 Kf6 Kg8 9 Qg7 mate but he sets a last trap for White instead). Now White must be careful: just after you have driven the king to the back rank is the dangerous moment. The natural move 7 Ke6 is wrong. Why? Look back to Fig. 16 if you do not know. Instead, play 7 Qb7 Ke8 8 Ke6 and mate next move.

7.3. Mate with King and Rook

Here again the principles are clear-cut. You must drive the enemy king to the side of the board, place your own king opposite to him to stop him escaping and give mate with the rook. For example, put the white king on f6 and his rook on d3 and the black king on h6; Rh3 is mate.

Fig. 39   Fig. 40

In driving the king back, we use two main ideas, 'reducing the rectangle' and the 'waiting move'.

Figure 39 shows a typical position in the ending. The black king is confined to the marked rectangle by the rook, which is protected by the white king. If it is Black's move he might play 1...Kc6; then 2 Rd5 reduces the rectangle by three squares; or if 1...Kb5 2 Kd5 Kb6 3 Rc4 again reducing the rectangle; you can see how in this way the king is driven back.

Suppose instead it was White's move: then we play 1 Ke5 and Black might reply 1...Kc6. We could reduce the rectangle by 2 Rd5 but there is another way of playing which shows the second idea in these endings. We could play 2 Rc4+. Now if Black plays 2...Kb5 3 Kd5 and we have cut a file off the rectangle: but he could play 2...Kd7 reaching Fig. 40.

In this position, if it were Black's move, he would either have to move to the back rank when the white king would follow up and prevent his escape, e.g. 1...Kd8 2 Ke6 Ke8 3 Rc8 mate, or else play 1...Ke7 and then White could drive him back with 2 Rc7+ and mate soon follows. But it is not Black's move — it is White's move; so White makes a *waiting move* which makes no real change in the position but passes the responsibility for moving over to Black.

To do this, White plays his rook somewhere on the c-file where it is still safe, e.g. 1 Rc1. Black must move: if 1...Kd8 or Ke8 2 Ke6 and if 1...Ke7 2 Rc7+.

Now go back to Fig. 38 but replace the white queen by a white rook. The win will take longer but cannot be stopped: we shall see how the ideas of reducing the rectangle and the waiting move are used in reaching it. Play might go 1 Ra4 (preventing the king from moving to the central squares on Black's fifth rank) Ke5 2 Kg2 Kd5 3 Kf3 Ke5 4 Re4+ Kd5 5 Ke3 (now Black is confined to the rectangle at the top left-hand corner of the diagram) Kc5 6 Rd4 (White can also play 6 Re5+ Kc4 7 Rh5 — the waiting move — Kc3 8 Rc5+ Kb4 9 Kd4 etc.) Kc6 7 Ke4 Kc5 8 Ke5 Kc6 9 Rc4+ Kb5 (or 9...Kd7 as in Fig. 40) 10 Kd5 Kb6 11 Rb4+ (or 11 Rc5, reducing the rectangle) Kc7 (or 11...Ka5 12 Kc5) 12 Rb1 (the waiting move) Kd7 13 Rb7+ Kc8 14 Rf7 Kd8 (or 14...Kb8 15 Kc6 Ka8 16 Rf8+ Ka7 17 Rh8 — the waiting move — Ka6 18 Ra8 mate) 15 Kd6 Ke8 (or 15...Kc8 16 Rh7 — waiting move — Kb8 17 Kc6 Ka8 18 Kb6 Kb8 19 Rh8 mate) 16 Rf1 (a waiting move) Kd8 17 Rf8 mate.

This can be short-cut slightly, but these variations show the general principles clearly, and should be studied closely.

You should set up king and queen or rook in various positions and practise until you can be sure of giving mate within fifteen moves with the queen and within thirty moves with the rook.

7.4. Refinement of the Forsyth Notation

In positions where few pieces are on the board, it is often possible to abbreviate the recorded position. Instead of Fig. 38 being recorded as '8; 8; 8; 3k4; 8; 8; 8; Q6K. White to move', it may be short-cut as '24; 3k4; 24; Q6K. White to move', where the '24' represents three ranks, each of eight vacant squares, in each case. This short-cut is useful in recording positions with few pieces left.

Exercise 13

1. White can mate in three moves.
2. White can mate in three moves. Give two variations, according to Black's reply to White's first move.
3. Black can mate in five moves.
4. How should White play?
5. Black can mate in three moves.
6. White can mate in seven moves.
7. White to move. Get a friend to take the black side and try to find the moves with the king that make it most difficult for you to mate him. Write down your moves as you make them, and when you have successfully mated him, reverse colours, and see if he can mate you in fewer moves! There are many solutions, one of which is given in the solutions at the back of the book, but you need only refer to this if you have found difficulty in mating in less than twenty moves.

Position 13.1

Position 13.2

Position13.3

Position 13.4

Position 13.5

Position 13.6

Position 13.7

7.5. Getting an Extra Queen

Suppose you are left with one piece and your opponent has none and you each have a few pawns. You can almost always use your extra piece to win some of his pawns, after which you force one of your pawns through to a queen with which you can mate him.

Fig. 41. White to play

In Fig. 41, White cannot win using the knight alone, since the black king can support the pawn from b7 or a7. White must bring up his king in support. Play can continue 1 Kd4 Kb7 2 Kc5 Kc7 3 Nc3 Kb7 4 Nd5 Ka2 5 Kc6 Kb8 6 Kb6 Ka8 7 K×a6 Kb8 8 Kb6 Ka8 9 Nc7+ Kb8 10 a6 Kc8 11 a7 Kd7 12 a8(Q), and the rest is easy. After 12...Ke7 13 Qf3 Kd6 White can mate in three more moves. Can you find out how?

Now add a black pawn at Black's h7 in Fig. 41. This time White must be more careful. If he plays 1 Kf4 Kc7 2 Kg5 Kc6 3 Nd4+ (otherwise 3...Kb5 and 4...K×a5) Kc5 4 Nb3+ Kb4 5 N-moves, K×a5; and the game is drawn, since White has lost his only pawn, and cannot mate with king and knight alone. White's plan must be to try and force a king-entry which will win the black a6 pawn, and shepherd his own to promotion, whilst using his knight to prevent the black h7 pawn from promoting.

Play could proceed 1 Kd4 h5 2 Nf4 h4 3 Kc5 Kc7 4 Nh3 compelling Black to make a decision as to whether he will try to defend his a6, or stake everything on an attempt to promote his h4. In the former case, there follows 4...Kb7 5 Kd6 Kb8 6 Kc6 Ka2 7 Kc7 Ka8 8 Kb6 Kb8 9 K×a6 Ka8 10 Kb6 Kb8 11 a6 Ka8 and now White must *not* play the natural move 12 a7. Why? Instead he should play, 12 Nf4 h3 13 a7 (Is 13 N×h3 a good alternative?) h2 14 Nd5 h1(Q) 15 Nc7 mate.

Should Black decide to stake everything on counter-attack he would choose 4...Kd7 5 Kb6 Ke6 6 K×a6 Kf5 7 Kb5 Kg4 8 a6 K×h3 9 a7 and now Black's best moves are 9...Kg3 or 9...Kh2. If 9...Kg3 10 a8(Q) h3 11 Qh1, after which we have a standard — and important — way of winning, by sitting in front of the pawn until the king can be brought up to capture it before proceeding to the king and queen mate. If 9...Kh2 10 a8(Q) h3 11 Qf3 Kg1 12 Q×h3, and wins.

There is a good way of working out the end-game chances after 4...Kd7 by 'counting' moves. We will explain this in section 8.7.

This example was not an easy one, largely because White had only one pawn left. The win is usually much simpler if there are a number of pawns on each side. Here is an example that is puzzling — until you see the method.

Fig. 42. White to move

White has got an extra bishop — but what can he do with it? It cannot take any of the pawns and might seem useless, but you can use it to force a way through the king. First, a waiting move to make the black king retreat. 1 Bg2 Kd6 2 Ba8 (2 Ke4 Kc6 doesn't get the king through) Ke5 3 Bb7 Kd6 4 Ke4 Kc7 5 Kd5 (White can also win by 5 Ba6 Kb6 6 Bb5 Kc7 7 Kd5 Kb6 8 Ke6 Kc7 9 Kxf6, but once the king has penetrated, White can frequently win more rapidly by sacrificing the bishop whilst gaining extra pawns) Kxb7 (or 5...Kb6 6 Ke6) 6 Kxc5 Kc7 7 Kxb4 Kb6 8 c5+ Kc6 9 Kc4 Kc7 10 Kd5 Kd7 11 c6+ Kc7 12 b4 Kc8 13 Kd6 Kd8 14 c7+ Kc8 15 b5.

(Why not 15 Kc6? When the black king is at the side of the board, then it is essential to take care) Kb7 16 Kd7 Kb6 17 c8(Q) and wins in a few moves, provided he avoids stalemate.

These examples should help to remind you that if you have material advantage it is usually best to exchange pieces but to keep the pawns on. If you have a disadvantage in material then you do the opposite — exchange pawns and keep the pieces on.

7.6. The King Must Work in the End-game

You will have noticed in all our examples how hard the king works in the end-game. In the earlier parts of the game the king has to stay in safety or he will be mated; in the end-game he can safely come out and he must do so. One of the most common mistakes in the end-game, made even by quite strong players, is not making enough use of the king; *it is just as important to 'develop the king' in the ending as it is to develop the other pieces in the opening.*

Exercise 14

1. Is ...Kb2 a good move? Give reasons. How should Black plan this ending?
2. How should White play?
3. How should Black play?
4. How should Black play? What should the result be?
5. How should White play?

Group Exercise 'B'

In this position, White has an extra knight for two black pawns. The position should be carefully examined, and an analysis of possible variations made to determine whether White can force a win, or whether he must be content to draw.

Position 14.1

Position 14.2

Position 14.3

Position 14.4

Position 14.5

Group Exercise 'B'

CHAPTER EIGHT

Pawn Endings

8.1. The Solitary Pawn

How small an advantage is enough for victory? An advantage of one pawn is usually enough when each side has several pawns; however, when you have king and one pawn against a lone king the position may be won or drawn according to circumstances. You must know when this ending is a win and when it is a draw; then when you are wondering whether or not to make exchanges you will know whether you are heading for a win, a draw or a loss.

8.2. The Unstoppable Pawn

In all pawn endings the question is 'Can you promote a pawn?' If you can — without the opponent doing so as well — the game is won; if not, you cannot win.

Fig. 43

The simplest case is that in which a pawn seeks promotion

67

unaided by its king. Figure 43 shows a typical position. White to move would play 1 a5 Ke6 2 a6 Kd7 3 a7 Kc7 4 a8(Q) and wins. If Black has the first move, play proceeds 1...Ke4 2 a5 Kd5 3 a6 Kc6 4 a7 Kb7 5 a8(Q)+ K×Q; drawn. Clearly White to move wins because he requires only four moves to promote, whilst Black needs five moves to reach the queening square. This is an example of solving the problem by counting — a method of frequent application in such endings (see section 8.6).

In the case of the unprotected pawn on its own, there is another way of working things out. In Fig. 43, the pawn stands on its opponent's fifth rank. A square is drawn, 5 by 5, with the pawn at a corner furthest from the enemy back rank. Had the pawn stood at a6 — i.e., the opponent's third rank — the square would be 3 by 3. Now, *the pawn can only be stopped by Black if he can move into the square*. With Black to move in the diagram, he can move into the square by Ke6 or Ke5 or Ke4 and draw the game; but if White has the move, he plays 1 a5 and since the square is now reduced to 4 by 4, Black cannot enter it and White cannot be prevented from promotion. Don't forget that the pawn's initial double-move affects the calculation if the pawn is still on its second rank — in this case, White promotes in only five moves, and the square becomes a rectangle 7 by 6.

8.3. The Opposition

Place the white king on e4 and the black king on e6. If White has the move, he cannot force his king through to the black back rank. If 1 Kd4 Kd6 2 Kc4 Kc6 3 Kd3 Kd5 etc., and the black king can always oppose White's entry. Nor can White prevent the black king crossing to d1 or f1. If 1 Kd4 Kd6 2 Ke3 Ke5 3 Kd3 Kf4 4 Ke2 Ke4 5 Kf2 Kd3 6 Ke1 Ke3 7 Kf1 Kd2 8 Kf2 Kd1. Similarly, if it is Black's move, the white king cannot be prevented from reaching Black's back rank, e.g., 1...Kd6 2 Kf5 Ke7 3 Ke5, etc. White is said to have 'the opposition'. Note that *a player has the opposition when his opponent has the move*, and has to give way along a file, rank, or diagonal, and that the opposition occurs when the kings have one square between them.

In the above example, we saw the vertical opposition — i.e., opposition along a file. Horizontal opposition, in which one king cannot prevent the other king crossing a file, is also important. Place the white king on e4 once more, but place the black king on c4. If it is White's move, Black has the opposition, and cannot be prevented from crossing the queen's file.

Note how Black uses the opposition in the first variation. Whenever White moves to the king's file, Black takes up the opposition on the same file, and compels White to give way again. This technique is most important in king and pawn endings.

8.4. The Supported Pawn

Fig. 44

In Fig. 44, the added pawn does not affect the opposition. If Black is to move, White has the opposition, and wins by penetrating to d7 or f7 with his king, and helping his pawn to promote. 1... Kd6 2 Kf5 Ke7 3 Ke5 (regaining the opposition) Kd7 4 Kf6 Ke8 5 Ke6 Kf8 6 e4 Ke8 7 e5 Kf8 8 Kd7 Kf7 9 e6+, and goes on to promotion.

If White is to move, Black has the opposition, and this enables him to draw. 1 Kd4 Kd6 2 e4 Ke6 3 e5 Ke7 (best) 4 Kd5 Kd7 5 e6+ Ke7 6 Ke5 Ke8 (best) 7 Kd6 Kd8 8 e7+ Ke8 9 Ke6 stalemate. This ending has to be played accurately by both sides. If, for example, Black plays 6...Kd8 in this last variation, White wins with 7 Kd6 Ke8 8 e7 Kf7 9 Kd7, and wins. This is because Black is unable to take up the opposition by 7...Kd8. When forced to retreat, Black must *move back along the file of the pawn*, and not diagonally, which surrenders the opposition.

White, on the other hand, must not surrender the opposition in the first variation by advancing the pawn prematurely. If he plays 1...Kd6 2 Kf5 Ke7 3 e4 (in place of 3 Ke5), Black takes the opposition by 3...Kf7 and the game is drawn after 4 e5 Ke7 5 e6 Ke8 (best), etc.

The side with the pawn should aim to penetrate with the king rather than press on with the pawn.

Now place the white king on e1, the black king on e8 and a white pawn on e2. White with the move can gain the opposition by 1 Kd2 Kd7 2 Kd3 Kd6 3 Ke4 Ke6 4 e3 (keeping this move in reserve has ensured White the opposition). Now Black must give ground by 4...Kf6 5 Kd5 Ke7 6 Ke5 (and not 6 e4 which surrenders the opposition), and goes on to win.

Black, having the move, can himself gain the opposition. 1... Ke7 2 Kd2 Kd6 3 Kd3 (a pawn move allows 3...Ke5 with the opposition) Kd5 (taking the opposition − 3...Ke5 4 Ke3 hands the opposition to White and loses) 4 Ke3 Ke5 and draws.

8.5. The Rook's Pawn

In many endings, the rook's pawn provides an exception to the general rule. Place White's king on h6, a white pawn on h5, and the black king on h8. White, with or without the opposition, can only draw. If 1...Kg8 2 Kg6 Kh8 3 h6 Kg8 4 h7+ Kh8 5 Kh6 stalemate. After Black has moved one square to the side, White normally takes advantage by moving one square diagonally forward in the opposite direction, but this cannot be done when he is already at the edge of the board.

Even if the defending king cannot reach g8 and h8, the ending will still be drawn if he is close enough. Transfer the black king to f7. White can either play 1 Kg5 when 1...Kg7 draws; or 1 Kh7 Kf8 2 h6 Kf7 3 Kh8 Kf8 4 h7 Kf7 stalemate. If in this line White plays 2 Kh8 Kf7 3 Kh7 Kf8 4 Kg6 Kg8 draws. There is no way through. Now put the black king on e6. White to move wins by 1 Kg7 but Black to move can draw with 1...Kf7.

8.6. Counting

Many endings come down to a race to queen a pawn. When this is so, instead of saying 'I do this, then he does that, then I do this. . .', you can often work out who will queen first just by counting how many moves each player will take. This method is quicker and much less confusing; of course you must be careful to see that there is no trick in the positions which throws the count out.

Turn back to Fig. 41, with the black pawn added at h7 and look at the position after 1 Kd4 h5 2 Nf4 h4 3 Kc5 Kc7 4 Nh3 Kd7. If White wants to win he has to accept a 'race to queen' between his pawn and the h4 pawn. To see if he can afford to risk this, he makes a count. After 4...Kd7 he can promote in six moves — two to take the pawn, one to move the king off the rook's file and three with the pawn. Black will take four moves to capture the knight; one to move off the file and his sixth move will take his pawn to h3. So provided White knows how to win with queen against pawn he can go in for the race without further calculation.

You can see that these races will often end up a queen v. pawn battle; we shall now find out when and how the queen wins against a pawn.

8.7. Queen against Pawn

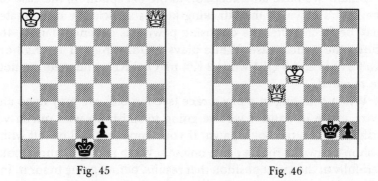

Fig. 45   Fig. 46

In Fig. 45, Black has a pawn on the seventh rank supported by his king. Can White, with the move, prevent the pawn queening and so win? To do so, White must force the black king to e1 and then bring up his own king to win the pawn. Play proceeds 1 Qd4+ Kc2 2 Qe3 Kd1 3 Qd3+ Ke1. White now moves his king towards the pawn with 4 Kb7. Play might go on 4...Kf2 5 Qd2 Kf1 (or 5...Kf3 6 Qe1) 6 Qf4+ Kg2 7 Qe3 Kf1 8 Qf3+ Ke1 9 Kc6, the manoeuvre being repeated until the white king reaches e3 or d3 when the queen captures the pawn, and mate soon follows.

You will not be very surprised to find that the rook's pawn is an exceptional case. Suppose Black has a pawn on h2, and White reaches the standard position with Black's king on g1, playing Qg3+. After ...Kh1, White cannot move his king towards the pawn, since stalemate would result, and the position cannot be won if the white king is far removed from the pawn.

You probably will be surprised however to find that the bishop's pawn is also exceptional. With the black pawn on c2, and king on b1, White's Qb3+ is again met by 1...Ka1! since the reply Qxc2 is again stalemate.

It is, however, quite simple to win against any pawn which has not reached the seventh rank. Place White's king on h8 and his queen on a8, with Black's king on a2 and a pawn on a3. White plays 1 Qa4 Kb2 2 Qb4+ Ka2 3 Kg7 and Black loses the pawn. Similarly, no stalemate manoeuvre is available when the bishop's pawn is on the sixth rank.

Finally we have an 'exception to the exception' in the case of the rook's pawn. If the attacking king is sufficiently near, mate may be forced after the opposing pawn has queened. Figure 46 shows the critical case. White plays 1 Qd2+ Kg1 (if 1...Kg3 or Kh3 2 Qd5 and 3 Qh1 wins) 2 Kf4 h1(Q) 3 Kg3, and mate cannot be avoided.

When counting in a pawn race (section 8.6), we may need an extra move in hand if we are going to finish up with queen v. bishop's pawn or rook's pawn. If your opponent will be left with bishop's pawn or rook's pawn on the seventh rank, you must look carefully at the exact position that results, before going in for it. In some cases it will be won — e.g. there may be other pawns which prevent the stalemate manoeuvre, or you may get a position where the king can be brought up at leisure to win the pawn — but you cannot assume the win in the general position as you can with other pawns on the seventh rank. Once more, we see the subtlety and richness of the ending, even when there is hardly any material left.

8.8. Endings with more than One Pawn

With additional pawns on each side, an extra pawn is more likely to lead to a win. There is a possibility of a second pawn being won, and a move with another pawn may prevent a draw by stalemate or enable the opposition to be gained.

Fig. 47. White to play

Fig. 48. White to play

In Fig. 47, White's correct play is first to advance the pawns on the king's wing, where he has one more than Black and to force a 'passed pawn': this is a pawn with no enemy pawn to stop it queening. This passed pawn will result in Black's king (who must watch it) being forced back and White finally sacrifices the pawn, using the time Black has to waste in taking it to go over and capture pawns on the queen's wing. Finally, White will queen one of his own queen's side pawns. You should notice how White copies Black's pawn moves on the queen's wing until finally Black runs out of pawn moves and has to retreat his king.

1 f4 (always aim to advance the pawn which is unopposed by an enemy pawn) g6 2 g4 b6 (if the black king moves, White starts the advance of his own king) 3 b3 a6 4 a3 b5 5 b4 Ke6 6 Kd4 Kd6 7 f5 g×f5 8 g×f5 Ke7 9 Kc5 Kf6 10 Kb6 K×f5 11 K×a6 Ke5 12 K×b5, and wins easily.

If it were not for the extra pawn in Fig. 48, Black would have the

opposition, and White to move would lose, e.g. 1 Kg3 Ke4 or
1 Ke3 Kg4. The pawn on a2, however, makes all the difference.
White plays 1 a3 (gaining the opposition) Kg6 2 Kf4 Kf6 3 a4
(regaining the opposition) Ke6 (or 3...Kg6 4 Ke5 wins) 4 Kg5
wins. Note that 1 a4 would be insufficient, for after 1...Kg6 2 Kf4
Kf6 Black has the opposition, and White can only draw by 3 Ke3
Kf5 4 Kf3, etc.

This example shows the great importance of not advancing
pawns without good reason — such action here throws away
victory, and this is only one of many similar cases. The old advice,
'When in doubt move a pawn', is thoroughly bad. Pawn moves are
most important. Once made, such moves can never be recalled, so
that *every pawn-move made must be with good reason*. There are, of
course, occasions when pawns have to be moved forward as fast as
possible — e.g. in a race to promotion.

The other point illustrated by this example is the importance of
the opposition: White's extra a2 pawn, just by allowing White to
win the battle for the opposition, turned a loss into a win. Such
endings often occur in practice.

In the following exercise, try to make use of the ideas you have
met in this chapter.

Exercise 15

1. What is the result with (*a*) White to move; (*b*) Black to move? Give reasons.
2. What is the result with (*a*) White to move; (*b*) Black to move? Give reasons.
3. What is the result with (*a*) White to move; (*b*) Black to move? Give sufficient
   analysis to prove your decision.
4. What is the result with (*a*) White to move; (*b*) Black to move? Give reasons.
5. What is the result with (*a*) White to move; (*b*) Black to move? Give reasons.
6. What is the result with (*a*) White to move; (*b*) Black to move? Give reasons.
7. White to move. How does he win?
8. How should Black play, and with what result? Give reasons.
9. Can White win? Give a line of play.
10. Black to move. How should he play, and with what result?
11. Black to move. Without moving the pieces, use counting methods to decide
    whether White or Black promotes first.
12. Use counting methods to decide how many moves each side will take to promote,
    and then examine the position after promotion to decide what the result should be.

Position 15.1

Position 15.2

Position 15.3

Position 15.4

Position 15.5

Position 15.6

Position 15.7

Position 15.8

Position 15.9

Position 15.10

Position 15.11

Position 15.12

13. (*a*) White to move; (*b*) Black to move. What is the result in each case? Give reasons.
14. (*a*) White to move; (*b*) Black to move. What is the result now? Give reasons.
15. White to move. What is the result? Give an analysis.
16. White to move. What is the result? Give reasons.
17. White to move. What is the result? Give a careful analysis.

Position 15.13

Position 15.14

Position 15.15

Position 15.16

Position 15.17

8.9. The End-game Matters

The biggest mistake that the average player makes is to think that the end-game is dull and does not matter. It is quite as interesting and important as the opening or middle game and all the great players have been experts in the end-game and have studied it deeply. It is true that it is not so complicated as the middle game, but for just this reason it is possible to make very deep and subtle calculations in the ending and there is a very great difference between the ordinary player and the master in end-game play. When you play an opponent of equal strength you will find, as you get better, that you often come down to an end-game; if you learn to win when you have a small advantage and not to lose with a small disadvantage you will greatly improve your results. So try to learn to understand and enjoy the ending.

The following exercise gives some more examples which can be of importance in practical play. Where possible, these should be studied in small groups of players, each group trying to find White's winning method, and then tackling the next position, before coming together to compare and discuss results with the Instructor.

Group Exercise 'C'

In each case White has a winning line. Find it. Make sure that you have also found Black's best defence.
1. White to move.
2. White to move.
3. (*a*) White to move. (*b*) What difference does it make if Black's king is on h8?
4. White to move.

Position 1

Position 2

Position 3

Position 4

8.10. En Passant

There is still one chess-move which we have not previously introduced.

In Fig. 49, White has a pawn on c5, and Black has just played 1...b5 from b7. Now, apart from the option on the first move, pawns can only advance one square at a time. Had the double-move not been available, and Black had decided to move his pawn, he would have played 1...b6 and White would have replied 2 c×b6. In such positions, Black is not allowed to avoid capture by making his double-move and by-passing the white pawn, and White is able to reply 2 c×b6 'en passant', which means 'as it passes by'. The white c5 pawn goes to b6, just as though the black pawn had only moved one square forward, and the black pawn is removed from the board.

The en passant move — recorded 'c×b6 e.p.' (or simply c×b6) — can be made whenever one side has a pawn on the fifth rank and a hostile pawn on an adjoining file makes its double-move alongside it. It is not a compulsory capture, and it must be made *immediately* after the opposing double-move, and not left to a later date. Note that if Black had moved the pawn to b5 from b6 instead of from b7, the en passant move would not apply, since it is not operative after a single-move by a pawn.

In Fig. 49, the e.p. capture makes all the difference between victory and defeat. Work out why.

Fig. 49.

Fig. 50.

Fig. 50 shows a typical example of the e.p. move in the ending. White cannot win by 1 Kf5 Kd7 2 Kg6 K×d6 3 K×g7 Ke7 4 K×h6 Kf7 (cf. section 8.5). He plays 1 d7+ Kd8 2 Kd6! If Black had no g7, this would be stalemate, but now he must move this pawn.

2...g6 3 h×g6 h5 4 g7 h4 5 g8(Q)mate — this can easily be checked by counting, White taking three moves to promote whilst

Black can only make two moves to reach h4 in the meantime (cf. section 8.6). This is clearly no defence, so Black must try 2...g5. If White replies 3 Ke6, the black pawn goes on to promotion, and after 3 Ke6 K×d7 Black wins — work it out. White, however, is able to play 3 h×g6 e.p. and a similar count shows that he wins. Black's g7 pawn is called a 'backward pawn', i.e. one that is back behind the neighbouring pawns of its own colour and is liable to be captured by an enemy pawn if it advances. We can see in this ending that this can be a serious weakness since it allows one white pawn to control two black ones; and we also see that the en passant capture stops one from using the double move to escape from 'backward' positions.

8.11. How to Lose!

This may seem a strange heading — surely we should be explaining how to win. All the same, a word about losing is worth while.

Many people playing over games by experts are puzzled by the fact that mate rarely occurs but that instead either White or Black 'resigns'. Why is this? It is because the loser realized that his position was quite hopeless and that it was a waste of time to continue. *Resignation in chess is really a compliment to one's opponent.*

Look at Fig. 50. Black knows he is in a desperate position, but sees one last chance. Perhaps his opponent will not remember the e.p. move. So he replies to 1 d7+ with 1...Kd8 and after 2 Kd6 plays 2...g5; when White replies 3 h×g6 e.p. he sees that there is no more chance and resigns.

Do not start thinking about resigning as soon as you get into difficulties; think how to get out of them instead. Only resign when you are sure that you have no chance left; when it is quite clear that your opponent knows how to win and that there is no reasonable chance left of his blundering away his advantage. You will learn to judge when such a position has been reached as you get experience — and of course you would be quite justified in continuing against a weak player in positions which would be hopeless against a strong one. One of the signs of a good player is knowing when and when not to resign. Finally, resign pleasantly when you do have to do so; it happens to everyone! Turn your king on its side, thank your opponent when you say the fatal words 'I resign' and give him credit for his good play instead of grumbling about your own mistakes.

8.12. Volume Two

If you have mastered this volume, you should have started to play on the right lines — but you will very soon find you need to know more. When you really understand these eight chapters and can put what you have learnt into practice — get Volume Two.

Solutions to Examples

Exercise 1

1. The black bishop.
2. The white bishop and right-hand pawn.
3. None.
4. The white knight.
5. The black bishop and the pawn next to the white queen.
6. The two nearest white pawns.
7. The black pawn on the next square.
8. None.
9. The black queen and rook.
10. The central white pawn.

Exercise 2

1. The white pawn on the left of the diagram can move one square forward – this is its only move.
2. The central white pawn can capture the black rook (but not the bishop).
3. The white pawn on the right of the diagram can only move one square forward.
4. The black pawn on the left of the diagram can capture the white queen, or move one square forward down the diagram.
5. The most central black pawn has no move.
6. The black pawn on the right of the diagram can move either one square or two squares forward.

Exercise 3

1. 7 bxc3	2. 7...Ne4	3. 8 Qg4	4. 8...g6
5. 9 Nf3	6. 9...c5	7. 10 dxc5	8. 10...Nd7
9. 11 Bd3	10. 11...Nxd2	11. 12 Kxd2	12. 12...Nxc5
13. 13 Rhe1	14. 13...Bd7	15. 14 Re3	16. 14...Qc7

Exercise 4

1. Position 10: rnbqrlkl; pp3pbp; 2p2npl; 4p3; P1P5; 2N2NP1; 1P2PPBP; R1BQ1RK1. White to move.
2. Position 7: 8; 3k1p1p; 5B2; K3R3; 1p1n4; Q3br1P; 1P1NP3; 5q2. White to move.
3. Position 12: 3b4; 8; 8; 3k4; 8; 1n6; 8; 6RK. White to move.

81

Exercise 5

1. (a) Bb6+, Qd5+, and Qh5+.
   (b) K×b6.
   (c) Qd5+ is bad because Black replies ...R×d5.
   (d) Black cannot take the queen or move the king. There remain three moves, putting material between the queen and the king.
   If 1...Rd5 2 Q×d5+ If 1...Ne5 2 Q×e5+.
   There remains 1...b5 which is the best.
2. (a) Bh6+, Nf5+, Ne6+.
   (b) 1 Bh6+ is met by 1...K×h6 or 1...N×h6. 1 Nf5+ is met by 1...g×f5.
   (c) No. Either the piece must be captured or the king must move.
   (d) After 1 Ne6+, Black must move his king to f6, g8 or h8.
   (e) 2 N×c7.
3. (a) 1...Nc6; in which case White wins a piece for a pawn by 2 d×c6, which is a good investment; 1...Kd6 which is safe; and 1...B×c1, the best move.
   (b) 1 Rc8+, when Black replies 1...K×c8.
   (c) 1 Nb5+, when Black replies 1...a×b5.
   (d) 1 d6+, when Black must now play 1...Kc6. White may reply 2 d×e7, or, even better, 2 Rc8+ Nc7 3 R×c7 mate.
4. (a) One only, by 1...Qa7+. Black cannot play 1...Ng4+, or 1...Ne4+, since this leaves the black king in check from the rook. Nor can he play 1...Rd2+, since that leaves the black king in check from the bishop.
   (b) After 1...Qa7+, the white king has four moves. If he plays Ke2 or Ke1, Black takes the queen; and if Kf1 or Kg2, Black takes the bishop, winning a piece and freeing his rook to move.

Exercise 6

1. ...Ra2.	2. Rh1.	3. Qg6.
4. ...Qg2.	5. ...Qh2.	6. Ra8.

7. ...Qa1 but not ...Qb2 which is met by ...N×b2.

8. Q×h7.	9. (a) R×h7. (b) ...Ra1.	10. Q×f7.

11. Rf7+, and after the black king moves to the back rank, White plays 2 Rg8 mate.

Exercise 7.

1. ...Re1.	2. Ne7.	Bf6.
4. h7.	5. Rg1.	6. ...Qg3.

7. ...Ba3.

8. f6, and the bishop is responsible for the mate. This is called 'discovered check'.
9. ...Qa1.
10. Nf7. This is called 'smothered mate', the black king being smothered by his own pieces which leave no escape square.

Exercise 8

1. Advantage — 5 units to 4½.	2. Advantage — 9 to 8.
3. Disadvantage — 9 to 10.	4. Equality — 7 to 7.
5. Advantage — 5 to 4.	6. Disadvantage — 3½ to 5.

7. Advantage — 3½ to 2.   8. Advantage — 10½ to 9.
9. Disadvantage — 8½ to 9.   10. Advantage — 9 to 8.
11. Advantage — 12 to 10.   12. Disadvantage — 10 to 10½.

In all of these, however, especially 1, 3, 9 and 12, the nature of the position might easily be such that the advantage would in fact be the other way.

Exercise 9

1. 2...Bxa3 gaining 5 units for 3½.

2. 1 Bxd5, and if 1...Bxd5 2 Qxd5 Qxd5 3 Rxd5, or if 1...Qxd5 2 Qxd5 Bxd5 3 Rxd5, but *not* 1 Qxd5 Bxd5 2 Rxd5, Q moves out of danger, and Black has gained 2 units. Correct is to take with the lesser piece first.

3. No. The black pawn is defended twice against being attacked twice, and White loses material by 1 Nxe5 Nxe5 2 Bxe5 Rxe5.

4. 1...Bxf3 wins a pawn. If White replies 2 Qxf3 Qxf3 3 gxf3 Rxf3 or 2 gxf3 Qxf3, etc.

5. No. 1...Bxf3 2 Rxf3 is an equal exchange, and Black must *not* now reply 2...Qxf3 3 gxf3 Rxf3; since although he captures a piece and a pawn for one piece — the queen — he loses three units, due to the relative values of the pieces.

6. Yes. White is attacking the knight with three pieces, and it is defended by only two pieces. After 1 Rxf7, Black's reply, 1...Rxf7, loses immediately, since White plays 2 Qxf7+ Kh8 (the only move) 3 Qxe8 mate.

7. Yes. The black d5 pawn is attacked three times and only defended twice. White plays 1 cxd5, and after either 1...cxd5 or 1...Nxd5; White recaptures twice, first with knight and then with queen, to gain an extra pawn.

8. No. 1 cxd5 cxd5 is an equal exchange. If White continues to capture with 2 Nxd5 exd5 3 Qxd5 he has lost 1½ units, the difference between the value of the knight and the two pawns obtained in exchange. Clearly, as in Position 5, the one white piece is better than the two black pawns, and the counting rule alone does not work.

9. Yes. The white e4 pawn is *not* protected adequately by the rook, since after 2 Rxe4, Black replies 2...Rd1+ followed by 3 Re1 Rxe1 mate. Threats to the king such as this possible back-row mate must always be taken into account.

10. (*a*) Yes. 1 Bb5 wins much material, for if 1...Qxb5 2 Nxb5 or if 1...Bxa3 2 Bxc6+ and 3 Rxa3. The queen cannot move off the a4-e8 diagonal, since that would leave the king in check.

    (*b*) With White's b2 pawn on b3 the situation is altered, because after 1 Bb5? Black has 1...Bxa3+ 2 Rxa3 Qxb5 winning a piece. The check has turned the tables; compare the example at Fig. 22.

11. The black bishop is protected twice, by queen and knight, but the queen has the double job of guarding both pieces at once, allowing 1 Rxf6 Qxf6 2 Qxd7 gaining two units.

12. Black's e5 pawn is only protected by the knight on c6 which White can immediately remove by 1 Bxc6. If Black now replies 1...dxc6 2 Nxe5 Qd4 attacking knight and e4 pawn, then 3 Nf3 gains time to protect the pawn.

13. No. Although the two rooks attack the knight which is only protected by the pawn, 1 Rxe5 dxe5 2 Rxe5 loses ½ unit and the counting rule breaks down.

14. Black plays 1...Qxf4 2 gxf4 Bh6 winning a pawn.

15. 1...Bg2 2 Rxh2 (the best chance) Bxf1+ 3 Kxf1 Bxh2. This is much better than 2...Bxh2 3 Nxh2. Note once again the power of the intermediate check which must be attended to.

Exercise 10

1. (*a*) King on c1, rook on d1.
   (*b*) 9...Nc6, which loses a pawn. 9...Qd7 losing much material. 9...Nbd7, which develops another piece, but makes it difficult to develop the QB — you should avoid choosing such moves. 9...Nfd7; open to the same objections, and moving a piece which is already developed. 9...Kf8, which can be met by 10 Bh6+ Kg8 after which Black will have great difficulty in developing his KR — a very bad situation. 9...Bd7, which develops another piece without disadvantage — this is the best move.
   (*c*) 9 Bh6, since Black cannot move his king across f8 where he would be in check.
2. After 8 Re1+, Black can play 8...Ne5; 8...Be7; 8...Ne7; 8...Qe7; 8...Be6; 8...Kf8; 8...Kd7. He cannot castle out of check. The first four moves all lose material. 8...Be6 is the natural move, since this develops another piece, and reserves the option of Black castling later on the queen's side. The other sensible move is 8...Kf8, so that 9 fxg7+ can be met by 9...Kxg7. Considerable experience is necessary to choose between these two moves, but on balance in such positions it is better to let the pawn go and bring your pieces into play, especially as the black king would be very exposed to attack on g7.
3. (*a*) No. White replies 2 0-0-0+, winning the rook.
   (*b*) 1...Bh4+ 2 K-moves (it may not castle out of check) Rxb2.

Exercise 11

1. The two black knights are decentralized, and the bishop obstructs an advance of the d-pawn. Better would have been 2...Nc6; followed by 3...Nf6 or 3...Bc5.
2. No. 6...exd4 7 cxd4 Qxe4 8 Re1, winning the queen for rook and pawn.
3. No. 11 Re1 again wins.
4. 9...Qf8.
5. (*a*) 11 Re1. This again shows the advantage of White castling, and the disadvantage of Black not having castled. 11 fxg7 is equally good.
   (*b*) 11 Qxd6 Bxd6 12 fxg7 or 11 fxg7 immediately. As White remains material ahead, it may be a good idea to commence exchanges by 11 Qxd6, and aim at a clear end-game advantage.
   (*c*) 11 f7+ and 12 Bxd8 or 11 fxg7 attacking queen and rook.
6. 10...Qf8.
7. Because it develops a piece towards the centre. Also it is good to offer exchanges when ahead in material.
8. No. 14 Re1 is still a winner!
9. Black threatens 15...Qxh2 mate.
10. By 16 Qh5+, as played, after which Black must move his king, and so forfeit the right to castle.
11. 18 Rad1, which is better than 18 Rfd1, since the KR is already developed. Now that the king and queen are on the d-file, White transfers threats to that file which previously applied along the e-file.
12. 18 Rg7 would have been even stronger. 18...Rf8 is not met by 19 Bxf6+ Qxf6 20 Qxf6 Rxf6, but by 19 Bxf8. If, on other hand, 18...Re8, 19 Bxf6+ Re7 20 Qf8+ Kd7 21 Nf5, and White smashes through.

13. 19 Ne6+, or 19 Nf5. The former is the more effective, combining threats to king and queen.
14. 21 Rxd6+ Bxd6 22 Qd7 mate.

Group Exercise 'A'

Game *'A'*
2...Nc6 is better.
3...a6 wastes time.
4...b5 weakens his position.
5...f6 is weaker than 5...exd4 and, if possible, 6...Nf6.
6...dxd5 is essential.
7...Ra7 fails to stop the mate, but the rook is lost if he saves the mate.

Game *'B'*
2...Qf6 brings out the queen too soon.
3...Nc6, 5...Ba5 and 6...Bb6 are preferable.
8...Qg6 is better, but the QR is lost to 9 Nxc7+.

Game *'C'*
2...Bd6 is bad, blocking the d-pawn.
3...Nf6 and 5...Nc6 are preferable.
7...Bc5 is fatal. Better is 7...Be5 or 7...Qf6 or 7...Qg5.
8...Qg5 is essential, but 9 Nxh6+ wins the queen.

Game *'D'*
4 Bb5+ wastes time. 4 exd5 is better.
10 Bxc5 loses material as it leaves Black with two threats. He should play 10 Re1 or Rf1, or 10 Ke2.

Game *'E'*
3...exd4 is better.
4...exd4 and if 5 Nxd4 Nf6 is much better. Black's development is hampered by the text-move.
5...dxe5 is better, but White wins a pawn by 6 Qxd8+.

Game *'F'*
2...Nf6 is better. Black should not be tempted to make pawn moves in preference to development of his pieces, even though he appears to trap a piece.
4 Bg3. This is not quite sound. 4 e3 is best.
5...h5 still aims to trap the bishop. If 6 exf4 h4.
6...Rh6. Fatal. Best is 6...d6 and if 7 Bg6+ Kd7 8 exf4 h4.

Game *'G'*
4...exd4 is better.
5...Bc5 was tempting but loses a piece to White's double attack. 5...Nc5 is better.
6...Bxf2+ actually loses a move, as the piece has to move again at move 8, better is 6...0-0.
9...f5 is no better, as explained later in Chapter 8.
10...Ne7 is also insufficient.
11...d6 is met by 12 Qf4 13 Qh6 and 14 Qg7 mate.
11...h5 is met by 12 Qf4 Kh7 13 Qg5 and 14 Qxh5+.

13...hxg5 is met by 14 Qxh5 followed 15 Qh4+ or Qh5+, and 16 Qh8 mate. In all these variations, mate can only be staved off by the sacrifice of Black's queen.

Game 'H'

3...d6 or 3...d5 are much better.

4...Ng8 immediately is preferable. The queen is subject to attack on e7.

6...Nc6 or 6...Qd8 are better.

At move 8, White can also play 8 Nxc7+ Qxc7 9 exd6 dis.ch. winning the queen.

Exercise 12

1. 1 Ng6+ hxg6 2 Rh4 mate. Cf. Fig. 34.
2. 1 Qxh7+ Kxh7 2 Rh5 mate. Cf. Fig. 34.
3. 1 Bb5+ axb5 (or 1...Bd7 2 Bxd7 mate) 2 Qxh5+ Bd7 3 Qxd7 mate. This mate against the 'uncastled' king uses a similar technique to that of Fig. 35.
4. 1 Rh5 and 2 Rh8 mate cannot be avoided. Cf. Fig. 36.
5. 1 Qxh6+ Kxh6 2 Rh4 mate. Cf. Fig. 34 — king caught on the rook's file once more. Won by W. A. Dixon (York, 1936).
6. 1...Qxc3+ 2 bxc3 Ba3 mate. This is a double-bishop mate that shows the great possibilities of these pieces along open diagonals. Won by Boden v. Schulten, 1853.
7. 1 Rxf7 (threatening 2 Qg7 mate or 2 Rxf8 mate) Rxf7 2 Rc8+ 3 R or Qxf8 mate. Mates of this type with the heavy pieces are of frequent occurrence. 1 Rc8 also wins quickly.
8. 1 Qe5. If Black moves his N, 2 Qh8 mate. If 1...f6 to prevent 2 Qxg7 mate, White continues 2 Qe7, again threatening 3 Qxg7 mate. If the knight moves now, White plays 3 Qxh7 mate. This example combines the essentials of Figs. 36 and 37 with the heavy piece mate of the previous example.
9. 1...Qxh3+ 2 Kg1 Rg3+ 3 fxg3 Rf1 mate. The heavy piece mate once more.
10. 1 Qe2 threatening 2 Qh5+ and 3 Qh7 mate. If Black replies 1...Bg5 2 Qh5+ Bh6 3 Bxh6, and mate follows in a few moves. This combination of queen and bishop to mate at h7 is again of frequent occurrence. Won by D. F. Wilson, Australia (Correspondence 1948/9).
11. White sees mating possibilities by Qg7, if only the queen can reach that square. He finds a method. 1 Rh8+ Kxh8 2 Qe8+ Kh7 3 Qxf7+ Kh8 4 Qg7 mate. This mate is again based on the idea of Fig. 37, but with the added point that the mate must be prepared by a sacrifice designed to transfer a vital piece to the key square without losing time by allowing the opponent a 'free move'.
12. 1 Rxg7+ Kxg7 (or 1...Kh8 2 Qxh7 mate) 2 Bh6+ Kxh6 (2...Kg8 or h8 3 Qxf8 mate) 3 Qg5 mate. These mates are again based on the weak black-coloured squares (cf. Fig. 36), together with a back-row mate, and a useful queen mate at the edge of the board. Won by Przepiorka against L. Steiner (Debreczen, 1925).

Revision Exercise

R1. 1...Nxg3+ 2 hxg3 Qh6+ 3 Bh3 Qxh3 mate. Cf. Fig. 34.
There is no good alternative for White. Won by Torre (Mexico) against Grünfeld.

R2. 1...Nxd5. If 2 exd5 Bxg5 3 Nxg5 Qxg5. If 2 Bxe7 Nxe7. In each case, Black wins a piece. This idea frequently occurs in play. The danger sign is that the black knight can unmask an attack on the bishop which is insufficiently guarded.

Since the text-move lost a piece, White should have played any other reasonable developing move.

R3. 2 Rd6 Q-moves 3 Bxf6 winning a piece. White has a long lead in development, and this has enabled him to mount an attack on the black f6, and to obtain sufficient control of the Q-file to penetrate effectively. Best may be 1. . .Nd5 followed by f6 or f5 giving Black more room for manoeuvre but White's better development gives him the advantage anyway.

R4. 2 Rxa8 Rxa8 3 Bxg7 Kxg7 4 Rxd5 winning two pieces for the rook.
Note that 2 Bxg7 would be met by 2. . .Rxa1 3 Rxa1 Kxg7 which is an illustration of the importance of playing moves in the right order. Black should have played 1. . .Rxa1 2 Rxa1 and only then 2. . . N or Bxd5.

R5. 2 Bf6+ Kg8 3 Qh6 and Black must give up his queen for the bishop to avoid mate. Cf. Figs. 36 and 37. White's move 3 is instructive – it prevents the king from escaping via f8, and is much stronger than 3 Qg5+.
Black had no saving move.

R6. 1. . .Rc8. Mate cannot be avoided on the white back rank except by 2 Rd1 Bxd1 after which Black has a simple win. Cf. Fig. 36. White should have moved rook along the back rank, giving up his d5.

R7. 2 Bxf7+ (which is better than 2 Qxd8 Kxd8 3 Bxf7 winning a pawn). If Black replies 2. . .Kxf7 3 Qxd8 wins the queen for a bishop. If 2. . .Ke7 3 Bg5+ and the queen can no longer be saved.
Black should have played 1. . .Nxe5.

R8. 1. . .Nxc3 2 Qxc3 Bxb5 or 2 Bxd7 Nxd1 in each case with gain of material.
The bishop, once attacked on b5, is only supported by a piece which can be exchanged off. This indicates the danger of an insecure guard. Cf. position R4 in this exercise. 1 Rc1 is a reasonable move, but there are many possible alternatives.

R9. 2 Qxh5 threatening mate at h7 or h8. If 2. . .gxh5 3 Bh7 mate. Black should have played 1. . .d4 to cut White's QB out of attack. Cf. Fig. 36. Won by Bird, a nineteenth-century English professional.

R10. 2 Qxd8 Rfxd8 3 Bxd7 winning a piece. Note that if Black plays 2. . .Raxd8 3 Bxe7 attacks both rooks, and wins further material. *Don't be afraid to exchange queens if it leads to material gain.* Stories about such exchanges being unsporting are only circulated by those who don't know how they can possibly win if their own queen is missing!! Botvinnik, the World Champion, made a habit of exchanging queens in the 1961 match against Tal, and he is not only a very great player, but a very sporting opponent.
Black should have played 1. . .Ra8.

R11. 1. . .Qxc7. Black sees that White cannot recapture by 2 Rxc7 without allowing mate by 2. . .Re1 and so gains a rook. The back-row mate is a constantly recurrent theme. Cf. position 6 in this exercise.
White should have played 1 g3 or 1 h3, making a loop-hole for his king.

R12. 2 Qh5+ (an example of an advantageous queen sortie, signposted by Black's last move, opening up the diagonal to the king). If 2. . .g6 3 Nxg6 (the point of the check) and 3. . .hxg6 loses much material by Qxh8, prefaced by Re1+ with mating threats. If Black plays 2. . .Ke7 3 Qf7+ Kd6 4 dxc5+ Kxe5 (or 4. . .Kxc5 5 Ba3 mate) 5 Re1 mate.
Black is so far behind in development that he has little chance of survival but he

should at least have attempted to make up for lost time. 1...Bd6 2 Re1 0-0 might be the best chance, but 3 Qh5 leads a very strong attack.

R13. 2 R×g7+ (White's pieces being massed for attack on the king, and Black's being cramped and ill-placed for defence) K×g7 3 Qg3+ Kh8 4 Qg6 (threatening 5 Q×h6 mate) Bf8 5 Qg8 mate. Black had no defence.

R14. 1...Rg3 threatening the queen and 2...R×h3+. Black wins at least queen for rook. If 2 R×g8+ Q×g8 is best. Cf.Fig 34 — use of the two outside files for mate. If White had played the alternative 1 Kf1 Rg3 2 R×g8+ Q×g8 3 Q×f4 (there is no adequate alternative) Rg1+ 4 Ke2 Qe8+ 5 Qe3 R×e1+ 6 K×e1 Q×e3 and wins.

R15. 2 N×f6 and various threats of mate can only be staved off by sacrificing the black queen. Try the alternative — the force of White's minor pieces working together is impressive. Cf. Fig. 35. Black had played 1...a6 to prevent 2 b5 and 3 Bb4+. His best chance would have been 1...Bd4 but White then wins by 2 N×d4 R×d4 3 Nc5 (threatening 4 Ne6+) Rd6 4 Ne6+ R×e6 5 B×e6 and the rook and two bishops will be too strong for the queen. Won by G. Abrahams, the well-known player and chess author.

R16. 1...B×d5 wins a piece, for if 2 Q×d5 Qg4 3 g3 (or 3 Kf1 Q×g2+ 4 Ke1 Qg1 mate) Qh3 and mate follows. Cf. Figs. 36 and 37.
White had to play⁻1 Ra6.

R17. 1...N×e4+ and White cannot reply 2 f×e4 without being mated by 2...Qg5+ 3 Kh2 Rh8 mate. Cf. Fig. 34. He must therefore move his king in reply to Black's first move, and loses his queen by 2...N×c5.
Best for White was 1 Qe3 but Black still has a strong attack after 1...Rh8.

R18. 2 Rb7 N×c6 3 Rfb1 Bh3 (there is no good move) 4 R×a7+ N×a7 5 Qb7 mate. Cf. Fig. 37.
Black had no defence.

R19. 2 R×b7 (threatening 3 Qa8 mate) K×b7 3 Bc6+ K×c6 (or 3...Kc8 or b8 4 Qa8 mate) 4 Qb5 mate. This is very similar to the last example of Exercise 12.
Black should have played 1...c5 giving protection to his bishop with the rook along the second rank.

Exercise 13

1 1 Qh2 Ke1 2 Ke3 and 3 Qf2 or Qd2 mate.

2. 1 Qe7+. If 1...Kg8 or Kh8 2 Kg6 and Q mates at g7, h7, d8, e8 or possibly f8. If 1...Kh6 2 Qa7, b7, c7 d7 (a waiting move) and mates by 3 Qh7.
But *not* 2 Qf7 with stalemate.

3. 1...Kc6 2 Kf6 Kd6 3 Kf7 Qg5 4 Kf8 (best) Ke6 5 Ke8 Qg8 mate or Qe7 mate.

4. 1 Rd3, e3, f3, g3 or h3 (the waiting move) Ka5 2 Ra3 mate.

5. Black can make *any* rook move. If White replies 2 Kd1 Black moves his rook to the e-file 3 Kc1 Re1 mate. If White plays 2 Kb1 Black moves his rook to the a-file 3 Kc1 Ra1 mate.

6. Black's play leading to the longest survival is given by 1 Rg1+ Kh3 2 Kf4 Kh2 3 Rg8 Kh3 4 Rg7 Kh2 5 Kf3 Kh1 6 Kf2 Kh2 7 Rh7 mate. Or 1 Rg1+ Kh5 2 Kf4 Kh6 3 Kf5 Kh7 4 Kf6 Kh8 5 Kf7 Kh7 6 Rh1 mate.

7. The following line is not a full analysis, but shows a speedy method of forcing mate against an active defence. 1 Ke5 Kc3 2 Ke4 Kc4 3 Rc8+ Kb5 4 Kd4 Kb6 5 Kd5 Kb7 6 Rc6 Kb8 7 Kc5 Kb7 8 Kb5 Ka7 9 Rc7+ Ka8 10 Kb6 Kb8 11 Rc1 Ka8 12 Rc8 mate.

Mate following analysis of Fig. 41

14 Qe4 Kd7 15 Qe5 or e6+ Kd8 or c8 16 Qe8 mate; or
14 Qe4 Kd7 15 Qe8+ Kd6 16 Qe6 mate; or
14 Qf6+ Kd7 15 Qe5 or Qe6+ as before; or
14 Qf6+ Kd7 15 Qf7+ Kd6 16 Qe6 mate.

Exercise 14

1. No. White replies 2 c4 and forces the exchange of Black's last pawn, after which the game is drawn. Black has two ways of winning — he can manoeuvre his bishop to win the c3 pawn and then the d4 pawn, or he can play the waiting move 1...Bg5 which forces White to abandon his pawn, or to advance it to c4, after which 2...dc×4+ leads to a pawn promotion in three more moves.
2. White plays 1 Ng4. If Black now moves his king, the white king penetrates, and wins black pawns. The alternative, 1...h2 2 N×h2 Kf6 3 Kd5 Kf5 4 Kc6 Kf4 5 K×b5 Kg3 6 K×c5 or K×a5 K×h7 7 b6 g4 8 b7 g3 9 b8(Q) Kh3 10 Q×g3+ and wins easily.
3. The situation is similar to that of Fig. 42. 1...Bh5 2 Kg3 Bd1 3 Kh4 Be2 4 Kg3 Kh5 5 Kh3 Bf1+ 6 Kg3 Bg2 7 K×g2 Kg4 and wins.
4. 1...f3+ forcing the exchange of White's last pawn, leads to a draw, even though Black loses both pawns in exchange. Other moves are less good. If 1...e3 2 Kf3 Kb7 3 Nc3 (not 3 K×f4 e2 and Black wins) Kc6 4 K×f4 Kc5 5 K×e3 and wins. If 1...Kb7 2 Kf2 (not Nc3 f3+ draws) Kc6 3 Nc3 e3+ (or 3...f3 4 g4 wins) 4 Kf3 Kc5 5 K×f4 Kc4 6 K×e3 K×c3 7 g4 Kc4 8 Ke4 Kc5 9 Ke5 Kc6 10 Ke6 Kc7 11 g5 Kd8 12 g6 Ke8 13 g7 and wins. Note that Black must take his opportunity immediately or the draw will no longer be possible.
5. White, a piece ahead, should welcome the opportunity of exchanging a piece. He plays 1 B×d5 K×d5 2 Bg7 Kd6 3 Ke4 Ke6 4 Be5 K moves 5 Kd5 and the king penetrates to win vital pawns.

Group Exercise 'B'

White wins, starting with 1 Nf3. He must not allow the black king to penetrate and attack a2 so White should work the knight round to d3 after which White plays Kf5. 1...Kd6 2 Ne1 Ke6 3 Nd3 f5+ 4 Kf3 g4+ 5 h×g4 h3 6 Nf4+ Ke5 7 g5 h2 8 Kg2 K×f4 9 g6 Ke3 10 g7 f4 11 g8(Q) f3+ 12 K×h2 f2 13 Kg2 Ke2 14 Qe6+ and wins.

If in this line 5...f×g4+ 6 K×g4 Kd5 7 N×b5+ Kd4 8 Nc2+ Kc3 9 N×a3 Kb3 10 b4 wins. However, after 1 Nf3 Kd6 White must play neither 2 Kf5 Kd5 3 K×f6 Ke4 4 N×g5+ Kd3 5 Nf3 Kc2 6 Kg5 Kb2 7 K×h4 K×a2 8 Kg5 K×b3 and Black's a3 pawn cannot be stopped, nor 2 Kd4 Ke6 3 Kc4 Kf5 4 K×b4 Ke4 5 Ng1 f5 6 Kc5 g4 7 b4 g3 8 b5 Ke3 9 b6 Kf2 10 b7 K×g1 11 b8(Q) g2 and because his own h3 pawn is in his way White cannot win against the g2 pawn, e.g. 12 Kd4 Kh8 13 Qb7 Kh7 14 Qc7+ Kh7 etc., or even simpler in this line, 6...f4 7 b4 f3 8 N×f3 K×f3 9 b5 g4 etc.

Exercise 15

1. (a) White wins — Black's king cannot move into the resultant 3 by 3 square.
   (b) Draw. Black's king moves into the 4 by 4 square.
2. (a)and (b). Draw in each case. Black's king is within the rectangle.

3. Black wins in each case.
   (a) 1 Kf2 (or Kh2 Kf3) Kh3 2 Kg1 Kg3 3 Kf1 g5 4 Kg1 g4 5 Kf1 Kh2, etc. If 2 Kf3 g5
   3 Kf2 g4 4 Kg1 Kg3 with the opposition.
   (b) 1...g5 with the opposition.
4. (a) Draw. Black has the opposition. 1 Kd3 (or 1 Kb3 Kb5) Kd5 2 c3 Kc5 3 c4 Kc6
   (best) 4 Kd4 Kd6 5 c5+ Kc6 6 Kc4 Kc7 (best) 7 Kd5 Kd7 8 c6+ Kc7 9 Kc5 Kc8
   (best) 10 Kd6 Kd8 11 c7+ Kc8 12 Kc6 stalemate.
   (b) White wins, having the opposition. 1...Kd5 2 Kb4 Kc6 3 Kc4, etc.
5. Draw in each case.
   (a) 1 Ke6 Kc7 2 K×d5 Kd7 and Black has the opposition.
   (b) 1...Kc7 (not 1...Kd7 2 K×d5 with the opposition) 2 K×d5 Kd7 with Black
   having the opposition.
6. Whichever moves loses. E.g. 1 Kf4 K×d4 and the pawn cannot be stopped.
7. 1 b4 (best) a6 2 a4 Kc6 (or 2...Kd6 3 Kd4 Kc6 4 Ke5 wins) 3 Kd4 Kd6 4 b5 a×b5
   5 a×b5 Kc7 6 Ke5 wins.
8. Black wins by 1...h5 2 Kc2 (or 2 Ke2 Kc3) Ke3 3 Kc3 Kf3 and queens two moves
   ahead of White.
9. Yes. 1 Ke5 (1 Kc5 is equally good) Kd8 (best) 2 Ke6 Ke8 3 d7+ Kd8 4 d5 (without
   this pawn the game would be drawn; now White has the opposition) Kc7 5 Ke7
   wins.
10. Black wins by diverting the white king with his passed pawn and winning the white
    pawns with his king. 1...h3 2 Kg3 h2 (or 2...Ke4 which also wins) 3 K×h2 K×f4
    4 Kg2 K×e5 5 Kf3 Kd4 6 Ke2 Ke4 7 Kd2 Kf3 8 Kd3 e5 9 Kd2 e4 10 Ke1 Ke3 and
    Black has the opposition.
11. Black promotes first. He takes eight moves — three with the king and five with the
    pawn — to White's nine moves — four with the king and five with the queen's rook
    pawn or five with the king and four with the queen's knight pawn. Black therefore
    wins. Note the alternative White promotions both of which must be examined.
12. White takes four pawn moves to promote — either by running the b4 pawn directly
    through, or by moving it to b7, and after...B×b7 2 K×b7 promoting the a7 pawn.
    Black also promotes in four pawn moves, and therefore reaches the eighth rank
    immediately after White, who will then have a queen on a8 or b8. However, after
    the promotions White plays 1 Qh8+ Kg4 2 Qg8+ Kf3 3 Q×g1 winning by a typical
    skewer.
13. (a) White wins. White takes four moves to promote, and Black's pawn reaches b2
    on the following move. Queen then wins against knight's pawn.
    (b) Drawn. Black promotes on the following move to White, and with queen each
    and no exceptional circumstances, a draw results.
14. (a) and (b). Drawn in each case. In the former, queen can only draw against
    bishop's pawn on the seventh rank; in the latter, each has a queen.
15. White wins. This is the exception to the rook's pawn drawing rule, due to the
    availability of the white king. White promotes in two moves, with Black's rook's
    pawn on a2. Play proceeds 3 Qf1+ Kb2 4 Qe2+ Kb1 (if 4...Ka3 5 Qd3+ Kb2
    6 Qd2+ Ka3 7 Qc3 Ka4 8 Kc4 wins) 5 Kc3 a1(Q)+ 6 Kb3 and wins.
16. White wins. On the third move, White promotes and Black's pawn reaches c3.
    Play proceeds 4 Qd4+ Kc2 5 Kf7 and advances to win the pawn and the game.
17. White wins. 1 f6 g×f6 2 g6!! (but not 2 g×f6 which leads to the case where the c-pawn
    on c2 draws against a queen) c4 3 g7 c3 4 g8(Q) c2 5 Qb8+ Ka1 6 Qa7+ Kb1

7 Qb6+ Ka1 8 Qc5 Kb2 9 Qb4+ Ka1 10 Qc3+ Kb1 11 Qb3+ Kc1 12 Kg2, etc. . . The black king can never leave the c2 pawn unprotected, since after Q×c2 Black's f6 pawn has a move which prevents the stalemate.

Group Exercise 'C'

1. The attacking position of the white king is decisive. 1 h5 g×h5 2 K×f5 Kg7 (2. . .Ke7 is no better) 3 Ke5 Kg6 4 K×d5 Kg5 5 Ke6 and White queens well ahead of Black. 3 Kg5 also wins in this line.
2. This position uses the same technique as position 10 in Exercise 15. White creates a passed pawn at g5 which is used to divert the black king from the defence of his pawns. 1 g5 h×g5 2 h×g5 Ke6 3 g6 Kf6 4 K×d5 K×g6 5 K×e4 Kf6 6 Kf4 with the opposition.
3. White gains the opposition by 1 h3 Kh8 2 h4 Kg8 3 h5 Kh8 4 g6 h×g6 (4. . .Kg8 5 g7 and *not* 5 g×h7+ Kh8 draws) 5 h×g6 Kg8 6 g7 Kf7 7 Kh7 wins. Note that 1 h4 only draws, since the pawn reaches g7 with check, and Black has the opposition. If Black's king starts on h8, White must play 1 h4 to obtain the opposition. This is a good example of the importance of exact calculation in pawn endings. It also shows the help that having a pawn on the second rank gives in gaining the opposition — you can choose whether to move it one or two squares.
4. Here White has two extra pawns. White can try 1 Kb5 Ka8 2 Kc6 or 2 Ka6 but these draw by stalemate. If he plays 1 Kd6 Black must not reply 1. . .K×b6 as this allows the a7 pawn to promote, but he can again play 1. . .Ka8 when 2 Kc6 or Kc7 is stalemate. The only way to win is to sacrifice the a7 pawn to obtain the opposition. White plays 1 a8(Q)+ K×a8 2 Kc6 Kb8 3 b7 Ka7 4 Kc7 and wins.

Index

93

LEARN CHESS

A Complete Course

Volume 2

Winning Methods

CONTENTS

PREFACE

This is a book in itself, although it is the second of two volumes. To help those who have read Volume 1 we sometimes refer back to it, but you need not have read the first volume to understand this one, provided you are not a complete beginner. If you find that we are assuming you know things that you don't, then the remedy is obvious; you need to go back and read Volume 1!

Chapters 1 to 4 in this volume examine thoroughly all the standard ways in which you can win (or lose!) material; Chapter 5 teaches you how to build up an attack against the king and Chapter 6 how to play the ending. Then we have two chapters on the openings and finally Chapters 9 and 10 look to the future.

There is a lot to learn and you will need to go through the book more than once. We suggest that first time through you tackle, say, the first third of the exercises — go on until you find you get stuck on two or three in succession, which probably means that they are too hard for you at this stage. Next time through you should be able to manage a good many more — it may be quite a long time before you can do the most difficult ones. Don't be too quick to look up the answers: you will learn more and get far more enjoyment if you keep those that completely defeat you to try another time.

Having been given the privilege of editing this new algebraic version of a chess classic, I took the opportunity of making a few minor amendments to the original text and, more importantly, of extending by three games the vital chapter on Making a Plan.

John E. Littlewood

CHAPTER ONE

Winning Material by Double Attack

1.1. What is a 'Double Attack'?

Any attack on two weak points at once in the enemy position is a 'double attack'; if he cannot defend himself against both threats at the same time, he may lose material. In Chapters 1 and 2 we shall give various standard forms of double attack.

1.2. Forks

When a piece, or pawn, is placed on a square where it attacks two (or more) enemy units at once, we say that it 'forks' them. All the pieces are able to 'fork' since they can all attack in at least two directions at once:

A rook can attack along a file and a rank.

A bishop can attack along two diagonals.

A queen combines these attacks.

A king can attack on all its next-door squares.

A pawn can attack on the two squares on which it can capture.

A knight can attack in as many as eight different directions if it is on a central square.

We shall deal with knight and pawn forks in Chapter 2; we shall look at all other forks in this chapter.

1.3. Double Attacks in Practice

In Fig. 1, both Black's bishop and his rook on f7 are unprotected. This is an invitation to White to find a move which attacks both at the same time. He can do so in two ways — by 1 Qc4 and by 1 Qh5.

1

If he plays 1 Qc4 Black can reply 1...Rf5 and save himself; but after 1 Qh5 Black has no way of protecting both rook and bishop. Both white moves are queen 'forks' but only the second is a useful one.

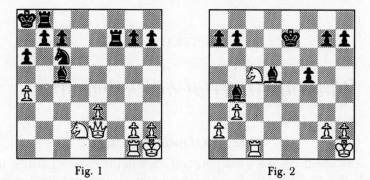

Fig. 1   Fig. 2

In reply to 1 Qh5, Black might try 1...Bxe3 (a bishop 'fork') so that if White replies 2 Rd1, protecting the knight, Black can then save the rook. Best for White then is 2 Qxf7 Bxd2 when White has won R for N and P and will at once win another pawn.

Figure 2 shows a position won by the Warwickshire player D. G. Horseman (British Championship, 1954). White saw that the two black bishops were unprotected and the king exposed and looked for a way of taking advantage of this. The winning move is 1 Nxb7. If Black replies 1...Bxb7 then 2 Rc7+ (a rook 'fork') regaining the piece and winning a pawn on balance. Black actually played 1...a5 and White replied 2 Nxa5 winning a second pawn, since 2...Bxa5 is met by 3 Rc5 forking the two bishops.

Fig. 3

In Fig. 3 Black has an unsupported rook. White plays 1 Qd8+ and wins it.

1.4. Signposts

Here are some signposts, or clues, to tell you when to look out for a double attack. *Look out* when:

(*a*) *Pieces or pawns are unguarded, or not well enough guarded*

When pieces are completely unprotected, look for a queen fork; if they are protected at all, however, a queen fork is not likely to be much good.

(*b*) *A piece or pawn can attack two pieces of greater value at once*

Here it does not matter if the pieces are protected — the capture will show a profit anyway. It is this that makes double attacks by pawns so dangerous (Chapter 2).

(*c*) *The king is in trouble*

Always look round to see if you can give a check which also has a second threat (Fig. 3 is a typical example). These forks are especially dangerous because the king must get out of check at once; this gives the enemy no chance to protect his other attacked piece or to make a counter-attack.

1.5. Successful Double Attacks

Now that we have seen what double attacks are and how to recognize them, we give a summary of the conditions needed for success

(*a*) *The double attack must be genuine*

There must be a real threat to take the pieces attacked. In Fig. 1, place a black pawn on b6 and Qh5 is not a true double attack since Q×c5 is not a threat (if you read Vol. I, use the rules given there in Chapter 4 and you should easily see whether a double attack is genuine or not. Remember that the weaker the unit making the double attack, the stronger the threat — because a capture is almost sure to show a profit).

(b) Protection against both attacks at once must be impossible

Sometimes one of the attacked pieces can be moved to protect the other; for example, in Fig. 1, 1 Qc4 is met by 1...Rf5 saving both pieces. Sometimes a third piece can be moved to protect the other two; put a black queen on b8 instead of the rook and now Qh5 is met by 1...Qf8 protecting both pieces. To give another example, in Fig. 2 put another white rook on f1 and a second black rook on d8; now 1 N×b7 would be met by 1...B×b7 2 Rc7+ Rd7 with advantage to Black. (Remember that you can't protect a piece against an attack by a weaker piece — you just have to move it or lose something.)

(c) No stronger counter-threat must be possible

This is true about all threats; beginners are always losing games because they only think of their own plans and do not look at counter-threats.

One more point; you can have a double attack even when you don't attack two pieces! This can happen when, instead of forking two pieces, you attack one piece and a vital square — or even two squares. For example, set up this position:

White K on h2, Q on d2, B on b2.

Black K on h7, R on a7, pawns on f7, g6.

White plays 1 Qd4 making a double attack on the rook and on the square g7 (threatening mate). Black must stop mate and White plays 2 Q×a7.

1.6. Practical Examples of Double Attacks

Exercise 1 gives a number of positions where there are chances of double attack. In the earlier examples, we give you some hints; in the later ones, you must find out what to do for yourself. We have put in some examples where the defender has a way of beating the double-attack — for example, by a counter-threat: you have been warned.

Exercise 1

1. A game begins 1 e4 c5 2 d4 c×d4 3 Nf3 e5 [see diagram, position 1.1]. Can White safely capture with 4 N×e5?

2. (a) Black plays 1...Ne4. How should White play?

   (b) Had Black a better move? [not easy to find!]

3. Black plays 1...N×e4. See if you can use the idea of the previous example to prove the move weak.

4. Is 1...B×f2 a good move?

5. Black's QB is unprotected. White to move.

6. Black has just played 1...Nb4 where it is unprotected. How does White take advantage of this fact?

7. Is 1 Rc8 a good move for White?

In the following examples you must find the unprotected piece, and work out means to win it. The fork may come after one or two preparatory moves, but loss of material cannot be avoided.

8. Black to move.

9. Black to move

Position 1.1

Position 1.2

Position 1.3

Position 1.4

Position 1.5

Position 1.6

Position 1.7

Position 1.8

Position 1.9

10. White to move.

Finally, some more difficult examples. In these, having found the double attack, examine all reasonable replies to see if some counter makes the double attack unsound.

11. White has played 1 Bb5+. What should Black reply? Give reasons.

12. White finds a way to win 2 pieces for a rook.

13. Can White win? Give an analysis.

14. Black to move —

    (a) White's QR can be made a target for double attack.

    (b) Does it make any difference if White's KB is at b3?

    (c) Does it make any difference if the 2 white bishops stand at b3 and b4?

15. Can White win a piece?

16. White to move.

Position 1.10

Position 1.11

Position 1.12

Position 1.13

Position 1.14

Position 1.15

Position 1.16

Position 1.17

Position 1.18

17. Which square would White like to occupy with his queen, and how should he play?
18. Black has just played 1...Nxe4. Was this good? [Compare Position 1.2.]

1.7. Discoveries

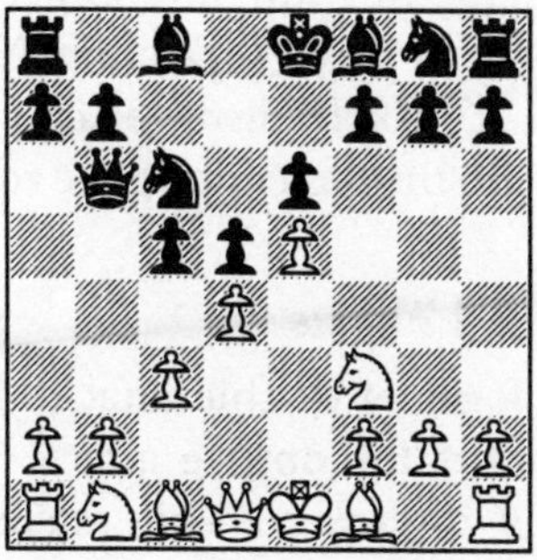

Fig. 4

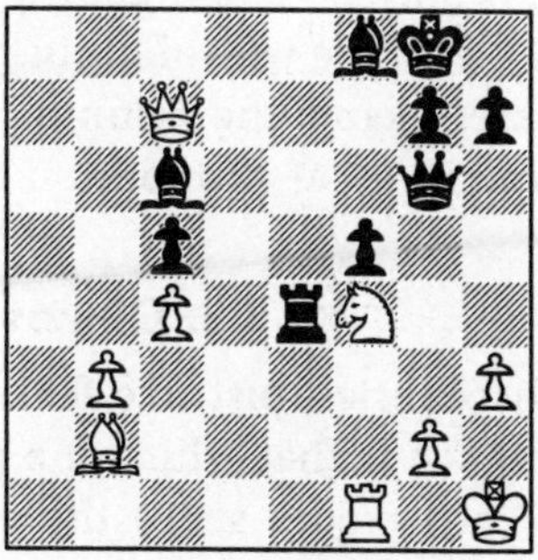

Fig. 5

In Fig. 4, White's QP is attacked and defended three times: Black cannot, therefore, win the QP. Suppose, however, that White plays 1 Bd3; now the QP is apparently only defended twice and Black can play 1...cxd4 2 cxd4 Nxd4 3 Nxd4 Qxd4 with an extra pawn.

However, Black's queen is unprotected; can White take advantage of this? If only there were no bishop on d3 he could play Qxd4 so he looks for a move which continues this threat with an attack on some other point. 4 Bxh7 Rxh7 5 Qxd4 would do nicely: unfortunately Black can play 4...Qxd1+ 5 Kxd1 Rxh7. We have to find (if we can) a threat so strong that Black has no time even for Qxd1+.

Can you see it? Attack on the king is the only thing strong enough to stop the queen being taken, so 4 Bb5+ Bd7 5 Bxd7+ Kxd7 6 Qxd4. The bishop check 'discovers' an attack on the black queen by the white queen, which had been hidden behind the bishop. Attacks like this from an ambush are called 'discoveries' and very often occur in play; you must always look for them when an attack is threatened by a piece hiding behind a piece or pawn of the same colour.

If Black is alive to the danger, he may reply to 1 Bd3 with 1...Bd7; and if White now plays 2 0-0, Black can gain a pawn by exchanges, since the bishop check is no longer available to White. Another example is shown in Fig. 5. In Chapter 5, we shall see that an attack by bishop and queen against the KNP is one of the standard ways of attacking a castled king. Here Black can see that, if only he could get rid of the defending knight and get his rook out of the way of his bishop, he could play Q×g2 mate! Now we are seeing the winning move: 1...R×f4 'discovering' the mating attack at g2 and leaving White no time to capture the rook.

1.8. Discoveries and Forks

Discoveries, just like forks, are a form of double attack. The difference is that while one piece makes the double attack in a fork, two pieces share the work in a discovery. This makes a discovery even more dangerous than a fork; not only can two pieces attack more squares than one, but you can't take both of them at once! You can beat a fork by capturing the forking piece — you can only deal with half of a discovery in this way.

This means that it is often possible to put one or even both pieces 'en prise' (i.e. where they can be taken) in a 'discovery' and still show a profit: many players miss chances through not understanding this. For example, suppose Black's a-pawn was at a6 in Fig. 4; White still plays 4 Bb5+, since after 4...a×b5 5 Q×d4 he has won a queen for a bishop.

Often the best move to make a discovery effective is a check by the front piece; this is so in many of the double attacks in Exercise 2, which underlines the rule *'Do not check unless it pays you'*. So often, beginners cannot resist a check — no doubt it might be a mate! A good player, however, only gives check when he sees an advantage from it; if a check does not help him, he keeps it till later, hoping to combine it with another threat to make a fork or a discovery.

The examples of Exercise 2 all depend on discovered attacks.

Exercise 2

1. Black played 1...Rb8. What should White reply?
2. White to move.
3. White to move.

4. White played 1 Re4. What should Black reply?
5. Find Black's masked threat. What should he play?
6. If only Black's knight did not stand on f6, White would lose his bishop or d4. How does Black play to win a piece?
7. White's queen is unprotected. How can Black play to take advantage of this fact?
8. Black to move.
9. White has a mating attack.
10. Black plays 1...g6. How should White take advantage of this move?
11. White has just played 1 Rf1. Black to move.
12. Black to move — analyse *very* carefully.
13. Black to move and win a piece.
14. Black to move: there is a preliminary move before the discovered attack threat is set up.

Position 2.1

Position 2.2

Position 2.3

Position 2.4

Position 2.5

Position 2.6

Position 2.7

Position 2.8

Position 2.9

| Position 2.10 | Position 2.11 | Position 2.12 |

| Position 2.13 | Position 2.14 |

1.9. Discovered Check and Double Check

If the king is the piece attacked by the hidden piece, the discovery puts him in check – a 'discovered check'. The discovered check gives you as it were two moves running with the front piece, since the enemy has to attend to the check immediately. Two moves running is usually enough to allow you to capture something, so a discovered check often leads to winning material. Here are two examples.

Fig. 6　　　　　　　　　　　　Fig. 7

Figure 6 shows a position that happens in the opening after the moves 1 e4 e5 2 Nf3 Nf6 3 N×e5 N×e4 (not best) 4 Qe2 Nf6 (this is very weak). Now White plays 5 Nc6 discovered check and whether Black plays 5...Be7 or 5...Qe7 White wins the queen by 6 N×d8(e7). In Fig. 7, White has a discovered check which gives him 'two moves running' with his rook; what can he do? At first we might think 1 Re6+ and 2 R×e8, but then Black plays 1...Kf7 and recaptures the rook: this shows us that a discovered check is not quite the same thing as actually having two moves running. However, a further look shows us that we can get at the bishop in two moves; so we play 1 R×b6+, K moves 2 R×b7 and White wins.

Things are still more dangerous when the front piece also gives check as it uncovers the hidden piece. Now the king is attacked by two pieces at once — double check: the only way out of this is to move the king, as any other move would leave him attacked by at least one of his enemies.

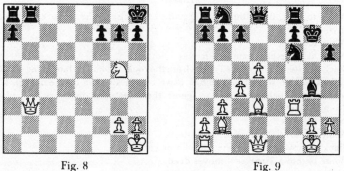

Fig. 8   Fig. 9

Figure 8 is a classic example of the possibilities of the double check. White plays 1 N×f7+ Kg8 and now looks for a discovery by his queen on the black king. In nearly every case the answer would be 2...R×b3 but White has one discovery where this reply is not possible — the double check. Accordingly he plays 2 Nh6+ and the king must move, even though both checking pieces are en prise. If Black replies 2...Kf8 3 Qf7 is mate. Therefore Black returns to h8 and White could force a draw by repeating the checks with the knight at f7 and h6 — a draw by perpetual check.

However, White has an attractive winning line. After 2...Kh8 he plays the surprising 3 Qg8+ and after 3...Rxg8 (the only reply) mates with 4 Nf7. It is easy to see why this is known as 'smothered mate'.

In Fig. 9, White has already sacrificed a knight to expose the black king. Now he makes use of the co-ordination of his rook and bishops to force home his advantage by means of double checks. He plays the unexpected 1 Rxf6 and Black naturally replies 1...Bxd1. Now White's masked attacks prove decisive by 2 Rg6+ Kh7 3 Rg7+ Kh8 4 Rh7+ Kg8 and 5 Rh8 mate. This attractive finish was played by Place (Paris, 1922).

We conclude this chapter with an exercise based on discovered checks — in some cases, double checks. Clearly the king is the piece against which masked attacks are to be launched. Find out along which lines they threaten, and then work out methods by which the threats may be put to decisive effect.

Exercise 3

1. White to play. Black threatens Q and N and also Qxh2 mate; can White do anything?
2. White to move.
3. White to move can mate in 3 moves.
4. Black threatens a discovered check from the rook, but only White's king stands on a black square, so that no piece or pawn can be attacked by the bishop. White consequently believes it safe to ignore the threatened discovery, and plays 1 Rhxh7. What should Black reply?
5. White to move.
6. White to move. Analyse 4 moves deep.
7. Black to move can force the win of a piece.
8. White to move. Analyse 4 moves deep.
9. White to move. In this position, the Oxfordshire player, Tylor, forced mate in 2 moves. Can you find it?

Position 3.1

Position 3.2

Position 3.3

Position 3.4

Position 3.5

Position 3.6

Position 3.7

Position 3.8

Position 3.9

CHAPTER TWO

Knight Forks and Pawn Forks

2.1. The Knight's Strength

The knight cannot work at long range along open lines as the queen, bishop and rook can: but it has one speciality. *The knight is an expert at forks.*

(*a*) It can attack any other piece without being at the same time attacked in return; it is the only piece that can treat the enemy queen in this way. Thus it can fork without being itself in danger.

(*b*) It has the advantage of weakness. A queen or rook attacked by a knight must move or material will be lost.

(*c*) Since it is not hindered by other pieces, it can move freely on a crowded board; and a crowded board offers plenty of chances of a fork.

(*d*) When the knight moves, it attacks a completely new set of squares. Compare it with the rook. A rook on e4 attacks squares on the king's file and on the fourth rank; move it to h4 and it attacks on a new file (the h-file) but along the same rank, changing only one line of action. Move a knight from e4 to (say) c5 and it attacks 8 entirely new squares. This increases its power to make new attacks and therefore to fork.

The great disadvantage of the knight is that it is a short-range piece. This means — as we saw in Chapter 5 of Vol. I — that we must post it in the centre and as near the enemy position as is safe: then it will be at its best in making forks and other attacks.

Finally, the one piece a knight cannot normally fork is an opposing knight since this would just result in an exchange.

2.2. The Knight Fork

It is worth studying carefully the different arrangements of enemy pieces that make a fork possible: this will greatly help you not to miss chances of a fork in play.

First, remember that all squares attacked by a knight at a given moment are of one colour — the opposite colour to the square on which the knight stands. This means that only *pieces which stand on squares of the same colour* as each other can be forked by a knight.

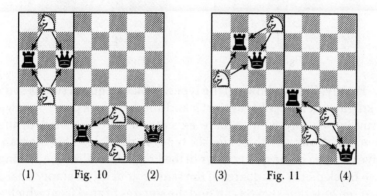

(1)   Fig. 10   (2)   (3)   Fig. 11   (4)

Figure 10 shows forks on a rank, and forks on a file work in the same way. You can see the rule: pieces are open to a knight fork if they are *separated by 1 or 3 squares on the same rank or file.*

We often get the first type with rook on e1 and king on g1 and the enemy knight giving check on f3; the second occurs with rook on a1 and king on e1 with Nc2+ — or with rook on h1 and queen on d1 and the knight forking at f2.

Figure 11 shows diagonal forks. Here again you can see the rule; pieces are open to a knight fork if they are *on the same diagonal and on adjacent squares or separated by 2 other squares.* Queen on d4, rook on a1 with Nc2 as the fork is a common example of type (4); queen on d2 and king on e1 with Nf3+ is a case of type (3).

Figure 12 shows our last types, where the pieces to be forked are not on the same rank file or diagonal. Here they stand *at the corners of a 4×2 or 5×3 box.* Those types are most easily overlooked, but you must know them. Q on d4 and K on e1 with the fork by

Nc2+ is a common example of (5) and Q on d5 with K on b1 and the fork by Nc3 is an example of (6).

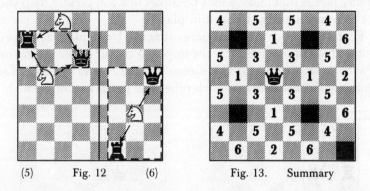

(5)   Fig. 12   (6)   Fig. 13.   Summary

Finally, Fig. 13 shows all the types. If Black's queen stands at d5 a knight fork is possible against it and another black piece or pawn standing on any white square except one of those shaded: the number shows which of the six types is possible. This diagram gives an idea of the great power of the knight fork. Practice putting two black pieces on squares of the same colour on an empty board and see how quickly you can find the squares (if any) from which a white knight can fork them.

It is just as important to know where pieces cannot be forked as to know where they can. Figure 13 will show you the rule. You are *safe from a knight fork with pieces separated by one square on the diagonal.* Another useful way of looking at this is that it takes 3 moves for a knight on one of the shaded squares to attack the queen on d5 in Fig. 13. For example, put a white knight on b3. You could go Nd4– c2–e3 attacking the queen: there is no faster route. Make sure you understand this; it is often very valuable to be able to get safety from a knight attack for several moves like this.

2.3. Practical Examples

In Fig. 14, White has just played 1 Rf4, threatening the knight. Black notices that both white rooks and his bishop are on 'fork-able' black squares, and that one rook and the bishop are unprotected. On d3 all the pieces would be forked, but the black knight

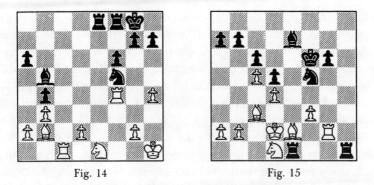

Fig. 14   Fig. 15

cannot get there easily, since that square is 2 squares away along the diagonal (cf. Fig. 13). On e2 both rooks would be attacked (type 4), and this square can be reached in 2 moves by 2 alternative routes. The route via d4 is useless because of 2 B×d4, but the second, via g3, does the trick, because 1...Ng3+ does not leave White time to move either rook out of danger. White replies 2 Kh2! and after 2...Ne2 Black wins 'the exchange' — rook for knight.

Note that if White had replied 2 Kg1 then 2...Ne2+ would attack both rooks *and* the king, and after a further move by the king, Black would play 3...N×f4, winning a clear rook. The attack on 3 or more pieces seen in this variation is frequently referred to as a 'family check'.

Now suppose the black knight had stood at c5 instead of at f5 in the diagram. How would Black have played then? He cannot get to e2 easily, but he can play 1...Nd3. This move attacks not only both rooks and the bishop, but, unfortunately, also attacks the white knight(!), so that White replies simply 2 N×d3. Can Black dispose of this enemy knight? The answer is clear. 1...R×e1+! 2 R×e1 Nd3 (types 5 and 6); and now, since both rooks and the bishop are unprotected, White must lose his bishop and Black has won two pieces for a rook.

Sometimes you have to drag an enemy piece to a square which allows you a fork. Look at Fig. 15. The fact that the white rook is unprotected and can be attacked by the black knight should make you ask the question 'Is there a fork?' The next question is 'Where can the knight attack the rook?' 1...Nh4 does not look promising as the black knight does not threaten any other white piece from there. What about 1...Ne3? That looks better because it is in amongst the white pieces; at the moment however it is hopeless because of K or N×e3. If only we could drag the white king to d1! Can we do it? Yes — by 1...R×d1+ 2 B×d1 R×d1+ 3 K×d1 Ne3+ 4 K-moves N×g2. Before we finally do it we must work out the profit and loss: we have given up 2 R's for R, B and N — a clear gain — and are left with an extra knight with an easy win. This combination should help you to see the importance of knowing the forking situations really well; an experienced player will think of a fork instantly he sees the rook on g2 and another piece on d1.

In the next exercise every position gives a chance for a knight fork. Find the best line and say which type of fork is involved.

Exercise 4

1. White to move. Give the next 2 moves.
2. Black to move. How does he win a pawn?
3. Black to move. How does he win the exchange?
4. White to move. Give the next 5 moves.
5. Black to move. Give the next 6 moves.
6. Black played 1...f5. Was this a good move? Give reasons for your answer.
7. Black to move. Due to the congestion of White's queen's-side pieces, Black can win the exchange.
8. Black to move.
9. Black to move can win a piece.
10. Black to move.
11. White has a strong passed pawn on c7, but must act quickly, since Black has drawing chances against White's exposed king if given time. White to move.

The following positions are taken from master-play. In each case the knight fork is decisive, but the positions require careful examination to find the combination played.

12. Black to play can win a piece. Give 2 main variations depending on White's second move.
13. White to play wins at least 3 pawns by threatening a succession of knight forks.
14. Black wins material.
15. White, seeing Black's king's-side pieces on black squares, discovers that he can win the QR after preparatory moves which threaten knight forks.
16. White to move.
17. White to move. The ex-world champion, Petrosian, played 1 N×f7 and Black drew by perpetual check. Can you do better?

Finally, a study by the great Russian endgame composer Troitsky, in which White offers a succession of rook sacrifices to force the win of the black queen after 8 moves:

18. White to play and win.

Position 4.1

Position 4.2

Position 4.3

Position 4.4

Position 4.5

Position 4.6

Position 4.7

Position 4.8

Position 4.9

Position 4.10

Position 4.11

Position 4.12

Position 4.13

Position 4.14

Position 4.15

Position 4.16

Position 4.17

Position 4.18

2.4. The Pawn's Strength

We have seen how a major piece usually has to retreat before a knight or bishop since exchange would mean material loss. This applies even more strongly in the case of a pawn, which is less valuable than any of the pieces. Every piece fears the pawns and a *pawn's chief strength is its weakness.*

Pawns are used for three main purposes:

(*a*) For controlling important squares, particularly those in the centre. The best squares to occupy for this purpose — *provided the pawns can be maintained there in safety* — are for White e4 and d4; other very good squares are f4, c4, e5 and d5.

(*b*) To provide a solid defensive barrier in front of their own king, and so make it difficult for enemy pieces to break through in attack — for this purpose, they are very well placed on their original squares (see Chapter 5).

(*c*) In attack. Pushing forward, they can sometimes drive enemy pieces away from the control of important squares; sometimes they can be used to smash the enemy defensive position in front of his king, and sometimes they can win material by advancing — as we shall see in the next paragraph.

What we must always remember, is that once moved forwards, the pawns can never return. This means that, whilst we must frequently advance our pawns to build up an attack, we must never advance them without careful consideration, and this is especially the case with the pawns in front of the king, which relies on their protection.

2.5. The Pawn Fork

In the case of a pawn fork, it is not necessary to find unprotected pieces to attack — 2 pieces one square apart on the same rank are an indication that a pawn fork may prove a possibility, whether they are protected or not.

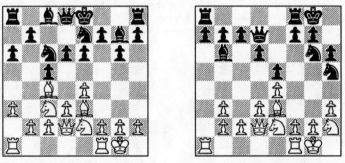

Fig. 16   Fig. 17

In Fig. 16, White appears to have a promising development, but there is one danger-signal — his QN on c3 and QB on e3 invite a pawn fork. Black is not allowed to make a double pawn-move by 1...d4; but he sees that he can gain time en route by attacking White's KB by 1...d5; after which 2 e×d5 e×d5 3 Bb3 d4 (the fork) and wins a piece.

In Fig.17, Black decides to play 1...f5. This is frequently a good move, opening up a line for his KR to operate against the opposing king, but, as with every move, it must not be played without careful examination — especially as to the effect of White exchanging pawns. Here it is ill-advised. White notices that after the exchange of pawns, Black will have 2 pieces on his 4th rank subject to a pawn fork, and so 1...f5? 2 e×f5 wins a pawn, since, if 2...Q or R×f5 3 g4 wins a piece.

The examples in Exercise 5 give chances of pawn forks: but look carefully at the positions — sometimes the player to be forked has allowed it deliberately having seen deeper into the position.

Exercise 5

1. White to move.
2. Black to move.
3. White to move.
4. Black played 1...b4. Was this a good move?
5. Black played 1...Be6. Was this a good move?
6. Black played 1...Nf5. Was this a good move?
7. Set up the position of 5.6 except that the black queen should stand at d7 instead of at h5. What should Black play in this case?

Position 5.1

Position 5.2

Position 5.3

Position 5.4

Position 5.5

Position 5.6

Position 5.7

CHAPTER THREE

Pins and Skewers

3.1. Pins

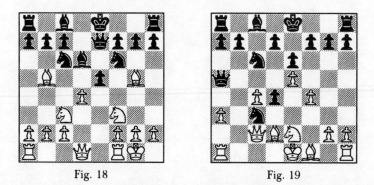

Fig. 18   Fig. 19

In Fig. 18, Black's KN is attacked by the white QB, and cannot move without loss of the queen. The knight is said to be pinned against the queen by White's bishop. Black's QN is pinned against his king by White's KB, and has no legal move. In addition to these pins, there is a dangerous possibility of a pin on the king's file, where Black has king, queen and KP in line. A situation of this kind, full of pins and threats of pins, can be very dangerous, and we shall see how White can gain a winning advantage here.

White plays 1 d×e5 B×e5 (if this pawn is not recaptured, a piece is lost next move because of the pawn-fork) 2 N×e5 Q×e5. The reply 2...N×e5 is not possible, since the QN is pinned against the king. Now White continues 3 Re1 winning queen for rook. The reply 3...Ne4 would allow 4 Qd8 mate, because of the pin of the QN.

Another strong line for White would be 1 N×e5 B×e5 (1...0–0

24

2 N×c6 wins 2 pawns for White) 2 d×e5. Black replies 2...Q×e5 3 Re1 wins Black's queen as before, but if the pawn is not captured, the KN is lost, since any move by that pinned piece would cost Black his queen.

1 d5, which is frequently a good move in such positions, is not so good here, as Black can save himself from serious loss by 1...a6! 2 Ba4 b5 3 d×c6 b×a4.

In Fig. 19, White's a-pawn is pinned against his QR by the black queen, and Black can play 1...Nb4! winning material by 2 a×b4 Q×a1+. Any move by White's queen to safety allows 2 Nd3 mate.

These examples show the characteristic feature of a pin — a piece of lesser value dare not move, because if it does a piece of greater value will be exposed to attack. You can think of a pin as a form of double attack, but where a fork attacks 2 pieces along different lines, a pin attacks them (so to speak) in succession; for example, the white bishop on g5 in Fig. 18 attacks the knight on f6, and threatens to take the queen beyond it if the knight moves away.

While the 'fork' (for reasons given in Chapter 2) is a typical weapon of the knight, the pin is a typical weapon of bishop or rook operating along the straight lines of the chessboard.

3.2. Dangers of the Pin

There is a very important point to learn at once: a pin against the king is different from a pin against any other piece. A piece pinned against the king *cannot* move (as Black's QN in Fig. 18); a piece pinned against any other unit *may* move, though normally it will not be able to do so without loss of material. This means that when you make a pin against any piece *except* the king, you must remember the danger of some exceptional circumstance arising in which it will pay your opponent to break the pin, despite the cost. Here are some examples arising from various openings:

A game begins **1 e4 e5 2 Nf3 d6 3 Bc4 Bg4** (Black pins the KN) **4 0-0 Nc6** (better is 4...Nf6 and 5...Be7 aiming at bringing his king to safety by Castling) **5 Nc3 Nd4 6 N×e5!! B×d1 7 B×f7+ Ke7** (forced) and now **8 Nd5 mate!** The pin has recoiled with a vengeance. Note how White's 3 minor pieces co-operate in the

final mating position — a tribute to the strength of a good development, and a clear case where the attack on the f7 pawn is very strong
in the face of weak play by Black. This variation was first exploited
by the Frenchman Légal over 200 years ago. Black should have
played 6...dxe5 but after 7 Qxg4 White is still well placed.

A second example is seen in a main variation of the Queen's
Gambit — an opening much used by experienced match-players,
but not recommended to the reader until he has learned a great
deal about positional play. After **1 d4 d5 2 c4 e6 3 Nc3 Nf6 4 Bg5**
Black often replies **4...Nbd7**. White now sees that Black's QP is
attacked twice, and only defended by the KP and the pinned KN,
and may try to win a pawn by **5 cxd5 exd5 6 Nxd5** (since
recapture by the knight would cost Black his queen). However,
6...Nxd5 7 Bxd8 Bb4+ and White has nothing better than **8 Qd2
Bxd2+ 9 Kxd2 Kxd8** leaving Black a piece ahead.

In the third example, we see a very common situation — the
case where a pin against the queen can be broken by a threat
against the enemy queen. **1 e4 c5** (the Sicilian Defence, another
popular line in match-play not recommended to the player who
has not learned how to handle positional play) **2 Nf3 Nc6 3 d4
cxd4 4 Nxd4 Nf6 5 Nc3 e6 6 Bg5 Bb4**. Now suppose White,
anxious to play **0-0-0**, moves **7 Qd2**. Black can reply **7...Nxe4!**
winning a pawn, for if 8 Bxd8 Nxd2 and if 8 Nxe4? Bxd2+ and
Black wins the queen. Notice in this last variation how useful it is
that the white N is pinned against *both* the queen and the king.

These 3 examples show failures of a pin against the queen. This
is not to say that such pins are generally bad — they are often very
good — but you must remember that such pins can be broken.
Also, remember that if the pin is broken, the queen is counter-
attacking the pinning piece in its turn, which, in the first example,
left White the move 7 Qxg4 after 6 Nxe5 dxe5.

3.3. Maintaining the Pin

A further important point to consider when wondering
whether to set up a pin, is whether or not you can maintain it. If
your pin is going to win material immediately, maintaining the pin
is of no importance, but this is not normally the case. If the pin

does not win material immediately, and the enemy can drive away the pinning piece easily without damage to himself, the pin will not harm him or benefit you; if, on the other hand, he cannot relieve the pin, so that one of your pieces is inconveniencing 2 of his for some time, and you may be able to bring up other units to attack the pinned piece, your pin is likely to prove valuable. For the same reasons, if you are wondering whether you should prevent a pin or not, you must ask 'Can the pin be maintained?', and only prevent it if it is likely to prove dangerous.

Timid players often prevent Bg5(g4) which would pin the KN against the queen, by playing h6(h3). Sometimes they are right to do so, but more frequently such prevention is wrong — so often, if this pin takes place, the bishop can be driven back by h6(h3) *after* it has moved to g5(g4) thus avoiding loss of time.

Here is an example of the kind of thing that often happens in play, and illustrates both effective and ineffective pins.

1 e4 e5 2 Nf3 Nc6 3 Bc4 Bc5 4 Nc3 Nf6 5 d3 0-0 (5...d6 before castling is wiser) **6 Bg5** (this is a good pin, for if Black replies 6...h6 7 Bh4 g5 8 Bg3 d6, White can continue 9 Qd2, followed by 10 0-0-0 and 11 h4 when Black's exposed king is in danger. Hence the preference for 5...d6 at the previous move, after which 6 Bg5 could be met by 6...h6 or by 6...Be6 7 Nd5 B×d5) **6...d6 7 Nd5 Bg4** (this pin is not so effective since White has not yet castled. In reply to 7...h6 aiming to relieve the pin, White has 8 N×f6+ g×f6 9 B×h6 — a constantly recurring theme in such situations — but 7...Be6 would be better) **8 c3** (to prevent 8...Nd4) **8...a6** (aimed to prevent 9 b4 and 10 a4, but unnecessarily timid; Black should play 8...Na5 and 9...c6, to force White's hand; now White obtains a strong initiative) **9 h3 Bh5** (9...Be6 is still preferable, to aim at 10...B×d5) **10 g4 Bg6 11 b4 Ba7 12 Nh4 a5 13 Qf3 a×b4 14 N×f6+ g×f6 15 B×f6 Qd7 16 N×g6 h×g6 17 Qg3 b×c3** (there is no saving continuation) **18 Qh4** and **19 Qh8 mate**.

The effective use of a pin is seen in a famous game played by the young American genius, Paul Morphy, in Paris in 1858. This game was played against the Duke of Brunswick and Count Isouard in the Duke's box at the Opera House during a performance of 'The

Barber of Seville', Morphy's opponents consulting over their moves. It seems difficult to imagine a game being played in similar circumstances these days!

Morphy was White, and the game went **1 e4 e5 2 Nf3 d6 3 d4 Bg4?** (defending the KP by pinning the KN, but this is a bad pin, because in threatening to relieve it, White forces Black to exchange his bishop with loss of time; 'defence by a pin' is often open to this objection) **4 dxe5 Bxf3** (since 4...dxe5 5 Qxd8+ — getting rid of the pin — 5...Kxd8 6 Nxe5 allows White to win a pawn) **5 Qxf3 dxe5 6 Bc4 Nf6?** (normally good, but not here) **7 Qb3** (a double attack on the f7 and b7 pawns) **7...Qe7 8 Nc3** (typical Morphy: he rejects 8 Qxb7 Qb4+, which would allow Black to escape at the cost of a pawn. He also avoids the tempting 8 Bxf7+ Qxf7 9 Qxb7 Bc5! 10 Qxa8 0-0 which would give Black a strong attack at the cost of the exchange: instead he plays another developing move and builds up his advantage) **8...c6 9 Bg5 b5?** (this move contributes nothing to Black's development, and weakens his defensive position; 9...Qc7 is best, but White is strongly placed; now Morphy shows that his lead in development justifies the sacrifice of a piece to press home his attack) **10 Nxb5! cxb5 11 Bxb5+ Nbd7 12 0-0-0** (threatening 13 Rxd7 or 13 Bxd7+; the black KN does not defend its partner adequately, because of the pin by the bishop on g5) **12...Rd8 13 Rxd7!** (a very instructive move, much better than the natural 13 Bxd7+; as played Morphy maintains the pin and brings his other rook into the attack — you should watch for this kind of sacrifice in your own games: you will also find similar ideas in some of the positions in Exercise 6) **13...Rxd7 14 Rd1 Qe6** (Black unpins his KN; now there are many ways of winning, but Morphy finds the quickest and most attractive) **15 Bxd7+ Nxd7 16 Qb8+! Nxb8 17 Rd8 mate.**

The logic of development in this beautiful game is borne out by the fact that the entire game has been repeated more than once in actual play.

3.4. Importance of Pins in Practical Play

Pins occur more often in play than any other tactical idea, especially in attacks on the king. It is very important therefore to be thoroughly familiar with them. Exercise 6 should help you in this.

All the examples in this exercise have pins as the main theme. If a pin exists, try to take advantage of it; if one does not exist, see if a useful pin is possible. Any piece or pawn that is shielding a more valuable piece is liable to be pinned, especially when it is the king that is shielded.

Don't forget to check that the pin really works; remember that sometimes the opponent can escape from the pin and turn the tables on you.

Exercise 6

1 White to move.
2. Black to move.
3. White to move.
4. Black to move.
5. Black to move.
6. White has pinned and attacked Black's knight. Black to move.
7. Black to move.
8. White to move.
9. Black to move, creates a pin and exploits it.
10. White to move.
11. Black to move.
12 Black has just played 1...Qb5. White to move.
13. White to move.
14. Black has just played 1...Q×h2. White to move.
15. White to move.
16. Black to move.
17. Black to move.
18. White to move.
19. Black has sacrificed a piece and allowed his king to remain in the centre of the board, so that he can maintain the pin on White's KN. White to move.

Position 6.1

Position 6.2

Position 6.3

Position 6.4

Position 6.5

Position 6.6

Position 6.7

Position 6.8

Position 6.9

Position 6.10

Position 6.11

Position 6.12

Position 6.13

Position 6.14

Position 6.15

Position 6.16

Position 6.17

Position 6.18

Position 6.19

3.5. Skewers

Fig. 20

Fig. 21

In Fig. 20, White attacks the queen with 1 Re5 and after the queen has moved, plays 2 R×a5 winning a piece. This is an example of a 'skewer'. Two pieces stand on the same rank, and an attack is made on one which is compelled to move to avoid loss, where-upon the second piece, previously screened from attack, is lost.

Figure 21 shows an important example of the use of a skewer in the endgame. Although White, to move, promotes first, Black wins. After 1 a8=Q h1=Q+ 2 king moves Q×a8 wins. If the white king had stood on some other diagonal, White, promoting first, would prevent Black from queening safely, and would himself win. This possibility must be taken into account in pawn endings when counting is used (see section 8.6 in Vol. 1).

The skewer takes its name from the way the effective attack on a piece takes place *through* another piece. The final sacrifice of the queen in the Morphy game of section 3.3, could be regarded as a skewer attack through the knight on the vital square d8.

Pins and skewers resemble each other very closely. Both are double attacks against the enemy units or points in the enemy position standing on one line – rank, file or diagonal – and are carried out by queen, rook or bishop. In each case, movement of the front piece would expose a unit or square beyond it to attack. However, there is an important difference.

The 'skewer' threatens immediate gain, and if the piece attacked moves out of the line of fire to prevent loss, the attacking piece is able to penetrate and do damage to some unit or at some point beyond it.

The 'pin' attacks a piece which screens one of greater value; there may not be a threat of immediate gain, but if the front piece moves, loss again results at a point previously screened from attack. The skewer has *immediate* effect, but a pin may be the basis of a series of moves each threatening to turn it to advantage, and so have a *long-term* effect.

Whilst a skewer is frequently directed at a piece which screens one of lesser value, this is not necessarily the case. As an example, place 2 black knights at d8 and d7 without protection, and a white rook on the queen's file attacking them. The front knight is lost unless it moves away, when the second knight comes under fire. This is a skewer attack on the second knight and is a form of double attack with two insufficiently protected pieces coming under fire. A skewer can also occur when a move by an attacked piece allows occupation of a vital square beyond it – especially if that occupation results in mate.

Exercise 7

In this exercise, all the examples are based on skewer possibilities. As with pins, look for points on one line which are subject to attack along that line.

1. White to move.
2. White to move.
3. How does White win?
4. White to move.
5. White to move.
6. White to move.
7. Black to move.
8. White to move.
9. White to move.

Position 7.1

Position 7.2

Position 7.3

Position 7.4

Position 7.5

Position 7.6

Position 7.7

Position 7.8

Position 7.9

10. Black to move.
11. Black has just played 1...Be5. White to move.
12. Black to move.

Position 7.10

Position 7.11

Position 7.12

Group Exercise 'A'

In these positions, material gain can be achieved by double attacks involving forks, pins, discoveries, etc.

1. White to move.	5. White to move.
2. White to move.	6. Black to move.
3. White to move.	7. White to move.
4. White to move.	8. White to move.

Position A.1

Position A.2

Position A.3

Position A.4

Position A.5

Position A.6

Position A.7

Position A.8

CHAPTER FOUR

More Ways of Winning Material

4.1. Undermining

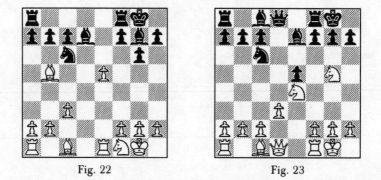

Fig. 22   Fig. 23

The simplest way to undermine a defence is *by capturing the defending unit.* In Fig. 22, White has just played 1 d×e5. Can Black recapture safely? Apparently it is safe to do so, since the pawn is twice attacked and only defended once, but now we run into an undermining combination. If the protecting piece can be captured after the recapture of the pawn, material may be lost. Thus, if 1...B×e5 when the bishop is defended by the knight, 2 B×c6 B×c6 3 R×e5 wins a piece and if 1...N×e5 so that the black QB is only protected by the knight, 2 R×e5 B×e5 3 B×d7 wins two pieces for a rook.

Notice that it pays to sacrifice the exchange temporarily in this second variation — the sort of sacrifice that frequently arises in undermining combinations — and that this sacrifice only gains material since the capture by the rook protects the white KB. If this bishop stood at a4, 2 R×e5 would be met by 2...B×a4 preserving equality.

Figure 23 shows another form of undermining. This time *the defending piece is attacked and* if it can be *driven away* material may be won. Here the white knights protect each other, and if the rear knight at e4 can be dislodged, the Kt at g5 will have insufficient protection. So Black plays 1...f5! winning a piece. He must, of course, examine the counter-threat by 2 Qh5, which threatens mate, but finds that 2...h6 3 Nh3 f×e4 4 B×h6! Qe8! (not 4...g×h6 5 Qg6+ Kh8 6 Q×h6+ Kg8 7 Qg6+, with a draw by perpetual check) leaves him a safe piece ahead.

The knight as a defender is particularly vulnerable to attack by a pawn in this way, since it cannot move and maintain its protection — unlike a bishop or rook, which, when attacked, may move away along the line of defence to avoid capture, and yet maintain its defence successfully.

The third way of undermining is by *diverting the defending piece.* You can do this when a defender has more than one job to do; if for example it has 2 pieces or squares to protect or has to protect a piece and defend against a mate. You make the piece do one of its jobs — then it is not there to do the other. We call such a piece 'overloaded' and overloading is important enough to be worth a section to itself.

4.2. Overloading

Fig. 24

Fig. 25

In Fig. 24, Black's queen appears to be adequately protected, but the rook is carrying out a second job — protecting the black king from 1 Rd8 mate. The rook is overloaded. White plays 1 Rd8+ R×d8 2 Q×c4 winning Q for R.

Notice the importance of the order of the moves. After 1 Q×c4? R×c4 Black's second rook takes over the protection of the back rank.

Now take away the 2 rooks standing at a1 and a8. 1 Rd8+ R×d8 2 Q×c4 still wins queen for rook, but 1 Q×c4! wins a full queen, since 1...R×c4 allows 2 Rd8 mate.

Now set up the position of Fig. 24 again, but move Black's g-pawn to g6. White wins by 1 Rd8+. 1...R×d8 2 Q×c4 or 1...Kg7 2 Q×c4 R×c4 3 R×a8. Black refuses to have the defence of his queen undermined, and declines 1...R×d8 for that reason, but leaves White with a 'skewer' combination against the rook on a8, by means of the queen exchange.

Back to the position of the figure, but remove the corner rooks and place Black's g-pawn at g6. Now 1 Rd8+ and Black loses material by 1...R×d8 2 Q×c4 — an undermining combination — or by 1...Kg7 2 Q×c8 — double attack.

Finally, no rooks in the corners, and with Black's pawn at g6, place White's KRP at h2. Now White has no winning line, for after 1 Rd8+ R×d8 2 Q×c4 Black counter-attacks with 2...Rd1+ 3 Qf1 R×f1+ 4 K×f1 with a drawn position.

This set of examples on Fig. 24 is worth careful study. Back row mating combinations are very common and these examples will help you to see the kind of thing that can happen. Also they will help you to see the importance of the order of the moves — what we call 'timing' in chess; the right moves in the wrong order ruin many games.

In Fig. 25, White has a number of pieces directed against Black's king's position. If Black's KN could be driven from f6, 1 Q×h7 would be mate. Also, the black KN is required to defend its fellow on d7 which is twice attacked and twice defended. White's greater threat is the mate at h7. He can win a pawn by 1 B×h7+ N×h7 2 N×d7 but far better is to maintain the greater threat, and make Black carry out its lesser task of protecting the QN. So White plays 1 N×d7. This wins a piece, for if 1...Q×d7 2 B×h7+ N×h7 3 Q×d7 or if 2...Kh8 3 Bf5+ Kg8 4 B×d7.

You will often find — though it is not always true — that when the same defender has to protect against two threats *it is better to carry out the lesser threat first.* (Then if the defender meets this lesser threat, he leaves you free to carry out your more important threat successfully.)

Fig. 26

Figure 26 shows a position that arose between E. Z. Adams and Torre at New Orleans in 1920, and is a classical example of an overload combination.

Adams saw that diversion of the black queen from its diagonal e8-a4, or of the rook on c8 from the back rank would allow a back-row mate. Both pieces can be overloaded. He played **1 Qg4!**. The overloaded queen cannot reply 1...Q×g4 2 R×e8+ R×e8 3 R×e8 mate. If Black replies 1...Qd8 2 Q×c8 wins. Black replied **1...Qb5**. Now White continued **2 Qc4!** (neither queen nor rook may capture due to overloading — and 2...R×e2 is met by 3 Q×c8+! and mate follows) **Qd7 3 Qc7!** (apparently the queen is safe from capture anywhere!) **Qb5 4 a4! Q×a4 5 Re4! Qb5 6 Q×b7!** and now Black resigned, since serious material loss could no longer be delayed. This is pure magic — but is built on a simple basic idea.

The following exercise is based on undermining and overloading combinations.

Exercise 8

1. Black to move.
2. Black to move.
3. Black to move.
4. White has just played 1 Qd2. His queen is overloaded. Black to move.
5. Black has just played 1...Qh4. White to move.
6. White has just played 1 Kg2. His rook on e1 is overloaded. Black to move.
7. White has played 1 Nd2. Black to move.
8. White has played 1 h3. His queen is overloaded. Black to move.
9. Black has played 1...Qe6. White to move.
10. Black to move.
11. White to move.
12. (*a*) White to move.
    (*b*) Now transfer White's QNP to b3. White to move.
13. Black's bishop is protecting the QBP and may be given the second task of preventing e6. White to move.
14. Black to move.
15. Black has played 1...a6. White to move.
16. Black to move.
17. White to move wins at least a pawn.

Position 8.1

Position 8.2

Position 8.3

Position 8.4

Position 8.5

Position 8.6

Position 8.7

Position 8.8

Position 8.9

Position 8.10

Position 8.11

Position 8.12

Position 8.13

Position 8.14

Position 8.15

Position 8.16

Position 8.17

4.3. The Trapped Piece

Another way of winning material is by *trapping a piece*. Here are the main ways in which you can do this.

(*a*) Drive an enemy piece — usually a bishop or knight — to the side of the board or somewhere else where it has no freedom to move and then attack it with a pawn.

(*b*) Lure one of the enemy pieces into invading your position (e.g. to take a pawn) and then prevent it escaping. Even the fast moving queen may be caught like this.

(*c*) Cut an enemy piece off from the rest of his men and then move across and take it at your leisure.

(*a*) and (*b*) occur mainly in opening or middle game positions and you must usually take advantage of your chance at once. (*c*) occurs mainly in the ending. Now there is often less hurry, as you may then be able to keep a piece trapped for some time.

The knight is the piece most in danger of being trapped, especially if it is at the side of the board where it has very few possible moves.

Here are two examples of type (*a*):

A game commences **1 e4 Nc6 2 d4 e6** (this allows White to occupy the centre unchallenged) **3 Nf3 Nf6 4 e5 Nh5?** (a common mistake among beginners — Black should not move his N on to the wing without careful consideration, and must always be aware of the danger of its being trapped there by pawns) **5 g4!** and wins a piece.

Again **1 e4 e5 2 Nf3 Nc6 3 Bc4 Bc5 4 c3 Bb6 5 d4 Qe7 6 0-0 Nf6!** (Black must not play 6...exd4 7 cxd4 Qxe4? 8 Re1 pinning the queen) **7 Re1 d6 8 a4 0-0 9 b4 exd4? 10 a5** and the bishop is trapped. Black should have played 8...a6 or a5 against this threat. b3(b6) is often a good square for the bishop — but you must watch that you do not get it trapped by a 'pawn storm' like this.

In Fig. 27, White has met a check by Black's queen with 1 Be3. Can Black now win the QNP safely with his queen? After 1...Qxb2 2 Rb1 Qa3 3 Rb3 Qa5 4 Bb6! and the queen is lost. This is a type (*b*) trapped piece, and is an instructive example. The QNP is often offered as a sacrifice in this way and you must think very carefully before you take it. You may get the queen trapped if you do; or — even if you can escape — you may lose a lot of time doing so and the gain in development may be worth more than a pawn to your opponent. It is sometimes right to make the capture — but take care.

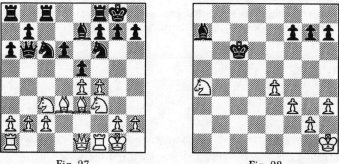

Fig. 27   Fig. 28

In Fig. 28 we see that White's knight has captured the QRP to obtain material advantage. Was it safe to allow his knight to become isolated so far from his own king and pawns? After 1...Kb5 2 Nc3+ Kc4 3 Nd5 and White is well-placed, but Black has seen that in the position of the diagram White can only move his knight to the squares c3 and b2 on the black diagonal. He therefore plays 1...Bd4 and picks up the knight in 2 more moves. This is a type (c) example, and shows the superiority of the bishop over the knight on an open board in the ending — it would prove far more difficult to limit the bishop's action in similar circumstances, due to its ability to move across the board in one move.

These and similar ideas are used in the following exercise, where material may be won by trapping and attacking a piece with units of lesser value. As you will see, the examples brin   in other ideas already met as well as that of 'trapping'.

Exercise 9

1. (*a*) Is 1...Nc6 correct?
   (*b*) Can Black play 1...Q×b2 safely?
   (*c*) Can Black win the pawn on d4?

2. White's last move was 1 Rb1. His QB has no mobility. Black to move.

3. Black's last move was 1...N×a2. White to move.

4. White's last move was 1 e3. Black to move.

5. Black is temporarily a piece up after his last move 1...N×b3. White to move.

6. Black's last move was 1...Kg7. White to move.

7. White has played 1 Be2 not realizing Black can win a pawn by isolating a rook at d6. Black to move.

8. Black has played 1...Q(a5)b6. He should have played 1...Q×e5. Why? White to move.

9. White's last move was 1 Ng5. Black to move.

10 Black's last move was 1...Qf4. White to move.

Position 9.1

Position 9.2

Position 9.3

Position 9.4

Position 9.5

Position 9.6

Position 9.7

Position 9.8

Position 9.9

Position 9.10

4.4. Promotion Themes

We have been considering how to win material in the most natural ways — by taking your opponent's pieces. There is another method; to increase your own strength by promoting a pawn. Nearly all endings depend on this, but it can also be important in the middle game or even the opening, so we include some examples here.

To get a queen for a pawn is such a big gain in material that you can afford to sacrifice a lot to achieve it. Here is another bit of 'pure magic' comparable with that of Fig. 26.

Fig. 29

This position occurred in the game Ortueta–Sanz at Madrid in 1934.

Black played 1...Rd2 2 Na4 R×b2! 3 N×b2 c3. If now 4 Nd3 c4+ 5 R×b6 c×d3! and the two connected pawns on the 6th rank win. White played 4 R×b6 hoping for 4...a×b6 5 Nd3, but Black played 4...c4! Now White is a rook and knight ahead, but is quite lost. He continued 5 Rb4 in order to meet 5...c2 with 6 R×c4, but the rook is overloaded, and Black achieved his final subtlety with 5...a5! and after 6 Na4 a×b4 White resigned.

Exercise 10

All the positions of this exercise enable decisive advantage to be obtained by play which threatens promotion of a pawn. The early examples are, of course, much simpler than the play required to force the win in Fig. 29.

1. Black to move.   5. Black to move.
2. Black to move.   6. White to move.
3. White to move.   7. White to move.
4. White to move.

Position 10.1

Position 10.2

Position 10.3

Position 10.4

Position 10.5

Position 10.6

Position 10.7

4.5. Winning Material – Summary

This chapter completes our survey of tactical means by which material advantage may be gained. Let us summarize the main categories:

(a) capture of unprotected material;

(b) advantageous exchanges;

(c) double attack along different lines – forks and discoveries;

(d) successive attacks on 2 points in one line – pins and skewers;

(e) undermining a protected unit;

(f) taking advantage of an overloaded unit;

(g) trapping and then capturing a trapped piece – the best piece of all to trap is the king!;

(h) promotion of a pawn.

4.6. Some Points to Remember

On working out how to win material, or in making any other tactical plan, there are some ideas which come up again and again. Many of these you may have used without realizing it; however, it is worthwhile trying to see when a general method is being used as it helps you to know what to look for in play.

Correct timing is one of the most important things in chess. When you have decided on a plan you must work out carefully the right order in which to play the moves. We have seen some good examples of this in our study of Fig. 24, and nearly all combinations except the very simplest need correct timing if they are to succeed.

Don't take moves for granted. A combination often fails because your opponent delays the obvious reply and puts in an awkward little move of his own first, such as a check or a counter-threat you dare not ignore. The Germans call this 'Zwischenzug' or the intermediate move. Figure 30 shows a simple example. White plays 1 B×d4? seeing that Black dare not take the bishop because of 2 Rc8+ and mate next move. However, Black first plays 1...h6! (the Zwischenzug), and after the white rook moves can safely play 2...N×d4 because he has an escape on h7 for his king.

Getting caught like this happens when you do not look carefully enough at your opponent's move. It is just as important not to
be too easily satisfied with your own — in fact '*When you see a good
move, look for a better one*': this is all part of not being a lazy player.

Fig. 30. 'Zwischenzug'   Fig. 31. Sacrifice to gain time

The sacrifice to gain time is an important tactical idea. Look at
Fig. 31. It is Black's move and his first idea is to play 1...Re1. He
does not mind 2 N×f3 B×f3 when he threatens ...Rh1 mate.
Unfortunately, after 1...Re1 White has 2 Qf7+ Kh8 3 Q×h7 mate.
Black is one move too late. He overcomes this by playing
1...Qh1+! 2 K×h1 Re1+ 3 Kh2 Rh1 mate. He gives up the queen
to gain that vital move.

Finally, the 'desperado' piece. If a piece is going to be taken
whatever happens, ask yourself 'Can it do any damage before it
dies?' We call such a piece a 'desperado' and you can often make
an effective last minute sacrifice of such a piece especially if
you can do so with check: remember that provided it does not cost
you valuable time anything you get may be a bonus if you were
going to lose the piece anyway.

From these chapters we hope you will get some idea of how
many tactical possibilities there are and how much there is to think
about in a chess position. Even the greatest players miss tactical
chances occasionally; a weak player misses them all the time. One
of the chief reasons for this is that he does not know the standard
tactical plans nearly well enough. You can do two things to
improve your own game so far as this goes. Practice through doing

examples such as these in this book — this will help a lot to get hold of the ideas. Even more important is to look for chances all the time in your games and to try to discover why you failed when you miss chances; in this way you will find out your particular tactical weaknesses. It is worth the effort.

We finish this chapter with a revision exercise in which various tactical ideas are used. The first few are easy; if you do not quickly see how to do them, read the chapter again and go through the various possibilities listed in it. Examples 6 to 17 are harder and if you can solve a number of them without help, you are on your way to being a good tactical player. Finally in 18 to 34 you can match yourself against the masters.

Revision Exercise R.1

1. Black's last move was 1...Nb4. White to move.
2. Black's last move was 1...Kf7. White to move.
3. White's last move was 1...Re1. Black to move.
4. White's last move was 1...Bb3. Black to move.
5. Black's last move was 1...Qxg3. White to move.
6. Black's last move was 1...Qe7. White to move.
7. White's last move was 1...Qxd6. Black to move.
8. Black has moved his king from e8 to threaten 2...Qxa6 without allowing a knight fork. White to move.
9. Black's last move was 1...Qf5. What is the effect of 2 Rd1 in reply?
10. White's last move was 1 b3. Black to move.
11. White's last move was 1 Qxa7. Black to move.
12. White's last move was 1 Qc6. Black to move.
13. Black's last move was 1...Qe7. White to move.
14. White's last move was 1 Kg2. Black to move.
15. White's last move was 1 Kh1. Black to move.
16. White has sacrificed a rook to break open Black's king's position. Black's last move was 1...Kxg7. White to move.
17. Black to move. He has a continuation leading to the win of at least a pawn and a much superior position.

Examples from master-play

18. White to move wins a pawn, with a good game.
19. Black to move wins at least 2 pawns.
20. Black to move.
21. Black to move.
22. Black has just played 1...Qe7. Why was this wrong?
23. Black to move.
24. White to move.
25. White to move.
26. Black to move.

27. White to move.
28. Black to move.
29. Black played 1...Qxe7. (a) How did White win? (b) What should Black have played?
30. White wins at least a pawn by a combination that threatens mate.
31. White to move.
32. Black to move.
33. White to move.
34. White, Rotlevi, had just played 1 g3 and his opponent, Rubinstein, one of the greatest of all chess players, brought off a combination of unsurpassed beauty and depth. White has 3 weak points: (i) his KRP, protected by the queen; (ii) his KB, protected by queen and N; and (iii) the N itself, which is under attack. Can you combine these factors to find Rubinstein's winning play?

Position R.1.1

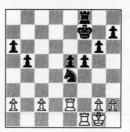

Position R.1.2

Position R.1.3

Position R.1.4

Position R.1.5

Position R.1.6

Position R.1.7

Position R.1.8

Position R.1.9

Position R.1.10

Position R.1.11

Position R.1.12

Position R.1.13

Position R.1.14

Position R.1.15

Position R.1.16

Position R.1.17

Position R.1.18

Position R.1.19

Position R.1.20

Position R.1.21

Position R.1.22

Position R.1.23

Position R.1.24

Position R.1.25

Position R.1.26

Position R.1.27

Position R.1.28

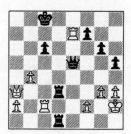

Position R.1.29

Position R.1.30

Position R.1.31

Position R.1.32

Position R.1.33

Position R.1.34

CHAPTER FIVE

Mating the Castled King

5.1. Introduction

The object of chess is mate. So far we have been seeing how to win material, which normally leads to mate in the end if you play properly: now we are going to look at situations in which mating attacks in the middle game are possible.

Mating attacks don't happen by accident, at least not in good games. They occur because there is something in the nature of the position which helps such an attack; you must learn to recognize the signs which tell you both that it is right to attack and what kind of an attack to make. In this chapter we shall examine in detail all the main types of attack against the castled king. This is not because the king is in greater danger after castling; quite the opposite. *The king is much safer when he has castled* and for this reason most players always castle if they can — so it is usually the castled king, not the king in the centre, that you have to try to attack. We shall show attacks against king's-side castling; the same ideas applies against queen's side castling as well. We show the black king being attacked; but needless to say, Black is equally capable of attacking White.

Before going on to a detailed analysis, there is one important general point to make; if you have read Volume 1 you will already have met it there. *Your attack is only likely to succeed if you can bring more pieces against the king than your opponent can bring to defend it.*

To do this you will probably need an advantage of one of two kinds. Either you will have to have more pieces in play, i.e. be *better developed*; or else you will have more pieces ready for the attack than are ready for defence; in the second case there will be room for more of your pieces than for the opponent's.

Don't rush through this chapter too quickly — there is a lot to learn; compare the examples with each other until you are sure you really understand them. If you would like to study sacrificial play based on the standard mating position in more detail, read *The Art of Checkmate*, by G. Renaud and V. Kahn.

5.2. Mating Attacks Dependent on the Position of the NP

(i) Attack on the KNP when the pawns in front of the king have not moved

Immediately after castling, the king stands behind 3 pawns, of which the BP is protected by the rook, and the RP is frequently protected by a knight at f3(f6). This formation, with the 3 pawns in a line, has no basic weakness, except (see section 5.4) for the possibility of back-row mates. On balance it is the best defensive position, especially when there is a knight on f6. However, the KNP, defended only by the king, is sometimes a weak point. Any 2 pieces can be brought to bear upon it along the file or diagonals, or by means of the knight move. Diagrams (*a*) and (*b*) of Fig. 32 show 2 such cases. Whilst a rook would also attack the KNP only the queen threatens mate, and may do so either along the KN-file or a diagonal. When operating along the file, it pins the KNP and allows a bishop or pawn to occupy f6 or h6 as in (*b*). Such attacks are frequently met by 1...g6; but, as we shall see, the formation

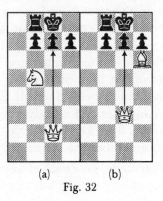

(a)   (b)

Fig. 32

Positions leading to (c) and (d)

Fig. 33

with a pawn on g6 is basically weaker than that with the pawns in line, and such a defence may therefore allow a new attack (see diagrams (*e*) to (*h*) below). Sometimes, as in (*b*), the defence 1...g6 will cost the exchange at once, and this quite often happens.

Examples of mates by the queen at g7 can be found in Volume 1 in Game C of Group Exercise 'A', the position in Fig. 37, in Exercise 12, No. 11 and in Revision Exercises Nos. 16 and 18. In this Volume, they occur in Fig. 5 and in Exercise 2, No. 8.

Sometimes the king-position can be broken open by direct sacrifice at g7. In the first position of Fig. 33, White plays 1 R×g7+ K×g7 (if 1...Kh8 2 Qf6 and the discovery wins) 2 Rg1+. Now, if Black plays 2...Kh6 3 Qh3 mate which we call type (*c*), whilst if 2...Kh8 3 Qf6 mate — type (*d*).

In the second position of Fig. 33, White plays 1 R×g7+ Kh8 2 Rg8+! (most other discoveries are met by 2...B×f6) K×g8 3 Rg1+ — type (*d*) again. Here the bishop controls the diagonal to h8, whilst the rook administers mate along the open file.

Other mates of this type are seen in Exercise 7, No. 5, in Vol. 1, and Exercise 3, No. 3, in this Volume.

(ii) The formation f7, g6, h7 — weakness on squares of one colour

You might think from this that the KNP is better placed at g6, guarded by the f7 and h7 pawns, but this creates new weaknesses. With pawns on f7, g6, h7 all the black coloured squares round the king are very weak and White can take advantage of this in a number of different ways. He can attack g7 with bishop and queen along a diagonal or he can get pawn or bishop at f6 and queen at h6 or he can get N at f6 and Q at h6 — all these combinations will be fatal for Black.

Look at Fig. 34 and see how in each case White wins because he controls all the black squares. Mates of this kind often occur in play and you should get thoroughly familiar with them. If you have Volume I, look back at these examples and classify them. Exercise 6, No. 7; Exercise 7, No. 3; Fig. 37; Exercise 12, No. 8; and Revision Exercise No. 16. And remember the principle:

When all the pawns are on squares of one colour, you attack on squares of the other colour.

Fig. 34

The general study of the strengths and weaknesses of various pawn-formations is beyond the scope of this book, but here you can see a simple and very important example of a positional weakness directly due to the pawn-formation. Unless Black can arrange some other satisfactory way of defending the black-coloured squares f6 and h6, this formation is wrong, and will nearly always give trouble. Now, however, put a black bishop on g7 — this guards f6 and h6 very well, and is itself hard to attack. This, therefore, is an excellent defensive position and one often adopted in master-play.

White, against such a formation, will aim to exchange off the black bishop, though his attacking chances may be less simple when his own black-squared bishop has gone. There are many fine games where White has offered the exchange of his QR for the black KB along the long diagonal, having calculated that he would then achieve decisive advantage by assuming control of the black- coloured squares.

(iii) The formation f7, g6, h7 — the NP is a target for attack and exchange

Coming back to the attack against the f7, g6, h7 formation, suppose that Black has countered the immediate threats of the kind shown in Fig. 34. We now see another weakness of the pawn at g6 — it is a *target for exchange*. By advancing his KRP or KBP to the fifth rank, White can exchange off the pawn, opening a file for rook or queen. Notice that with the pawn at g7 it is much harder to open a file like this — your pawn has to get to the sixth rank instead of the fifth rank, and when it gets there, Black's pawn may push past you, blocking the position. To push from g6 to g5 is more dangerous, since no other pawn will give protection, and the advanced pawn may be lost. Against a pawn at g7, you may have to push one pawn to f6, force . . .g6 and then push another pawn to h5 to open a file — a long process.

(iv) The KNP captured or exchanged — attacks along the rook's-file

If you manage to open the h-file you will have new chances of attack. If Black recaptures at g6 with the BP you may be able to take the KRP; if he recaptures with RP, then Fig. 35 shows the kind of thing that may be possible.

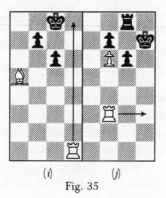

(i)   (j)

Fig. 35

Here we see the white rook giving mate on the opened h-file. Notice again the weakness of the black squares in Fig. 34 (*i*). Now let us make (*i*) a little more complicated, by adding a white queen at h3, a black bishop at g7, black knight at g5, and the black queen at e7. It looks as if White must move his queen to prevent capture, after which Black would continue 1. . .Q×e5. White actually plays 1 Qh8+! B×h8 2 R×h8 mate, and a 'brilliant' sacrifice has been effected through a knowledge of a standard mating position.

(v) The pawn advance — pros and cons

One special case where pawn-advances like this are nearly always good, is *when players have castled on opposite sides.* Here you are not removing any protection from your own king, so there is nothing to be lost. In the first of the two game-positions we now give to complete this section, you will see that the players have castled on opposite sides.

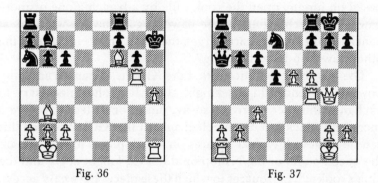

Fig. 36   Fig. 37

In Fig. 36, White plays 1 h5 and Black has no good reply. If 1...c5 attacking the rook, 2 h×g6+ Kg8 3 Rh8 mate. Nor is 1...Rh8 any better. White must not be diverted from his plan by 2 B×h8 but continue 2 h×g6+ Kg8 3 R×h8 mate. Finally, 1... Kg8 2 h×g6 and mate is still unavoidable, since Black cannot reply 2...f×g6 the KBP being pinned. This is an example of a type *(i)* mate.

In Fig. 37, White has sacrificed a piece to divert the black queen from the defence, and now forces the win by direct attack. He plays **1 f6** (type *(a)* threat) **g6** (1...N×f6 2 e×f6 is no better) **2 Qg5** (type *(e)* threat) **Kh8 3 Qh6 Rg8**. Now, the natural 4 Rh4 is met by 4... Nf8. White must act more rapidly. **4 Q×h7+! K×h7 5 Rh4 mate** (type *(j)* mate). White made use of three of our mating types in this attack; it is a great help in thinking of a combination like this and in working it out correctly to be thoroughly familiar with all these standard possibilities.

5.3. Mating Attacks Dependent on the Position of the RP

(i) Attack on the KRP when the pawns in front of the king have not moved

So far we have been considering attacks centring round Black's KNP. First we attacked the pawn itself at g7, trying to win it, to sacrifice a piece for it or to force it to advance to g6. Then we looked at attacks based on the weakness of the black-coloured squares when the pawn stood on g6 and finally there were attacks based on forcing open the rook's file by advancing one or more pawns and exchanging off the pawn at g6. Now we will look at attacks on the other natural target, the pawn on h7 — assuming the other pawns to be at f7 and g7.

The first thing to notice is that the KRP has a natural and very powerful defender in the knight at f6. It is often necessary to exchange this piece, drive it away, pin it, or deflect it, before a successful attack can be launched against the KRP. Provided this can be achieved, typical squares on which pieces are placed are the queen on h5 or d3, bishop on d3 or c2, knight at g5, and the king's rook at h1 — squares to which these pieces have easy access.

(k)

Fig. 38

Figure 38, type (k), shows a direct attack on the KRP by queen and knight. White plays 1 Q×h7 mate. The mate is equally effective if the queen is protected on h7 by a bishop or rook, and examples of both are of frequent occurrence. Note that the mate owes itself in part to the presence of the black rook on f8; if this rook is moved to e8 and Black's queen stands on d8 1 Q×h7+ Kf8 2 Qh8+ Ke7 3 Q×g7 wins 2 pawns, but it is not mate. If, on the other hand, the rook stands on e8, and the black bishop is at e7, 1 Q×h7+ Kf8 2 Qh8 is mate, since the king cannot escape via e7. Further, if the rook is on e8 sometimes 1 Qh5 will threaten both

2 Q×h7+ and 2 Q×f7+ and Black will not be able to stop both.

You can find examples of mates of this type in Vol. 1, Ex. 6, No. 8, and in this Volume Ex. 4, No. 13.

If you have a more effective development, you can quite often make a successful sacrifice of a piece for the KRP. Figure 39 shows a typical situation; you should notice that White has been able to drive the black knight away from f6 by e5 so that it no longer protects the rook's pawn.

Fig. 39

White plays **1 B×h7+!** There are several important variations. If Black replies **1...K×h7 2 Ng5+ B×g5 3 h×g5+ Kg8** (if 3...Kg6 4 Qh5+ Kf5 5 g6+ Ke4 6 Qf3 mate — a king driven up the open board has little chance of survival) **4 Qh5** (type (*l*) threat) **f5 5 g6!** and mates next move. If Black plays 2...Kg8 3 Qh5 (type (*k*) threat) Re8 (3...B×g5 transposes into the previous variation) 4 Qh7+ Kf8 5 Qh8 mate. If Black varies with 1 B×h7+ K×h7 2 Ng5+ Kg6 (2...Kh6 3 N×f7+ wins at least the queen) 3 h5+ Kf5 and White has 2 mates on the move. Finally, Black may decline the sacrifice with **1...Kh8** but White has not only won a pawn — he can continue his attack unabated with **2 Ng5 g6 3 N×e6 f×e6 4 B×g6 Kg7** (4...Rf5 is a little better, but insufficient) **5 Qg4 Rh8 6 Bf5+** (not 6 Q×e6 Nd×e5!) **Kf8 7 B×e6 Qe8** and White mates in two moves by an overload combination.

Look back again at Fig. 39. White has no more pieces in play than Black has, but he has more room for his pieces and has used this to bring more pieces to attack the king than Black can get to his defence. This is why the attack succeeds. Incidentally, you do not always need to play h4. If the black bishop were not at e7 then your own bishop at c1 would be enough protection for the N at g5.

As in the case of the KNP an attack on the KRP may prove well worthwhile even if it only forces Black to weaken the pawns in front of his king. Suppose, for example, that White has a bishop at d3 and plays Qh5 threatening mate. Black then plays 1...g6 and drives the queen away. Was White's manoeuvre a waste of time? Not necessarily, because Black now has a weaker formation (f7, g6, h7) and White may be able to use one of the attacks discussed in section 5.2.

(ii) The KRP captured or exchanged — attacks along the rook's-file

When the KRP has been captured or exchanged, there are attacks along the file somewhat similar to those of Fig. 35, though in these cases the KNP still stands at g7.

In type (*l*), with 2 major pieces — rooks or rook and queen — on the file, White plays 1 Rh8 mate. In types (*m*) and (*n*), the king cannot escape from the rook's-file, since g8 is controlled by a white piece, and the mate is effected by rook or queen along the h-file.

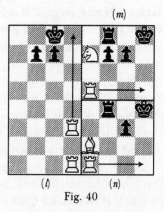

(*m*)

(*l*)   (*n*)

Fig. 40

An interesting example of type (*m*) occurs in the Ruy Lopez opening (Chapter 7). Play can proceed **1 e4 e5 2 Nf3 Nc6 3 Bb5 a6 4 Ba4** (White cannot win a pawn by 4 B×c6 d×c6 5 N×e5 because of 5...Qd4) **Nf6 5 0-0 Nxe4 6 Re1 Nc5 7 Nc3 Nxa4** (safer is 7...Be7) **8 Nxe5 Nxe5 9 Rxe5+ Be7 10 Nd5 0-0 11 Nxe7+ Kh8 12 Qh5 d6?** (12...g6 is best, but White has a strong attack — e.g. 13 Qh6 d6? 14 Rh5! gxh5 15 Qf6 mate) **13 Qxh7+! Kxh7 14 Rh5 mate.**

We have had examples of types (*l*), (*m*) and (*n*) before in Volume 1, Exercise 7, Nos. 2 and 9; Exercise 12, No. 1; and Revision Exercise No. 1.

(*iii*) The formation f7, g7, h6 — the second best formation

We finish section 5.3 with the case where the KRP has been advanced to h6 — i.e. the formation f7, g7, h6. Although on the whole not quite so strong as the formation f7, g7, h7 it has certain advantages, and is of frequent occurrence in practical play. If the pawn formation in front of the king has to be weakened, h6 is generally much less damaging than g6 (unless there is a bishop to go to g7 to guard the black squares). You can see why — with the KNP at g6, the squares f6 and h6 are both unguarded by pawns, but with the KRP at h6 all the third rank squares are guarded.

The advantages of the formation f7, g7, h6 over f7, g7, h7 are:
- (*a*) there is a bolt-hole for the king, so that back-rank mates (see section 5.4) are less likely;
- (*b*) White cannot maintain a bishop or knight at g5.

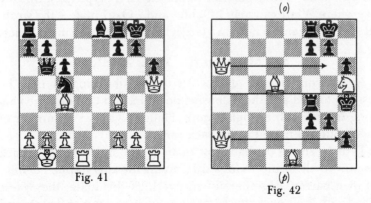

Fig. 41

(*o*)

(*p*)

Fig. 42

Of the 4 main disadvantages, the first 2 arise from the fact that the pawn on h6 is a target, having advanced beyond its fellows:

(*a*) White may be able to advance his KNP and exchange it for the black RP (taking care that Black cannot bypass it by...h5), thus opening a file.

(*b*) A piece may be sacrificed for the pawn — if QB and queen both attack the pawn, the sacrifice may prove fatal for Black. In Fig. 41, White plays B×h6, and after 1...g×h6 2 Q×h6, mate cannot be avoided (type (*l*). 1...g6 is met by 2 Q×g6+, the KBP being pinned, and 1...Na4 2 Bc1! Nc3+ 3 Ka1 leads to unavoidable mate.

(*c*) The third disadvantage is the weakening of the KNP. With pawn at h7 the NP, if hard-pressed, can advance to g6 where it will be guarded by 2 pawns. However, with the KRP at h6 a pawn forced to advance to g6 will only be guarded by one pawn, so that a sacrifice is more likely. Also, since the pawn at h6 would then have no pawn-support, it might be easily lost.

(*d*) The square g6 is itself weakened by the advance of the KRP to h6, being only guarded by the KBP. This may be worse than at first appears, since the BP is frequently pinned by the KB, when the square has no protection at all. We have already seen this in Fig. 41, in the variation 1...g6 2 Q×g6+. Figure 42 (*o*) shows another example; White can play 1 Qg6 threatening 2 Q×g7 mate and also 2 Nf6+ Kh8 3 Qh7 mate. If the king moves to h8 to avoid this pin, it may prove possible to pin the KNP; type (*p*) shows the case where White can play 1 Q×h6+ and 2 Q×g7 mate — the weakness of the advanced KRP as a target being once more in evidence.

5.4. Mate on the Back Rank

Apart from frontal attacks on the castled king, it may be possible to outflank the defensive position, and threaten the king along the seventh or eighth rank. Figure 43 shows a number of possibilities of mate on the back rank.

Type (*q*) shows the back row mate in its simplest form — Black has moved all his pieces forward, leaving the king trapped behind his own pawns. Beginners often overlook this mate; they press ahead with their own attack, take no notice of counter threats and suddenly they are mated. The danger of back-row mate is greatest when the pawns in front of the king are unmoved; you learn this one – and then you are caught by types (*r*), (*s*) and (*t*)! An important example of type (*s*) can be seen when Black's pawns stand at h7, g6, f7 and he has a bishop at g7, and king at g8; whilst

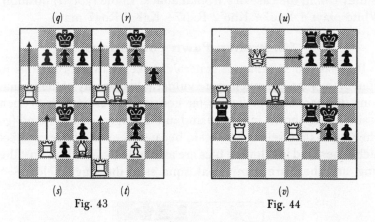

Fig. 43   Fig. 44

White's rook is at e1 and bishop at, say, f4 White plays 1 Re8+ Bf8 and now the old weakness on the black-coloured squares proves fatal, for White plays 1 Bh6, attacking the pinned bishop, and mate cannot be avoided. Note that 2 Bd6 also wins the bishop, but is not as good as 2 Bh6, since it does not take full advantage of the weakened squares in the king's-position.

You can see examples of these mating types in Volume 1, Exercise 7, No. 1, and Revision Exercises Nos. 6 and 11; and Volume 2, Exercise 1, No. 15; Exercise 6, No. 12; and Exercise 7, No. 11.

Figure 44, type (*u*), shows the use that can be made of a pin in conjunction with back-row mate. White plays 1 Q×f7+ R×f7 (or 1...Kh8 2 Q×f8 mate) 2 Ra8 mate. This has something in common with type (*o*).

If you want to see the finest 'back-row mate' combination ever played look back to the Adams–Torre position of Fig. 26; we gave this as an example of an overload combination, but the overloading is caused by back-row threats, so you can equally well think of it as a back-row attack.

We finish with an attack on the seventh instead of the eighth rank. You can nearly always win something if you can get two heavy pieces 'on the seventh' because you have outflanked the pawns; they cannot protect either the king's position or each other as they can in the case of a frontal attack. In the type (*v*) position, White plays 1 R×g7+ Kh8 2 R×h7+ Kg8 3 Rbg7 mate.

5.5. Broken Pawn Formations

It is easy to see that, in general, broken pawn formations in front of the king are much more vulnerable than any of the formations of connected pawns so far considered. Examples of such positions are shown in Fig. 45 and in Fig. 46, types (*x*), (*y*) and (*z*). The pawns themselves are weak, because they no longer protect each other, and in addition files are available for attack against the king, and there are many weak squares in the king's field.

Fig. 45

Figure 45 is a typical example. White has opened a file against the black king by advancing his KBP and sacrificing it at f6, and a second pawn-sacrifice on the g-file has opened the way for his QR. White plays 1 Rg1+ Kh8. Now, how is the attack to be continued? The natural attacking move 2 Qh5 is met by 2...Qd5+!, forcing the exchange of queens. If White has nothing immediate, Black may reach a won ending, but White has not yet made use of his extra developed piece, the KR at f4. This piece being well-placed for attack, and the partially exposed king point the way to success. White plays 2 Q×h7+! K×h7 3 Rh4 mate — type (*c*).

You will quite often find that a sacrifice of this kind is possible when you have got the queen and the rooks all in the attack. These pieces are so powerful that heavy sacrifices are worth while to open up the king completely to them.

In this example, you should note that Black's extra pawn at f6 is actually a handicap. If it were not there, 2 Q×h7+ K×h7 3 Rh4+ would be met by 3...Qh6 winning. This interference by useless pawns is typical of positions of this kind; but remember that if White had not been able to mate, these very pawns would have won the ending for Black, so don't sacrifice recklessly.

5.6. Some Other Mates

Figure 46 shows 4 more mates that may occur when the position in front of the castled king has been opened up, and the bishops and rooks are free to operate along open lines, whilst the knights can occupy weakened squares.

Types (*w*) and (*z*) show mates with 2 bishops — the former more frequent against the king castled on the king's-side, and the other against a king which has castled on the queen's-wing. Type (*z*) examples occur in Volume 1 in Exercise 7, No. 7; Exercise 12, No. 6; and Revision Exercise No. 15.

Type (*x*) involves the use of 3 minor pieces, though the 2 bishops may operate from long range. It is associated with the

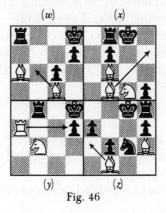

Fig. 46

great English chess-master, Blackburne, who was one of the

greatest players in the world round the turn of the century. Volume 1 examples are Group Exercise 'A', Game 'G', and Revision Exercise No. 9.

Type (*y*) is a mate with rook and knight, which can be easily overlooked, since the king appears in little danger from a solitary rook on the seventh rank, until the N moves to f6 to attack the square h7 and prevent the king's escape via g8. There is an example in Volume 1, Exercise 6, No. 9.

5.7. Summary

This has been the most difficult and important chapter in the book so far, and it is worth while summarizing the main points:

(*a*) How you attack the king's position depends on how the pawns are placed in front of the king.

(*b*) *The best formation,* all things considered, *is with the 3 pawns unmoved at f7, g7 and h7.* Except for back-row mates, this has no weakness, and is the most flexible. When hard-pressed, it can be transformed to f7, g6 and h7 or to f7, g7 and h6.

(*c*) Against the formation f7, g7, h7, the attacker will usually have to exchange the N on f6 or drive it away if he is to succeed. He can mount his attack against either g7 or h7.

(*d*) *The formation f7, g6 and h7 is usually weak unless there is a bishop on g7.* Against this formation, White attacks either along the unoccupied black squares, or by advancing BP or RP in order to exchange the defending NP and open a file.

(*e*) The formation f7, g7 and h6 is better than f7, g6, h7 unless the latter has a bishop at g7. White may be able to attack by the sacrifice B×h6 by playing to g6 when the KBP is pinned, or by advancing his KNP to g5.

(*f*) Broken pawns in front of the king are nearly always defensively weak.

(*g*) A pawn advance to break up the enemy king position is very often good when the players have castled on opposite wings.

(*h*) Look out for back-row mates when the king has no outlet.

(*i*) Doubled rooks or rook and queen on the seventh rank are very strong in attack.

There are a lot of examples from modern masterplay in the

next exercise; try them all. They will help you to absorb this chapter and will show you how you are getting on. Don't be discouraged if you find some of them hard; some of them *are* hard!

Exercise 11

These examples illustrate 'mating patterns'.
1. Black to move.
2. Black to move.
3. Black to move.
4. White to move.
5. Black to move.
The remaining 40 positions are nearly all from master play.
6. White to move.
7. White to move.
8. White to move.
9. White to move.
10. Black to move.
11. Black to move.
12. White to move.
13. Black to move.
14. White to move.
15. Black to move.
16. White to move.
17. Black to move.
18. Black to move.
19. White to move.
20. Black to move.
21. White to move.
22. White to move.
23. White to move.
24. White to move.
25. White to move.
26. White to move.
27. White to move.
28. White to move.
29. White to move.
30. Black to move.
31. White to move.
32. White, who was winning fairly easily, now played 1 Rha7. Why was this a fatal blunder?
33. White to move.
34. White to move.
35. Black to move.
36. In this position Black played 1...d2.
    (*a*) Why was this a fatal mistake?
    (*b*) How should Black have played?
37. Black played 1...Bc6. Can you find a better move?

38. Black has just captured a pawn on e4 and appears to have a good game, but is, in fact, lost. Why?
39. Black to move.
40. White to move.
41. White to move. In analysing this position, make quite sure that you have allowed for the *best* defence.
42. White to move.
43. White to move.
44. Black to move. How can he break up White's king-position decisively?
45. White has just played 1 h3. How does Black win? This is a good example to test your imagination and analytical powers.

Position 11.1

Position 11.2

Position 11.3

Position 11.4

Position 11.5

Position 11.6

Position 11.7

Position 11.8

Position 11.9

Position 11.10

Position 11.11

Position 11.12

Position 11.13

Position 11.14

Position 11.15

Position 11.16

Position 11.17

Position 11.18

Position 11.19

Position 11.20

Position 11.21

Position 11.22

Position 11.23

Position 11.24

Position 11.25

Position 11.26

Position 11.27

Position 11.28

Position 11.29

Position 11.30

Position 11.31

Position 11.32

Position 11.33

Position 11.34

Position 11.35

Position 11.36

Position 11.37

Position 11.38

Position 11.39

Position 11.40

Position 11.41

Position 11.42

Position 11.43

Position 11.44

Position 11.45

CHAPTER SIX

Winning the Ending

6.1. The Endgame Matters

Too many players — especially young ones — think that the endgame is dull and unimportant: they reckon to win or lose in the middle game. This is a wrong attitude. As you get better you will find more and more games are not finished by winning attacks; then endgame skill settles things — so start to get some now. You should study the ending and you will find that it is just as interesting as the opening and middle game — all the greatest players have excelled in and enjoyed endgame play.

Chapters 7 and 8 in Volume 1 dealt with the simplest types of endgame — the basic mates with queen or rook and the easier types of pawn ending. Here we will tackle some harder problems but even so only show you some of the most important types of ending and the main principles of play. When you want to learn more, read one of the books dealing just with endings; look at 'books to read' in Chapter 10 for some of these.

6.2. Two Pawns Unsupported by the King

Two pawns on adjacent files can protect each other against the enemy king even when their own king is too far away to help. In Fig. 47 (a), Black plays **1...Kb7** and White replies **2 b6**. Now, Black cannot capture by 2...K×b6 since the BP promotes, but must play **2...Kc8** after which White brings up his king to force promotion of a pawn.

Figure 47 (b) shows that pawns may be safe from capture even

when separated. Black to play must continue **1...Kg8**, for 1...Kf7
2 h7 wins for White. After 1...Kg8 White must not advance either
pawn, but move his king once to effect promotion.

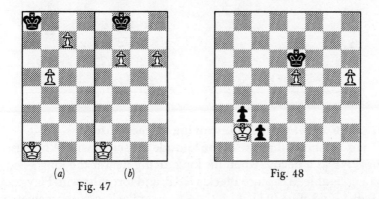

(*a*) (*b*) Fig. 48

Fig. 47

Figure 48 shows a position where White cannot leave the black
pawns unattended, and yet can win with his separated pawns,
which prove stronger than Black's united passed pawns. White
plays **1 h6 Kf7** (if 1...K×e5 2 h7 wins, the king being outside the
pawn's square) **2 h7 Kg7 3 e6! K×h7 4 e7** wins.

Now place the white pawns on the fourth rank instead of the
fifth rank. White can no longer win, but in fact loses! Play may
proceed **1 h5 Kf6 2 Kc1** (or 2 h6 Kg6 3 e5 K×h6 4 e6 Kg6, winning
the second pawn) **Kg5! 3 e5 K×h5 4 e6 Kg6** and wins. The
principles on which these king and pawn endings are based are:

(1) *The king never dares to take the back pawn — because the other one
queens.*

(2) *He can only capture one pawn if he remains in the square of the
other pawn.*

6.3. Positions with Equal Pawns

Positions with equal pawns are not necessarily drawn. Two
important cases are illustrated overleaf.

In Fig. 49, White wins because his pawns are further advanced,
and Black's king cannot come to the rescue. White plays **1 g6!** and
the pawn must be captured. If **1...h×g6 2 f6! g×f6 3 h6**, and if

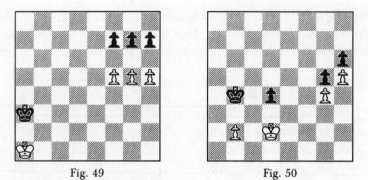

Fig. 49   Fig. 50

1...f×g6 2 h6! g×h6 3 f6, winning in each case.

Fig. 50 shows the case of the 'outside passed pawn'. White uses his QNP as a decoy, when his king, being nearer the king's- side pawns, is able to capture Black's KRP, and force the win. Play proceeds **1 Kd3 Kb3** (if 1...Kc5 2 b4+, with similar lines to the main variation) **2 K×d4 K×b2 3 Ke5 Kc3 4 Kf6 Kd4 5 Kg6 Ke4 6 K×h6 Kf4 7 Kg6 K×g4 8 h6** winning. This idea often comes up in play.

6.4. Minor Piece Endings

These are endings in which only bishops, knights and pawns take part. We shall look at those cases in which neither side has more than one minor piece left. If you understand these, then you will have a good idea of how to play in the more complicated cases when there are several minor pieces left on the board.

6.5. Knight Against Pawns

Fig. 51   Fig. 52

In Fig. 51, White cannot afford to lose his pawn, since king and knight alone only draw. Black plays **1...Kc4** in an attempt to win the pawn in exchange for his own. Play continues **2 Nxe4 Kb4** and now **3 Nc3**. If **3...Kxc3** 4 a5 wins. Note that 3 Nc5? Kxc5 only draws. *The pawn must be protected from the rear.* This is the same idea that we saw in the king and pawns ending when the king did not dare to take the back pawn because the front one queened.

Now place the white king on b4, his knight on c6, and his pawn on a6, with Black's king on c8. This position might occur a few moves later in the same game. Black would now play 1...Kc7 and White must not reply 2 a7 which looks natural, since 2...Kb7 draws. If 3 Kb5 Ka8 and now 4 Ka6(b6) is stalemate, whilst a knight move loses the pawn. Correct is 2 Kb5 Kc8 3 Kb6 and Black can resign. You have to be careful in all endings with the rook's pawn because of these stalemate chances and should not advance it to the seventh rank until you are sure this wins.

If you have just a knight against two pawns then you cannot win; Fig. 52 shows how careful you must be sometimes even to draw. Your only chance is to blockade the pawns with the knight and then come up with the king. Here, White must play **1 Nh3!** (1 Ne2 d3 2 Nc3 e3 3 Nd1 e2 wins for Black). If now **1...d3 2 Nf2 d2 3 Nd1** and White will win both pawns. If **1...e3 2 Nf4** and the pawns are again blockaded and lost. Black to play in the diagram would win by **1...d3 2 Nh3 e3 3 Nf4 d2!** In general, the pawns cannot be held by the knight alone if they can both reach the sixth rank in safety.

6.6. Bishop Against Pawns

In general, a lone bishop can draw against 2 pawns whether the latter are connected or isolated, and may be able to hold 3 connected pawns if they have not advanced too far.

In Fig. 53, Black has 2 advancing pawns, and the kings are too far removed to take an active part in the struggle. White to move draws by **1 Bc1 e3** (1...f3 2 Be3 blockades the pawn and draws easily — this should be White's aim in such endings) **2 Kf6 e2 3 Bd2 f3 4 Be1** and again blockade forces the draw.

With both pawns on the sixth rank, Black wins. Place the black pawns at e3 and f3, and whatever White plays, 1...f2 wins.

Fig. 53

If the king is available in defence, even pawns on the sixth rank are unlikely to win. Place White's king at f1 and his bishop at a3 with Black's king at e4, and black pawns at e3 and f3 Black cannot win. For instance, **1...e2+ 2 Kf2 Kd3 3 Bb4** and draws; or **1...f2 2 Ke2 Kf4 3 Bc5 Ke4 4 Bxe3 f1=Q+ 5 Kxf1 Kxe3** or, finally, **1...Kd3 2 Ke1 f2+ 3 Kf1 Kd2 4 Bb4+ Kd1 5 Ba5** draws.

As you will see from the last two sections, the bishop finds it much easier to deal with passed pawns than the knight. This is because it is a far-ranging piece, whilst the knight is a 'short-stepper'.

The bishop is never too far away to reach the pawns and it can control them from a distance. The knight on the other hand must come right down to the scene of action and then the pawns are likely to harass it. We shall look again, in section 6.10, at the relative strengths of bishop and knight in the ending.

6.7. General Remarks about Minor Piece Endings

Usually you can win with one extra pawn in endings where each side has a minor piece and pawns. We shall see, however, that this is not so frequently true for 'bishop of opposite colour' endings (section 6.9).

Here are the main things that you should try to do:

(a) *Bring your king into the fray as quickly as possible.* This is essential in almost all endings.

(b) *If you have the extra pawn, try to force a passed pawn.* You can support this with your king and minor piece and force the opposing king to retreat. Then you should be able to promote your pawn, win the opponent's piece for it, or get your king in amongst the enemy pawns.

(c) *If you are a pawn down, try to exchange off pawns.* If you can reach a position where your opponent has just one pawn left, then you can give up your piece for it and draw. With the extra pawn you avoid pawn exchanges (except to help to get a passed pawn) but try to exchange the pieces; endings with pawns only are the easiest to win if you are a pawn ahead.

Even with equal pawns, minor piece endings are not necessarily drawn. If you have better placed pawns or king or a more effective minor piece the game may still be won. Isolated pawns (those with no neighbour to protect them) are usually a weakness; a king in better play than the enemy's may easily be decisive. You will learn with experience to recognize these and other signs of good and bad endgame positions.

6.8. Knight and Pawns Against Knight and Pawns

The knight, being a short-stepping piece, takes a number of moves to cross the board. In endings with pawns on both sides of the board you have to watch carefully for chances to sacrifice pawns (as, for example, in Fig. 49), or even the knight, to rush a pawn through to queen before the opposing knight can be brought to the scene of the action.

The knight is very effective against isolated pawns. First of all, it may be able to win such a pawn — but there is another less obvious reason, which applies perhaps even more in the middle game than in the ending. *The knight has a very strong post on the square immediately in front of an isolated pawn,* especially if the pawn is near the centre of the board. The isolated pawn cannot advance and it gets in the way of the king or other pieces, whih might drive the knight back.

You will not absorb points like this fully until you have come across them in practice many times; look out for them and you will gradually make them part of your game. Meanwhile, here is a straightforward example showing how one sets about winning with an extra pawn:

Fig. 54

In Fig. 54, Black, to move, has an extra pawn. In a correspondence game, play proceeded **1...f6 2 g×f6 g×f6** (Black has established a passed pawn which he aims to promote after due preparation) **3 Kb2 Kf7** (both sides aim to bring their kings rapidly to the scene of action) **4 c3 Ke6** (note that the king aims at the centre, rather than directly to gaining the KRP; if 4...Kg6 5 Kc2 Kh5 6 Kd3 Nc5+ 7 Ke3 K×h4 8 Kf4, and though Black can win, White's centralized king makes the process more troublesome than in the main variation) **5 Kc2 f5 6 Kd3 Nd6 7 Nd2** (exchange of knights leaves a won pawn-ending for Black, and 7 Ne3 f4 8 N-moves Kf5 helps Black towards promotion) **Ke5 8 Ke3 f4+ 9 Kf3 Kf5 10 a4 Nf7** and White resigned. He is driven further back by the knight check and loses his KRP for nothing, for if 11 Nc4 Ne5+ 12 N×e5 K×e5 13 Kg4 Ke4 14 h5 f3 wins.

6.9. Bishop and Pawns Against Bishop and Pawns

The bishop can only move on squares of one colour, hence we get the most important question in bishop endings — 'What coloured squares are best for the pawns?'

Beginners almost always give the wrong answers to this question. They want to keep their pawns on the same coloured squares as their own bishop so that it can protect them; they also want (if it does not contradict their first rule) to keep the pawns on squares of opposite colour to the enemy bishop.

There are two reasons why this is wrong: (*a*) the pawns get in the way of the friendly bishop, (*b*) with bishop and pawns all on squares of one colour, you have no control over squares of the opposite colour and the opponent can stop you making any headway.

Figure 55 shows an extreme case where this lack of control of squares of one colour leaves a draw, even though Black is no less than 5 pawns ahead! White just moves his bishop up and down the diagonal, and takes any black pawn that moves.

Now take away the black pawns at f6, e5 and d4 and move the pawn back from b2 to b3 and Black wins — with or without the move — by ...c2 since he controls certain white as well as black squares.

Fig. 55

All this leads us to the expert's rule: 'If it is safe to do so (i.e. without early loss of pawns), *keep your pawns on opposite coloured squares to your own bishop, and on the same-coloured squares as the opposing bishop.*'

Of course, if both bishops operate on squares of the same colour, the two parts of this rule are contradictory; in that case, it is usually right to be guided by the first part of the rule, and keep your pawns on squares of *opposite* colour to the bishops. If you carry out this plan, both bishops will have equal freedom to move among the pawns; and if the pawns advance, both sides can control the squares to which they move; but whilst these two factors balance out, you have some control over squares of both colours, denied to your opponent; and your pawns are safe, whilst your opponent's pawns may be subject to attack if he places them on squares of the same colour as the bishops. This is particularly the case if the pawns become locked, when it is almost always better to be the player with the pawns on opposite-coloured rather than on the same-coloured squares.

Figure 56 shows a case where this difference in the coloured squares on which the pawns stand enables White to force a winning king and pawn ending.

Fig. 56

White plays **1 Kd3 Bd6** (1...Ke6 — the natural move — allows 2 Ke4 Bg5 3 Be5 Bd8 4 Bf4, winning a pawn; or 2...Bd6 3 Bg7 winning a pawn; so that Black's pawn-weaknesses allow White to get a superior king-position for the resultant ending) **2 Ke4 Bh2 3 Bc1** (but *not* 3 Be5? B×e5 4 K×e5 Ke7!, with the opposition, and the game is drawn; White must improve his king position before exchanging bishops) **Kg7 4 Kd5 Bd6 5 Ke6 Bh2 6 Bb2+ Kh7** (or 6...Kf8 7 Kf6 Bf4 8 Ba3+ Ke8 9 Kg6 Be3 10 Bb2 Ke7 11 Be5 Kd8 12 Bg7 and wins) **7 Be5!** (for now the king and pawn ending is won for White) **B×e5 8 K×e5 Kg7 9 Ke6 and wins.**

When bishops are of 'opposite colour', the inability to force an exchange of pieces, and even more, the difficulty of controlling squares of the colour of the opposing bishop, make it very hard to win. Other factors being equal, an advantage of one pawn is rarely decisive, and even a 2-pawn advantage may not result in victory. In Fig. 57, White has no way of winning. **1 d5 Ke5,** with blockade, and **1 e5+ B×e5 2 d×e5+ K×e5** both draw.

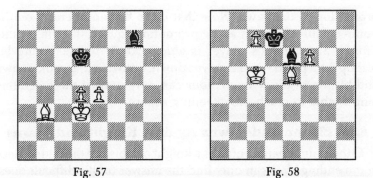

Fig. 57   Fig. 58

When the pawns are separated, White has greater winning chances. In Fig. 58, White wins by **1 Kb6 Bd5** (or 1...Kc8 2 Kc6 Bf7 3 Kd6 Bh5 4 Ke7) **2 f7 Bxf7 3 Kb7**, etc.

The win can be forced if there are at least 2 files between the pawns, except in certain cases where the rook's pawn is involved.

When there are queens or rooks as well as opposite coloured bishops on the board, the game is much less likely to be drawn. Now there may be strong attacking chances against the king, since it is hard for the defender to meet threats on squares of the same colour as the attacker's bishop.

Understanding these properties of 'opposite-coloured bishops' is a great help in knowing when to exchange pieces. Suppose you have a knight and a 'white-coloured' bishop against a knight and 'black-coloured' bishop; if you are a pawn down, you should try to exchange knights to reach a draw with bishops of opposite colour; but if you are a pawn ahead, you should exchange bishop for knight, or knight for bishop to reach an ending with real winning chances. If, on the other hand, both players have rook and bishop, and White is a pawn ahead, what should be his normal policy in regard to exchanges? If bishops are of the same colour, he should try to exchange rooks, but if of opposite colour, the rooks should be retained.

To conclude this section, we note one important exception to the rule that an extra piece and pawn win. Place White's king at h5, a white bishop at d3 and a white pawn at h6 with Black's king at h8. There is no way in which the black king can be winkled out of the corner to force promotion of the pawn. Note that if the bishop operates on the same- coloured squares as the promotion-square, the win is quite simple. Sometimes a player is able to draw by sacrificing his bishop for a pawn when 2 pawns down, knowing that rook's pawn and bishop of the wrong colour can only draw if the defending king is able to reach the queening square.

6.10. Bishop and Pawns Against Knight and Pawns

Other things being equal, is a knight or a bishop the better piece in the ending? We can only find the answer to this difficult question by looking at the weak and strong points of the two pieces.

We have already seen that the bishop is most effective along open diagonals, unhampered by pawns; the knight is at its best on a crowded board where it can hop about more easily than any other piece. In the ending, therefore, an 'open board' favours the bishop, while the knight is better when the position is blocked by the pawns.

This advantage of the knight is increased if there are useful squares (especially those in the centre — see section 6.8) on which it can be posted with safety from attack. Once more we see why it is wrong for the player with the bishop to keep his pawns on squares of the same colour; if he does so, he will impede the movement of his bishop, and give the knight strong squares of the opposite colour from which to operate.

On the open board, the bishop's advantage is increased if the players want to operate on both flanks. This is especially true in unbalanced positions, where there is an extra pawn for White on one side of the board and for Black on the other. Now the bishop can help his own pawns to advance and at the same time defend against the advance of the enemy pawns; the short-ranged knight cannot manage both tasks at once. Summarizing:

In favour of the bishop	In favour of the knight
Open positions	Blocked positions
Unbalanced positions	Positions with strong central points for the knight

Overall, there is little to choose between the two pieces —

players of the last century thought a knight rather better than a bishop, but modern masters have a slight preference on balance for the bishop. For practical purposes they may be considered as of equal value. Here are two positions which illustrate the strengths and weaknesses of the two pieces.

Figure 59 shows a position which is symmetrical except that White has a bishop and Black a knight, but even with the move Black will lose. E.g. **1...g3 2 hxg3 hxg3 3 Bxg3! Nxg3 4 b6 axb6 5 a6!** (but *not* 5 axb6? Nf5! 6 b7 Nxd4+ and 7...Nc6 winning) or **1...Nf6 2 b6 axb6 3 a6** or, finally, **1...h3 2 b6 axb6 3 a6 g3 4 Bxg3! Nxg3 5 a7!** promoting a pawn in each case. In this type of position, the knight is always at a disadvantage.

Fig. 59   Fig. 60

Figure 60 (from the game Zubareff–Alexandrov, Moscow, 1915) shows the other side of the picture. The pawns are more blocked, White has complete control of the black squares with powerful points at d4 and f4 for his knight, and, largely because of his control of the black squares, White's king can penetrate the black position. White played first to establish his knight at f4 tying the bishop down to the defence of 2 pawns, after which a waiting move forced the penetration of Black's position by the white king.

Play continued **1 Nb3 Bg4 2 Nd4 Bh3** (not 2...Kd7 3 Kb6) **3 Ne2 Bf5 4 Nf4 Bg4.** Now White plays his waiting move **5 b4** and after **5...Kd7 6 Kb6 Bf3 7 Kxa6 Kc6 8 Nxe6** Black resigned.

Compare the ending with that in Fig. 56 and see how the entry of the king was decisive in both cases.

6.11. Rook Against Pawns

A rook can win against 2 connected passed pawns which have not advanced beyond the fifth rank when the kings are too distant to affect the play.

Fig. 61

In Fig. 61, White wins by **1 Rd7 d3 2 Rd4** and both pawns fall. Now advance both pawns to the sixth rank. This time Black promotes a pawn no matter how White plays. For example, **1 Rd7 d2** (or 1...e2) **2 Rd3 e2** and promotes, or **1 Rc3 e2 2 Rc1 d2** or **1 Rc1 d2 2 Rd1 e2** and Black has a theoretical though difficult win with queen against rook.

Lone rook against a pawn protected by the king is quite a common ending; you get it when the opponent gives up his own rook to stop your last pawn from queening. It is usually a win, even with your own king far away, if the pawn has not got beyond the fifth rank; however, exact play is often necessary. A study of such positions is beyond the scope of this book; later on you will have to learn how to win them.

6.12. Endings where Both Sides have a Rook

Apart from the king, the rook is the last piece to come into active play, and it frequently remains for a long time in comparative safety on its own back rank. For this reason rooks often survive after all the other pieces have been exchanged, and rook and pawn endings are the most frequent of all in practical play. They are also very tricky, and provide innumerable difficulties and subtleties which have caused even the greatest players to go astray. It will only be possible here to examine a very few positions, and to give general guidance on the principles to be adopted when they are encountered.

First, let us consider two cases where there is only one pawn on the board, but each side has a rook.

Fig. 62 shows the famous Lucena Position, named after a Spanish player who lived 500 years ago. White has reached the queening square with his king and is not in check. In such positions the win can be forced, by driving the black king a file further from the pawn, and by forming a bridge to protect the

Fig. 62   Fig. 63

white king from checks by the rook along the pawn's-file. White plays **1 Rd4 Rb1 2 Re4+ Kf7 3 Kd7 Rd1+ 4 Kc6 Rc1+ 5 Kd6 Rd1+ 6 Kc5 Rc1+ 7 Rc4** and wins. Note the importance of checking the king to the bishop's file at move 2 — had the king remained at e8 Black would now play 7...Rxc4+ 8 Kxc4 Kd7 and 9...Kxc7.

In attack, you should *advance the king* to the queening square, rather than press straight on with the pawn. Place White's king at c5 and rook at h6, with a pawn at d5. Black's king stands at d8 and his rook at g1. White to move, must force the black king away from d8 and d7, and this cannot be done by 1 d6, when Black simply checks from the eighth rank, and White can make no further headway. Correct is **1 Kd6! Rg8 2 Kc6 Rg1 3 Rh8+ Ke7 4 d6+ Ke6 5 Re8+ Kf7 6 Re2** and White forces the Lucena Position.

If Black varies with 2...Re8 3 d6 Rf8 4 Rh7 Kc8 5 Ra7 Kb8 6 Rb7+ Ka8 7 Rb4, and the way has been cleared for the pawn.

In defence also, try to get your king to the queening square. You use your rook in two ways. Try first of all to stop the advance of the enemy king — keep your rook, if you can, on the third rank to act as a barrier. Once the enemy pawn has got to the sixth, you use a different plan; move your rook down to the seventh and eighth rank and start checking the king as it tries to advance.

In general, if the defending king is in front of the pawn, or even if it is close to it before the pawn has advanced far, the ending of rook and pawn against rook should be drawn, the winning positions being somewhat exceptional.

Fig. 63 shows a common situation in the ending. White to play wins by 1 Ra8 employing skewer technique. Black to move can draw by 1...Kb7! to discount this possibility. Now White can force his king to g6, but promptly has it checked away again. The white rook is badly placed in front of the pawn. White should aim to *place the rook behind an advancing pawn*; if a rook blocking its advance moves away, the pawn promptly advances, and the mobility of the defending rook is reduced.

It would take a whole book to go properly into the problems of endings where each side has a rook and a number of pawns. All we can do is to set out certain general principles that usually apply:

(*a*) As in all endings, *the king must play an active part* in attack or defence.

(*b*) The best position of all for a rook is on the seventh rank, hemming in the enemy king; often this is enough to win the game, other things being equal, and it may well be worthwhile to give up a pawn to establish an unassailable rook 'on the seventh'. Another strong position (for either attacker or defender) is behind an advancing pawn.

(*c*) Try to *defend by counter-attack*. The rook is bad at passive defence so keep it as active as possible. An excellent position is on the seventh or eighth rank (as in Fig. 63); then, as the enemy king moves up the board in attack, you can carry out a long series of checks from behind, and possibly also mop up some pawns that he has left unguarded in his rear.

(d) Endings with all the pawns on one side of the board are usually drawn, even when one player has an extra pawn. With pawns on both sides of the board, the player with an extra pawn usually wins.

This is because we use the extra pawn to establish a passed pawn and then the defending king and rook are needed to stop its promotion. If there are pawns on the other side of the board your king will then be free to move in and attack them; however, if all the pawns are on the same side of the board the defending king may be able to prevent this penetration while still keeping the passed pawn under control.

So, *if you are a pawn down, try to exchange off all the pawns on the other side of the board.*

(e) Except for the case of bishops of opposite colour, endings with rooks on the board are harder to win when you are a pawn ahead than any others. It is therefore a very good principle to *exchange off rooks when you are ahead in pawns, but keep them on when your opponent has extra pawns.*

6.13. Other Endings

We have only introduced you to endgame theory. There are many endings that we have not discussed at all, such as those with queen and pawns or with rooks and minor pieces and we have only given the basic principles of those we have discussed. Remember that the endgame is both interesting and very important and play as hard in the ending as you do in the rest of the game; you will get a lot of extra wins if you do.

In the following positions, which are suitable for group working, we do not tell you the result, find this out for yourself as part of the exercise.

Group Exercise 'B'

1. Black to move.
2. Black to move.
3. (a) White to move; (b) Black to move.
4. White to move.
5. Can White win in this slightly modified version of Position 4?
6. Black to move.

7. White to move.
8. Black to move.
9. White to move.
10. Black to move.
11. Black to move.
12. White to move.
13. White to move.
14. White to move.
15. White to move.
16. Black to move.
17. Black to move.
18. White to move.
19. Black to move.
20. Black to move.
21. (*a*) Black to move; (*b*) White to move.
22. White to play and win. This position was composed by Dr. Emanuel Lasker, World Champion from 1894 to 1921.
23. White to move. This difficult position shows how intricate an ending can be.

Position B.1

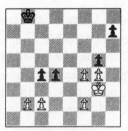

Position B.2

Position B.3

Position B.4

Position B.5

Position B.6

Position B.7

Position B.8

Position B.9

Position B.10

Position B.11

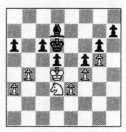

Position B.12

Position B.13

Position B.14

Position B.15

Position B.16

Position B.17

Position B.18

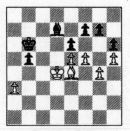

Position B.19   Position B.20   Position B.21

Position B.22   Position B.23

CHAPTER SEVEN

The Openings
1 e4 e5

7.1. How to Play the Openings

All young players want to learn the openings; what is a sensible way to start? First, we can decide on what is *not* a sensible way — and that is to memorize lines of play.

Books specializing in the opening list many thousands of variations and these are being changed and added to all the time; so there is too much to learn by heart and anyway you would be out of date before you had finished learning. And what do you do if your opponent plays a line that is not 'in the books'?

The only satisfactory way to learn is to *understand the principles* of the openings you play, so that you know what you are trying to do. In this chapter we try to explain these for a number of recognized openings. We give two examples in each case, one showing how the opponent can be met satisfactorily by a better defence. We also indicate briefly other things that might happen and put some questions to help you to think about the opening for yourself. Of course this does not give anything like a complete analysis of even the simplest openings; but it gives you some idea of what each opening is about. Then, later on, when you study books on the opening, you will be able to understand the lines they give and not just memorize them.

You must start by playing openings in which the ideas and methods of play are reasonably straightforward: even the greatest players started in this way. These are the openings in which the objects are rapid development, immediate control of the centre and an early attack on the enemy king. Everyone would play them except that in masterplay defence is so good that Black can too easily find a way to draw. For this reason, masters tend to play more subtle and complex openings in which the way to equalize is harder to find. This does not apply, however, to the ordinary player and especially not to the young player. You should play the simpler and more adventurous openings, from which you will learn how to use the pieces. Much later on you can go on to the more difficult openings — if you play them now you won't understand what you are doing and you will learn nothing except how to be a dull player.

Play the openings beginning 1 e4 e5. This chapter looks at these from both White's and Black's point of view; in Chapter 8 we suggest what to do when Black meets your 1 e4 with some other move and — when you are Black — what to do when White opens with some move other than 1 e4.

Finally, there is a lot of meat in this chapter; don't get indigestion! When you study any section first play through the main lines (those in heavy type) and don't bother about the notes. When you have got the general hang of the main lines, then you can look at the comments in brackets without getting confused.

7.2. The Scotch Game
1 e4 e5 2 Nf3 Nc6 3 d4

As we know, one of the main objects in the opening is to occupy the centre. The quickest way, 1 e4 e5 2 d4, actually loses time. After 2...exd4 3 Qxd4 Nc6 White has to lose a developing move by moving his queen a second time. The Scotch Game, so called from its successful adoption by the Edinburgh players in a correspondence game against London in 1824, delays d4 one move to avoid recapturing with the queen when the pawns are exchanged.

The normal continuation is **3...exd4 4 Nxd4**. White now has more space available, having a central pawn whilst Black has none, but he has lost a little developing time, having played two moves with his knight. Black can use his slight gain in time to attack White's centre and equalize.

Here is an example to show what might happen if Black played weakly. After **4...Nf6 5 Nxc6 bxc6 6 e5 Nd5 7 Bc4 Nb6 8 Bb3 Bc5** (this natural move is not as good as 8...Ba6 which prevents White castling; 9 Nc3 d5 10 exd6 Bxd6) **9 Qg4 0-0?** (better is 9...g6 10 Bg5 Be7 11 Qf3 Nd5 12 Bh6, though Black is still rather uncomfortable) **10 Bh6** (Fig. 64) **g6 11 Bxf8**, with advantage.

Try to see why White got the better of this. First, White's advantage in the centre allowed Black's knight to be driven away; then *having no pieces to defend his king*, Black castled. Notice also White's Qg4. This is often good when the enemy knight has been driven back and the king's bishop has come out; but remember that Black may attack your queen by ...d5, discovering his QB.

Here is a line showing Black's counter-attack holding its own. **4...Nf6 5 Nc3 Bb4 6 Nxc6 bxc6 7 Bd3 d5 8 exd5 cxd5 9 0-0 0-0 10 Bg5 Be6** (Fig. 65). Both sides have developed, and the game is about even.

Fig. 64. White has the advantage   Fig. 65. Equal game

Now learn more about the Scotch Game by trying out the following suggestions:

(*a*) Decide why 3...d6 is not a very good move.

(*b*) Examine the exchange 4 Nxd4 Nxd4 5 Qxd4 and decide whether it is a good idea from Black's point of view.

(*c*) Play some games in which Black plays 4...Bc5 (another good defensive method), and see how you get on.

(*d*) Play some games in which White plays e5 safely — as in the first variation — and find for yourself some of the advantages and disadvantages of this move in practical play.

(*e*) Try out the wild line 4...Qh4 5 Nb5 Qxe4+ 6 Be2 and see whether you can justify White's sacrificial play by strong attacking chess.

We don't give any answers to these suggestions in this book: they are put in to help you to *develop your own ideas about the openings*.

7.3. The Four Knights Game
1 e4 e5 2 Nf3 Nc6 3 Nc3 Nf6

f3(f6) and c3(c6) are nearly always good squares for the knights in the opening, but the best squares for the bishop are less obvious and depend much more on how things go. Because of this, people often say 'knights before bishops', and in the 'Four Knights' all the knights came out before any other piece is moved. This is a sound but dull opening. By defending his KP with the third move, White leaves Black few chances of an early counter-attack but equally this move does little to worry Black. Choose a more aggressive opening — you will learn more that way and get more exciting positions.

We only give one line of play here, showing a good way of developing for both players. This goes **4 Bb5** (4 d4 exd4 5 Nxd4 transposes into the Scotch Game; and 4 Bc4 is met by 4...Nxe4! which is examined under 'Two Knights Defence' in section 7.6)

Fig. 66

Bb4 5 0–0 0–0 6 d3 d6 7 Bg5 (threatening Nd5) **Bxc3 8 bxc3 Qe7** (the manoeuvre from moves 8–10 allows Black to relieve the pin on his KN and, at the same time, bring his QN to a more effective post) **9 Re1 Nd8 10 d4 Ne6 11 Bc1 Rd8** and Black has equality (Fig. 66).

7.4. The Giuoco Piano
1 e4 e5 2 Nf3 Nc6 3 Bc4 Bc5

Despite its name, the Giuoco Piano, or 'Quiet Game', can give rise to hair-raising variations.

The opening aims at rapid development, and occupation of the centre, combined with pressure on the f7 square, the weakest defensive point in the initial set-up.

4 c3 (this is the most energetic move, aiming to obtain a strong centre by 5 d4: alternatives 4 d3, 4 Nc3 and 4 0–0 are all quite sound, but pose less difficult problems for Black) **4...Nf6** (this, in turn, is the most energetic reply: it is almost invariably good to develop the KN to this square early in the game, as it mounts a counter-attack in the centre, and allows an early Castles for Black) **5 d4 exd4** (the move 5...Bb6? allows 6 dxe5 Nxe4 7 Qd5! with the double threat of 8 Qxe4 and 8 Qxf7 mate — a very common trap which is frequently possible after Black's KN goes to e4 in the king's-side openings) **6 cxd4**.

Here we will branch out into the two lines 6...Bb6 and 6...Bb4+.

6...Bb6 7 Nc3 (White can do better with an immediate 7 e5, since the reply 7...d5, which is frequently good in similar positions, allows 8 exf6 dxc4 9 d5! Na5 — 9...Nb4 10 Qa4+ wins — 10 fxg7 and Black's position is disorganized and exposed: e.g. 10...Rg8 11 0–0 Rxg7 12 Re1+ Kf8 13 Bh6! wins) **7...0–0?** (Black should challenge the centre with 7...Nxe4 8 Nxe4 d5 — another common manoeuvre in such positions — when he should be able to hold his own in the resulting complications; once this chance has been missed, Black has no further opportunity of equalizing with ...d5 and White's control of the centre quickly ensures victory) **8 e5** (Fig. 67) **Ng4** (if now 8...d5 9 Bb3! and 10 Nxd5 or if 8...Ne8 9 Bg5! Ne7 10 Nd5! wins — Black has no room for manoeuvre) **9 h3 Nh6 10 Bg5 Qe8 11 B×h6 gh×6 12 Nd5! Kg7 13 Qd3!** (threatening 14 Nf6 followed by 15 N×e8 or 15 Q×h7 mate) **Rh8 14 Qf5! d6 15 Qf6+ Kg8 16 Q×h6! Qd8 17 Nf6+ Q×f6 18 e×f6** and **19 Qg7** mate.

Before proceeding to the second variation, discuss this play, see how you can improve on Black's play, and decide what you would then do if you were faced with these improvements as White. Now to the second line.

6...Bb4+! 7 Bd2 (7 Nc3 N×e4 8 0–0 leads to very complicated play, in which Black wins a pawn, but White gets a strong attack.

Fig. 67. White is winning

Fig. 68. Black has held his own

One possible continuation is 8...B×c3 9 d5 Ne5 10 b×c3 N×c4 11 Qd4 f5! 12 Q×c4 d6 with approximate equality; work out how White wins against the move of any of the black knights to d6 on move 11) **B×d2+ 8 Nb×d2 d5!** (the usual correct way to counter in the centre) **9 e×d5 N×d5 10 0–0 0–0** (Fig. 68) and Black has held his own fairly well. Notice how comfortably the black knight is placed on d5 in front of the isolated pawn.

The Giuoco Piano is one of the most interesting openings and you will learn a lot, as Black and White, by playing it frequently.

Questions and Suggestions

(*a*) Why is the non-developing move 4 c3 (taking the best square away from the QN) justified in this opening?

(*b*) Why would 5 d3 be a feeble move, and what should Black answer?

(*c*) After 6...Bb4+ 7 Bd2 Bxd2+ 8 Nbxd2 can you see another way in which Black can play ...d5 instead of making the move immediately at move 8?

(*d*) If 6...Bb4+ 7 Nc3 Nxe4 8 0–0 Bxc3 is followed by 9 bxc3, is 9...Nxc3 a good move?

(*e*) What is Black's best ninth move in variation (*d*)?

(*f*) Why does White play 9 d5 instead of capturing the bishop?

7.5. The Evans Gambit
1 e4 e5 2 Nf3 Nc6 3 Bc4 Bc5 4 b4

The Evans Gambit is an exciting offshoot of the Giuoco Piano, named after a British sea-captain. A gambit is a chess opening in which material (usually one or more pawns) is given up for an advantage in position. Here White sacrifices the QNP to decoy the black KB from the centre, and to gain open lines along which to deploy his pieces. In particular the attack is directed once more at f7 square.

The gambit is usually accepted by **4...Bxb4** (though it may be declined by 4...Bb6) **5 c3 Bc5** (the natural move, but more dangerous than 5...Ba5, since White can now gain time on the bishop) **6 d4 exd4 7 0–0 dxc3 8 Nxc3**. Now Black has two extra pawns, but White's lead in development and better centralization make it very difficult for Black to set up an adequate defence. **8...Nf6** (best here is 8...d6; but White maintains the attack with 9 e5 dxe5 10 Qb3 Qe7 11 Nd5 Qd7 12 Rd1 etc.) **9 e5 Ng4 10 Qd5 Qe7** (defending the mate and KB) **11 Bg5** (Fig. 69) **Qf8** (if 11...f6 12 exf6 gxf6 13 Rae1) **12 Qe4 Nh6 13 Nd5 Bb6 14 Rab1! Ba5 15 Rb5 a6 16 Rxa5 Nxa5 17 Nxc7** mate.

Safer for Black is the line **5...Ba5 6 d4 d6** (intent on completing his development, rather than gobbling up a number of pawns) **7 Qb3 Qd7** (if 7...Qe7 8 d5 and 9 Qa4+, forking the king and KB) **8 dxe5 Bb6** (threatening to eliminate White's KB by 9...Na5, whereas 8...dxe5 would be risky, opening up the d-file for later attack by White's rooks, and giving White an excellent diagonal for his QB by Ba3. It is usually wrong to open up lines when your opponent is better developed, especially if he is attacking you). This position leads to most interesting middle-game possibilities (Fig. 70). The last variation demonstrates a valuable technique in meeting a gambit — *accept the material, and then be prepared to return it* in order to blunt the attack and aim at a preferable ending.

One possibility from the position of Fig. 70 is **9 Bb5 Nge7 10 exd6 cxd6 11 Ba3 Qg4 12 0-0 Be6 13 Qc2 0-0-0 14 Nbd2,** with equal chances.

The Russian Grandmaster Tal, World Champion 1959-61, stated that he would try the Evans Gambit against Botvinnik in

Fig. 69. Although he is two pawns up, Black is losing

Fig. 70. Black has quite good chances

the World Championship if he got a chance, so don't think it isn't sound enough for you to play! It gives very good practice in both attack and counter-attack; if Black can beat White back he can often get a very strong attack himself. Also there is a lot to be found out in the Evans — so you might make a discovery.

Questions and Suggestions

(a) Find out what White threatens if he substitutes 7 Qa4 for 7 Qb3 in the last variation.

(b) If Black replies 7...exd4 in (a), and White replies 8 Nxd4, find out how Black should continue, and decide which side stands better.

(c) Another variation is 5...Ba5 6 d4 exd4 7 0-0 Bb6 8 cxd4 d6 9 Nc3. What compensation has White for his sacrificed pawn?

If Black now plays 9...Nf6 decide what White should reply.

(*d*) Play a number of games to try out the variation of (*c*).

(*e*) In the Evans Gambit Declined where Black plays 4...Bb6, determine whether White can safely win a pawn by 5 b5.

(*f*) One variation of the Gambit Declined continues 5 b5 Na5 6 Nxe5 Nh6 7 d4 d6 8 Bxh6 dxe5 9 Bxg7 Rg8 10 Bxf7+ Kxf7 11 Bxe5. Whose position do you prefer? Play some games with this variation also.

7.6. The Two Knights Defence
1 e4 e5 2 Nf3 Nc6 3 Bc4 Nf6

Black can avoid the dangers of the Giuoco Piano and the Evans Gambit by playing 3...Nf6 — but this has complications of its own. White has three main lines 4 Nc3, 4 Ng5 and 4 d4 which we will look at in turn.

4 Nc3 is not so good as the other two; however, in ordinary school or club play you may often meet it so we give some examples here. The trouble with the move is that Black can reply 4...Nxe4! with a good game e.g. 5 Nxe4 d5 (recovering the piece with a pawn fork and counter-attacking in the centre) 6 Bd3 dxe4 7 Bxe4 Bd6 8 0–0 0–0 9 d4? exd4 10 Nxd4 Nxd4 11 Qxd4? Bxh2+ 12 Kxh2 Qxd4. 6 Bb5 and 6 Bxd5 also give Black a good game. After 4...Nxe4 White might try to expose the black king by 5 Bxf7+ Kxf7 6 Nxe4 but after 6...d5 7 Neg5+ Kg8 Black's control of the centre and open lines gives him the advantage, e.g. 8 d3 h6 9 Nh3 Bg4 (or even 9...g5, threatening a pawn fork) 10 Be3 Qf6 11 Nhg1 Rd8 threatening 12...e4, with advantage to Black. Notice that you must not play the sacrifice ...Nxe4 if you have a bishop of your own at c5 since then Nxe4 will attack your bishop and you won't be able to recover the piece.

4 Ng5 is an interesting move. White has only two pieces out so it ought to be wrong for him to make an attack like this: on the other hand it is not easy tactically to meet his threat. A conflict of ideas like this usually leads to dangerous positions for both players. Here is a line in which White's attack succeeds. **4 Ng5 d5! 5 exd5 Nxd5? 6 Nxf7** (6 d4 is probably even stronger but the knight sacrifice gives White a powerful attack) **Kxf7 7 Qf3+Ke6 8 Nc3 Nb4 9 Qe4 c6 10 a3 Na6 11 d4** (Fig. 71) **Qf6?** (11...Nc7 is best) **12 Nxd5 cxd5 13 Bxd5+ Kd6 14 dxe5+Qxe5 15 Bf4** wins.

Fig. 71. A difficult position: Fig. 72. Another difficult position,
chances about equal   rather in Black's favour
in practical play

Black is better advised to let the pawn go and play **5...Na5! 6 Bb5+ c6 7 dxc6 bxc6 8 Be2 h6 9 Nf3** (Fischer has successfully experimented with the bizarre looking 9 Nh3!?) **e4 10 Ne5 Bd6 11 d4 exd3 12 Nxd3 Qc7** and Black's long lead in development fully compensates for the sacrificed pawn (Fig.72).

The alternative line **4 d4** is best met by **4...exd4 5 0–0** (if 5 e5 d5! and now 6 Bb5 Ne4 7 Nxd4 Bd7, with a satisfactory game for Black). Now the immediate counter by 5...d5 is insufficient, because of the exposed position for Black's king. For example, 6 exd5 Nxd5 7 Re1+ Be7 8 Nxd4 Nf6 9 Bb5! Bd7 10 Bxc6 Bxc6 11 Qe2! Qd7 12 Nf5! Nd5 13 c4 Qxf5 14 cxd5 wins.

Much better for Black is **5...Nxe4 6 Re1 d5 7 Bxd5! Qxd5 8 Nc3 Qa5 9 Nxe4! Be6 10 Neg5 0–0–0 11 Nxe6 fxe6 12 Rxe6 Bd6** and the stronger attacking player should win (Fig. 73). It is interesting to note that by giving back both sacrificed pawns, Black just manages to escape from the attack along the e-file.

The 'Two Knights' is a sound and interesting opening; play it sometimes but not always when you meet 3 Bc4. There is so much to be learnt from the Giuoco Piano that you should be ready to defend this as well.

Fig. 73. Equal chances

Questions and Suggesions

(a) 4 c3 is a good move in the Giuoco Piano. Why is it of no use against the Two Knights Defence?

(b) After 4 Ng5 d5 5 exd5 Nxd5 6 d4, decide whether 6...Nxd4 is a good move.

(c) Examine the line given in the text commencing 4 Ng5 d5 5 exd5 Nxd5 6 Nxf7 and see if you can improve upon the play for White and/or Black. In particular, examine the game resulting from 11...Nc7 (instead of 11...Qf6?). The 'book' gives 12 Bf4 Kf7 13 Bxe5 (or 13 dxe5), and chances are supposed to be about even. Which side do *you* prefer and why?

(d) In this same variation, another interesting alternative is 9 a3 (instead of 9 Qe4) Nxc2+ 10 Kd1 Nxa1 11 Nxd5 Kd6 12 d4 c6 13 Bf4! Try this out with White and with Black and see what you can make of the position in each case.

(e) In the 4 d4 line, examine 4...Nxd4 and 4...Nxe4 as alternatives to 4...exd4. Why are they less often played?

(f) Take the black pieces, and try out the variation 4 d4 exd4 5 Ng5.

7.7. The Danish Gambit
1 e4 e5 2 d4 exd4 3 c3

The Danish Gambit is an offshoot of the Centre Game — 1 e4 e5 2 d4 exd4 3 Qxd4 Nc6 4 Qe3 Nf6 5 Nc3 Bb4 6 Bd2 0-0 7 0-0-0 d5!, in which Black takes advantage of the loss of time by White's queen by means of the usual recipe of counter-attack in the centre, coupled with superior development. To prevent this, White offers a pawn and sometimes two pawns to obtain the same sort of advantages as in the Evans Gambit — a lead in development, superior centralization, and an attack on f7, e.g. 3...dxc3 4 Nxc3 (or at once 4 Bc4 cxb2 5 Bxb2 with complex play) Nc6 5 Nf3 Bb4 6 Bc4 d6 7 0-0 with difficult play for both sides.

The Danish Gambit is less promising than most of the gambits, and we do not therefore recommend it for White, but as Black, you should know how to defend against it. The simplest counter is an immediate **3...d5!** **4 exd5 Nf6** (4...Qxd5 is also playable) **5 Nf3 Nxd5 6 Qxd4** (6 Nxd4 leaves Black slightly ahead in development) **Nc6 7 Bb5 Be7!** **8 0-0** (if 8 Qxg7 Bf6 9 Qh6 Qe7+ 10 Be3 Bd7, followed by 11...0-0-0. Now Black has a very good position for his sacrificed pawn, being better developed and having open lines for his pieces) **8...0-0 9 Bxc6 bxc6 10 Re1 Bb7** (Fig. 74), followed by **11...c5** and Black has good attacking chances. This is a good example of a standard way to equalize against gambit openings.

Fig. 74

7.8. The King's Gambit
1 e4 e5 2 f4

The King's Gambit offers the white KBP for two reasons. One is to gain more central control than Black; the other is to open the f-file for the white KR, yet another way of attacking f7. The disadvantage of 2 f4 is that it does nothing to help White's development. There are two main variations after **2...exf4**, the King's Knight Gambit (3 Nf3) and the King's Bishop Gambit (3 Bc4). **3 Nf3** is probably the strongest and we shall look mainly at this.

Our first variation shows what can happen if Black plays weakly. After **3...Nc6 4 Bc4** Black must not play the routine developing move **4...Bc5**, since his KP has been decoyed from e5 and White is able to gain time by attacking the bishop with **5 d4 Bb4+** (losing more time) **6 c3 Ba5 7 Bxf4 d6 8 0-0 Bb6** (afraid that White might play 9 Qa4, threatening 10 d5, with gain of a piece – Fig. 75). Now White's open lines and superior development enable him to settle the game by **9 Ng5 Nh6 10 Bxf7+! Nxf7 11 Nxf7 Kxf7 12 Bg5+**, winning the queen.

Fig. 75. An ideal King's Gambit position; White has got his pawn back and is winning easily

Fig. 76. Equal chances

The oldest method of meeting this attack is to try to retain the pawn by 2... exf4 3 Nf3 g5. This is quite good but very difficult for an inexperienced player. The game might continue 4 Bc4 g4 (4...Bg7 5 0-0 d6 6 d4 Nc6 7 c3 h6 is safer). White then has a strong central position in exchange for his pawn and chances are even) 5 0-0 gxf3 winning a piece, but leaving White a strong attack against his undeveloped position. For example – 6 Qxf3 Bh6 (6...Qf6 is best but White still has value for his piece) 7 d4 Nc6 8 Bxf4 Nxd4 9 Qh5 Ne6 10 Be5 winning the rook, since 10...Bg7 allows 11 Bxg7 Nxg7? 12 Qxf7 mate.

Once more Black is well advised to accept the gambit pawn to equalize in development, by playing an early . . .d5. The game might go **2. . .exf4 3 Nf3 d5 4 exd5 Nf6 5 Bc4** (if 5 Nc3 N×d5 or 5 c4 c6) **Bd6 6 0–0 0–0 7 d4** (Fig. 76), with equal chances.

Similarly 3 Bc4 may be met by 3. . .d5 4 B×d5 Nf6 5 Nc3 Bb4, with active counterplay for Black.

Questions and Suggestions

(*a*) Using general principles, can you see a good alternative for Black to 2. . .exf4?

(*b*) Do you think 2. . .d6 is a good move? What are your reasons?

(*c*) After 2. . .Nc6 why would 3 f×e5 be a mistake? Suggest White's best alternative.

(*d*) Consider the line 2. . .exf4 3 Nf3 g5 4 Bc4 Bg7 5 0–0 d6 6 d4 Nc6, and decide whether 7 d5 would now be a good move, giving reasons for your conclusion.

(*e*) Suppose the variation in (*d*) continued 7 c3 Bg4 8 g3 f×g3, what would you play as White? Look at the pressure down the f-file.

7.9. The Vienna Game
1 e4 e5 2 Nc3

Like the King's Gambit, the Vienna aims at opening the f-file by f4. In the Vienna, however, White plays 2 Nc3 first in order to make it harder for the Black to play . . .d5. The trouble about 2 Nc3 is that it is not a direct threat to Black's centre and, although it is a tricky opening to meet if you don't know anything about it, Black has several ways of equalizing. Usually he plays one of his knights out on the second move.

2. . .Nc6 allows the Vienna Gambit 3 f4 e×f4 4 Nf3 g5; Black should not be afraid of this, as he should at least hold his own. It is safer for White to play **3 Bc4**, but after **3. . .Nf6** energetic play in the centre gives Black full equality — e.g. 4 d3 Bb4 5 Nf3 d5 6 e×d5 N×d5, with a satisfactory game.

If, on the other hand, Black plays passively, White gets a strong attack, as in the line **3 Bc4 Nf6 4 d3 Bc5 5 f4 d6 6 f5 0–0? 7 Bg5**

Bd7 8 Nd5 (Fig. 77) **Na5 9 N×f6+ g×f6 10 Bh6** and wins the exchange, because of the threat of 11 Qg4+. It doesn't take an outright blunder by Black to lead to a lost position in the early stages — passive play soon allows White to show the power of the attack.

The most aggressive way to meet **2 Nc3** is by **2...Nf6**. Now **3 f4** is met by **3...d5!** (3...e×f4? 4 e5 gives White marked advantage, as shown in Game 'H' of Group Exercise 'A' in Volume 1) **4 f×e5 N×e4 5 Nf3**. (The alternative 5 d3 may lead to wild complications

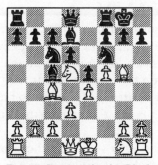

Fig. 77. Passive play by Black
has allowed White to get
a winning position

Fig. 78

by 5...Qh4+ 6 g3 N×g3 7 Nf3 Qh5 8 N×d5 N×h1 9 N×c7+ Kd8 10 N×a8 Be7 11 Bg2 Bh4+ 12 Kf1 but 5...N×c3 6 b×c3 d4! is less hair-raising and sounder) **5...Bb4 6 Be2 0–0 7 0–0 Nc6** (Fig. 78) and Black has equalized comfortably by straightforwardly developing and maintaining pressure on the centre. It is often good for him to play ...f6 fairly soon after castling to get rid of the strong white pawn on e5.

Questions and Suggestions

(*a*) Examine the alternatives 3...Nc6 and 3...d6 in the line which starts 1 e4 e5 2 Nc3 Nf6 3 f4.

(*b*) After 3...d5 4 f×e5 N×e4 5 d3 analyse the results of (*i*) 5...Qh4+, (*ii*) 5...Bb4.

(*c*) Try out the line 2...Nf6 3 f4 d5 4 f×e5 N×e4 5 d3 Qh4+ in a number of games, taking White and Black alternatively, and test your attacking and defensive powers.

(*d*) If the game commences 2...Nc6 3 Bc4 Nf6 4 d3 Bc5 5 f4 d6 6 f5, decide on Black's correct plan of campaign.

(*e*) Examine the interesting line 2...Nc6 3 Bc4 Bc5 4 Qg4. Do you think this early queen move is correct? Who has the better game? Is 4...Qf6 a good reply?

7.10. The Ruy Lopez Opening
1 e4 e5 2 Nf3 Nc6 3 Bb5

This opening is called after a Spanish bishop of the sixteenth century — who did not invent it! It is a different kind of opening from any we have yet examined. Instead of trying to attack f7, White tries merely to put pressure on the centre; in this way he hopes to force Black into a cramped positon and later on to build up an attack. 3 Bb5 helps towards this end by threatening the black knight, which protects the centre.

The Ruy Lopez is much harder to play well than those previously discussed and you should not adopt it until you are a more experienced player. Meanwhile, however, you must be prepared to defend against it: a good defence is the 'Open' variation which gives free play for the pieces and an interesting game for both sides.

Here is an unusually short win by White, showing how Black's game can collapse if he underrates White's pressure in the centre. Black played **3...a6** (this does not lose a pawn, for after 4 B×c6 d×c6 5 N×e5 Qd4 Black regains the lost material with a good game) **4 Ba4 Nf6 5 0-0 N×e4 6 d4 d5?** (This move is very weak; he should play 6...b5 first to get rid of the pin) **7 N×e5!** (Fig. 79) **Qd6** (if 8...Bd7 9 N×f7 K×f7 10 Qh5+ g6 11 Q×d5+ and 12 Q×e4, with a winning game) **8 f3 Nf6 9 Re1** (now a succession of discoveries decide the issue) **Be7 10 Bf4 Ng8 11 N×c6 Q×f4 12 N×e7+ b5** (on 12...Kd8 13 N×d5 Qd6 14 Re8 mate) **13 N×d5+**, resigns. Note the latent power of White's KB and KR if Black opens files or diagonals leading to his king before he has castled.

Although Black came to grief in our last example, the line is a good one if played correctly. Let us go back and see how Black gets on with proper play. **5...N×e4 6 d4** (if 6 Re1 Nc5! 7 B×c6 d×c6 8 d4 Ne6 9 N×e5 Be7 10 c3 0–0, with equality) **b5! 7 Bb3 d5! 8 d×e5 Be6.**

White's plan now will be to build up a king's-side attack based on his strong KP; as Black you should develop quickly and perhaps try later to use your extra pawn on the queen's side. One of the many continuations is **9 c3 Bc5 10 Nbd2 0–0 11 Bc2 f5 12 e×f6 N×f6 13 Nb3 Bb6 14 Nbd4 N×d4 15 N×d4 Bd7 16 Bg5 c5** (Fig. 80) and the position is about equal.

We have only touched on a fraction of the Lopez theory; this is a very difficult and much analysed opening — don't try to play it until you are really experienced.

Fig. 79. White's threats in the centre are too strong

Fig. 80. An equal game

Questions and Suggestions

(a) The variation 3...a6 4 Ba4 b5 5 Bb3 Bc5 leads to a position resembling the Giuoco Piano. Is it better or worse for White?

(b) Try out the interesting defence commencing 3...Bc5 in a number of games.

(c) Examine the position after 3...a6 4 Ba4 Nf6 5 d3 Bc5. Can White win a pawn by 6 B×c6?

(d) Decide why 8 d×e5 is usually played rather than 8 N×e5 N×e5 9 d×e5 in the line recommended in the text.

(e) After 3...a6 4 Ba4 Nf6 5 0–0 N×e4 6 d4 there is a very interesting line 6...e×d4 7 Re1 d5 8 N×d4 Bd6 9 N×c6 B×h2+ 10 Kh1 Qh4 11 R×e4+ d×e4 12 Qd8+ with a slightly better game for White. See if you can understand why these moves were played.

7.11. Petroff's Defence
1 e4 e5 2 Nf3 Nf6

This opening, named after a Russian player of the nineteenth century, bases its plan of action on immediate counter-attack on the white KP. You can play it if you want to avoid the Lopez; however, you will learn more by trying to defend the Lopez so we suggest that you only play the Petroff occasionally. White has two main methods — to capture the KP and to advance in the centre with 3 d4.

Fig. 81

In the first line, Black must take care not to fall into the trap 3 N×e5 N×e4? 4 Qe2 d5 5 d3 Nf6 6 Nc6+, winning the queen. He should play 3...d6 4 Nf3 N×e4 5 Qe2 Qe7 6 d3 Nf6 7 Bg5 Be6, with equality. **3 d4** leads to livelier play. Black may proceed **3...e×d4 4 e5 Ne4 5 Q×d4 d5 6 e×d6 N×d6 7 Bd3 Nc6 8 Qf4** (Fig. 81) and both sides have chances.

7.12. Philidor's Defence
1 e4 e5 2 Nf3 d6

This opening takes its name from the great French player of the eighteenth century who first developed an organized technique on which the foundations of modern positional play have been based, but it is rather too passive — and too hard to play well — for you to use it yet. As White you should occupy the centre and watch for tactical chances arising from Black's cramped position.

An example of what can happen with inferior Black play is 3 Bc4 Be7 4 d4 e×d4 5 N×d4 Nd7? (5...g6 seems the best try here) 6 B×f7+! K×f7 7 Ne6! (Fig. 82) Qe8 (if 7...K×e6 8 Qd5+ Kf6 9 Qf5

Fig. 82. A catastrophe in Philidor's
Defence; Black is lost

Fig. 83. Black has a solid
defensive position

mate) 8 Nxc7 Qd8 9 Qd5+ Kf8 10 Ne6+ Ke8 11 Nxg7+! Kf8 12
Ne6+ Kf7 13 Qh5+ followed by 14 Qf5 mate.

Sterner defence is shown in the variation **3 d4 Nf6 4 Nc3
Nbd7 5 Bc4 Be7 6 0-0 0-0 7 Qe2 c6 8 a4!** (Fig. 83) (an important
move which prevents Black's freeing manoeuvre of 8. . .b5. If now
8. . .h6 9 a5! b5 10 axb6). From the diagram White will aim to
complete his development by Rd1, h3 (to prevent the exchange of
his QB at e3 by the black N), and Be3 Black's position is not bad
though he is still rather cramped for a comfortable defence.

7.13. Summary

We have looked at eleven openings in this chapter. Which
should you play? For various reasons, you should wait till you are
more experienced before playing the Four Knights, the Lopez or
Philidor's Defence. The Scotch and the Danish are worth an
occasional game, but no more; Petroff's Defence is also something
to play occasionally.

This leaves five openings which fall into two groups; Giuoco
Piano, Evans Gambit and 'Two Knights Defence', all beginning
with 1 e4 e5 2 Nf3 Nc6 3 Bc4, make up one group, while the King's
Gambit and Vienna, each with an early f4, make up the other. We
suggest that you play all these openings, with Black and White.
When you have mastered them you will have learnt a lot about the
'open game' and will be reaching the point where it will be worth
tackling the Lopez. At this point you will need to study a more
advanced book.

CHAPTER EIGHT

Further Openings

8.1. Positional Play

We have tried to show you how to play in positions in which there is free play for the pieces — what is called 'the open game'. In this you must develop quickly, know how to seize chances of winning material and how to build up an attack against the king and be able to play the endgame properly. All this is essential if you are ever to be any good at chess — but it isn't the whole game: if it were, most master games would be drawn.

There are more subtle ideas in chess which depend on taking advantage of a better pawn formation than the opponent's. Badly placed pieces may be regrouped but it is much harder to correct bad pawn formations, since a pawn move can never be taken back by retreating the pawn.

We have seen examples already, e.g. in the 'bad' bishop of section 6.10 and in the weak pawn formations in front of the castled king in Chapter 5. There are many other bad (and good) formations and much of the experts' play is based on trying to get, and then to use, the better pawn formation; play of this kind is called 'positional play'.

Study of pawn formations and positional play comes after you have thoroughly mastered the open game. One very good reason for this is that after a player has got the better of things from good positional play he usually has to open the game up and win by good tactical play; so, if you haven't learnt how to play the open game you won't be able to use positional advantage even if you are able to get it.

We therefore think you should play the openings that lead to an open game — those that begin 1 e4 e5. However, your opponents may not agree with us — so you must be ready to meet other openings. In this chapter we try to deal with this problem: we give lines for you to play as White if your opponent doesn't reply 1...e5 when you open 1 e4 yourself and lines to play as Black if your opponent doesn't play 1 e4 when he is White. The lines we suggest are those that lead to an open game so that you can reach positions of a kind that you know how to play. Later on you will have to learn other methods — but not yet.

8.2. The Centre Counter Game
1 e4 d5

In this defence, Black makes an immediate counter-attack on White's KP. The move is premature, since exchange of pawns draws Black's queen to a square where it is subject to attack by the QN, and has to lose time before Black can continue his development.

2 exd5! Qxd5 3 Nc3 Qa5 (the usual move, though 3...Qd8 can also be played: at a5 Black hopes to place his queen on a square where it is safe from further attack for some time, and from which it is available to join an attack if White plays weakly) **4 d4 Nf6 5 Nf3 Bg4 6 h3 Bxf3** (6...Bh5 7 g4 is good for White) **7 Qxf3 c6 8 Bd2** (or 8 Bc4). White is slightly ahead in development, and his 2 bishops are slightly better than Black's bishop and knight.

Alternatively, Black may play 4...e5, when White continues his development with 5 Nf3 Bb4 6 Bd2 Bg4 7 Be2 exd4 (or 7...Bxf3 8 Bxf3 exd4? 9 Bxb7 dxc3 10 bxc3! and wins) 8 Nxd4 Qe5 9 Ncb5 Bxe2 10 Qxe2 Bxd2+ 11 Kxd2 Qxe2+ 12 Kxe2 with a useful lead in development.

Black may choose to play the opening on gambit lines with 2...Nf6; and White does well to continue his development rather than try to maintain the pawn with 3 c4 c6! 4 dxc6 Nxc6 when Black has compensation for the sacrificed pawn. We recommend 3 d4 Nxd5 4 Nf3, with c4 in reserve to gain further space in due course (compare with 8.7).

Fig. 84 shows the typical position after 4 d4 in the main line.

Fig. 84. White has a slight advantage.

Although slightly inferior, this defence is not unsound, and White must not expect to get more than a slight lead in development, which should be achieved by simple and rapid developing moves. From time to time, players adopt this defence as a surprise weapon, perhaps hoping that White will overreach himself by expecting too much from the position.

8.3. The French Defence
1 e4 e6

Like the Scotch Game, the French Defence derives its name from its adoption in a correspondence game in the early nineteenth century — this time between London and Paris.

The French Defence has clear-cut positional objectives. Black aims to play 2...d5 without having to recapture with his queen in the event of a pawn-exchange; further, if play continues naturally **2 d4 d5** he tempts White to advance his pawn to e5, and then aims to attack the white pawns on d4 and e5. If we look at the advantages and disadvantages of these pawns, we shall get an idea of the vital part that pawn-structure plays in an opening in which the pawns get locked as here. Both advantages and disadvantages arise from the fact that the pawns are far advanced. The advantage to White is that he has more space; he has taken away f6 from the knight, and we have seen in section 5.3 (i) how this can give rise to the sacrifice B×h7+, against the castled king, whilst Black will find it difficult to develop his QB adequately. On the other hand, the pawns, being far advanced, can be attacked more readily, and Black will try to force White back on the defensive by such moves as ...c5, followed by ...Nc6, ...Qb6, ...f6 and ...Nge7-f5, all bearing down on the QP and the KP. This gives rise to a difficult positional game beyond the scope of this book.

Fig. 85

White's simplest plan is to adopt the Exchange Variation **3 exd5 exd5**, when the pawn-formation is symmetrical, and each side is free to develop pieces to natural squares. Play can continue, for example, **4 Bd3 Nf6 5 Nf3 Bd6 6 0–0 0–0 7 Nc3**, with an easy development for both sides (Fig. 85). However, as in the Four Knights Game, the symmetrical nature of the position makes it rather hard to build up an attack, and it is fairly easy for Black to achieve a position with equal chances.

We suggest that you play the Exchange Variation at first. Later on, as you become a stronger player, you should go over to one of the lines which involve e5, and you will then have to study a more advanced book to see how such positions should be handled.

8.4. The Caro-Kann Defence
1 e4 c6

This defence, developed some eighty years ago by two Central European players after whom it is named, has only been adopted with any regularity by leading players since the First World War.

More recently it became a favourite weapon of Flohr and of the ex- World Champion, Botvinnik, who played it with great success when regaining the title from Tal in 1961. While the Caro-Kann can be an aggressive defence in the hands of a great player, it is used more by ordinary players as an attempt to avoid trouble and secure a draw. You should not play safe in this way — you will never learn anything if you do; so don't play the Caro-Kann.

The general object of the defence is similar to that of the French Defence — to play . . .d5 with the possibility of recapturing with a pawn instead of with the queen. It has the advantage over the French of not shutting in the QB, but the disadvantage that . . .c6 obstructs the normal development of the QN and that Black may later have to lose a tempo to attack the centre with . . .c5. We

Fig. 86

recommend that at first you adopt a similar line of play to that in the French, by playing the Exchange Variation followed by simple development on the following lines: **2 d4 d5 3 exd5 cxd5 4 Bd3 Nc6 5 c3** (the alternative 5 Nf3 Bg4 6 c3 leads to much the same sort of position) **Nf6 6 Bf4 Bg4 7 Nf3 e6 8 Qb3 Qc8 9 Nbd2** and White has a good free game (Fig. 86).

Later on, you will probably find that this simple method does not make things difficult for Black. When this happens you must study the defence further and choose an alternative line.

8.5. The Sicilian Defence

1 e4 c5

This is the most popular reply to 1 e4 by players who prefer not to play 1...e5. The idea of the defence is to bring pressure to bear on d4 and to build up a queen's side attack: let us look at bit more closely at this.

First suppose White plays d4. He will not play it at once since 2 d4 cxd4 3 Qxd4 Nc6 gains time for Black; however, 2 Nf3 Nc6 3 d4 cxd4 4 Nxd4 is standard play. Black will then put further pressure on d4, e.g. by ...g6 and ...Bg7, and will also use his QR and Q to bring pressure on the c-file against the white QBP. White will counter this by an attack against Black's castled king position. These rival attacks give rise to very critical positions; White often wins with his attack, but if he fails Black may get the better endgame.

If White tries to avoid this struggle by holding back his QP at d3, Black will get a good game by advancing the queen's side pawns: so, as White, you must accept the challenge and be prepared to 'mix' things if you want to win.

Your plan should be to develop quickly, keeping a firm hold on the centre — in particular you must not allow Black to play ...d5 if you can possibly help it. Having developed, then build up a king's side attack.

There is a bewildering array of possible systems within the Sicilian Defence, so you cannot therefore expect Black to follow the particular line we give here which is just to show how the game may develop. Faced with different moves — as you will be — you must follow the general policy of development followed by attack on the king.

Play may proceed **2 Nf3 Nc6** (2...d6 and 2...e6 are common alternatives) **3 d4 cxd4 4 Nxd4 Nf6** (4...Nxd4 5 Qxd4 brings the queen to a strong central square) **5 Nc3** (*not* 5 Nxc6 bxc6 6 e5? Qa5+, winning the KP by double attack) **5...d6** (Black has several chances of playing ...e5 in the opening of which this is one. The weakness of the move is that his QP is left in a weak position and his d5 is unprotected by pawns, referred to respectively as a 'backward' pawn and a 'hole'. Once again, you need to gain more experience before you resort to such a committal move. In reply, as White, you must not exchange knights which strengthens

Fig. 87

Black's position but must move away with your knight) **6 Bc4 e6** (6...g6 is not good because of the reply 7 N×c6 b×c6 8 e5!: when 8...d×e5? 9 B×f7+ wins the queen and 8...Ng4 9 Bf4 Qb6 10 Qf3 and White stands well) **7 0–0 a6** (to prevent 8 Ndb5, and intending later to play ...b5-b4 to drive away White's QN from the protection of his KP) **8 Bb3** (this move avoids counter-play by ...Ne5, which would now be met by 9 f4 and removes it from the dangers of discoveries by the black queen after Black's next move) **Qc7 9 Be3 b5 10 a3** (Fig. 87) and, having prevented...b4, White is ready to complete his development by 11 Qe2 and 12 Rad1, or to launch a king's-side attack with pawns by 11 f4.

When you are ready to play some defence other than 1...e5, try the Sicilian. It leads to positions in which both sides have to play energetically and gives plenty of scope for the imagination. But give 1...e5 a good long run first.

8.6. The King's Fianchetto Defence
1 e4 g6 or 1 d4 g6

A Fianchetto consists of the development of a bishop at b2(b7) or g2(g7). When the KB is so developed we have a King's Fianchetto, and this method of development by Black, without an immediate challenge to White's centre, has been given new life recently by the researches of the Yugoslav and Austrian grandmasters Pirc and Robatsch, each of whom has developed a defensive system starting with this Fianchetto (Pirc's move-order being 1 e4 d6 2 d4 Nf6 3 Nc3 g6).

Black's plan — playable equally against 1 e4 and 1 d4 — is to tempt White to advance a number of pawns and occupy the centre and then to counter-attack with his own pawns and break up this centre. White's general line should be to occupy as much of the centre as he can do with safety but not to be too greedy.

It is dangerous to play all 4 central pawns to the fourth rank — i.e. to c4, d4, e4, and f4 — since 4 moves have been played without developing a piece, and Black is often able to mount a strong attack against this pawn-formation. We recommend, therefore, that White should be content to play e4, d4 and f4 only, giving himself a marked advantage in space without too much risk.

Play might proceed **1 e4 g6 2 d4 Bg7 3 Nc3 d6 4 f4 Nf6 5 Nf3 0–0 6 Bd3 Bg4** (6...Nc6 and 6...Na6 are interesting alternatives) **7 h3 Bxf3 8 Qxf3 Nc6 9 Qf2** (Fig. 88). This is how the game began between ex-British Champion Jonathan Penrose and Robatsch, using his own defence, at Hastings, 1961-2. White has a firm grip on the centre, and later on may get a king's-side attack with f5. Penrose kept his advantage in space throughout the game, and finally won with the attack (see Chapter 9 for the complete game).

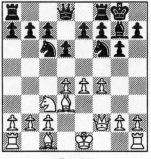

Fig. 88

A word on how to handle positions when you have a strong central pawn formation with, say, 3 pawns involved.

In general, the pawns are at their best when placed parallel on the fourth rank — (a) they occupy or control all the central squares, and (b) they constantly threaten to advance. White's general plan should be to try and maintain them where they are, and only move them when forced so to do, or when their advance leads to clear advantage for him. Black's counter-play must be based on attacking them, and trying to force White to exchange them, or to advance them at a time which offers him no advantage.

8.7. Alekhine's Defence
1 e4 Nf6

This defence was introduced into master-play by Dr. A. Alekhine, World Champion for many years between the two World Wars. Like the King's Fianchetto Defence, it aims to tempt the white pawns forward on to squares where they will be liable to counter-attack by Black. It is not bad for White to make these pawn advances but at this stage we advise you to concentrate simply on developing your pieces.

So, we suggest **2 Nc3 d5** (the usual counter 2...e5 allows White to transpose into the Vienna Game) **3 exd5 Nxd5 4 Bc4 Nb6**

Fig. 89

5 Bb3 c5 (threatening 6...c4, winning the bishop) **6 d3**, with an easy development and equal chances (Fig. 89). If Black assumes that White's play has failed to challenge the centre adequately he may be in for a shock; for example, 6...e5 (immediate development by 6...Nc6 would be wiser) 7 Qh5 (possible since apart from the double threats to KP and KBP Black's KN has been diverted to the queen's-wing) 7...Qc7 (if 7...Qe7 8 Bg5! and Black cannot play 8...f6 since this pawn is pinned) 8 Nb5 Qe7 9 Bg5 Qd7 10 Bxf7+! Qxf7 11 Nc7+ and wins the queen and the queen's rook! This variation shows the great power of a long lead in development.

8.8. The Queen's Gambit
1 d4 d5 2 c4

Unlike the king's side gambits, the Queen's Gambit is not a real sacrifice of material, since Black cannot safely hold on to the offered pawn. Nevertheless you should take the pawn, but not try to keep it: in this way you will get an easier type of game than if you decline it. The gambit declined leads to difficult positional play while accepting it leads to more open positions.

After **2...dxc4** White usually continues **3 Nf3** to prevent 3...e5. Other lines are less good. For example 3 Qa4+ can be met by 3...c6 4 Qxc4 (Black threatened to retain the pawn by 4...b5) Bf5 5 Nf3 Nf6 6 Nc3 Nbd7, with equality.

An immediate 3 e4 is met by 3...e5! (returning the pawn for an easy development) 4 dxe5 Qxd1+ 5 Kxd1 Nc6 6 f4 and now that White's queen cannot check at h5, Black plays 6...f6, disrupting White's advanced pawns.

The main line continues **3...Nf6 4 e3 e6** (Black must not spend time protecting his pawn by 4...b5, since White obtains the advantage by 5 a4 c6 6 axb5 cxb5 7 b3! cxb3 8 Bxb5+, regaining the pawn with a superior development) **5 Bxc4 c5!** (attacking White's centre and removing a possible weakness in the form of a vulnerable pawn on the open c-file which is now open for White's major pieces). **6 0-0 a6** (Fig. 90). This is the standard position. White tries to make use of the open files on the queen's wing, and to complete his development by e4, freeing his QB for action. Black must also aim to complete his development rapidly, so that all his pieces are available for defence or counter-attack in the middle-game. Play may continue **7 Qe2** (bringing the KR to d1 and striving for e4 once his QP is adequately protected) **b5 8 Bb3**

Fig. 90   Fig. 91. Development nearly complete
in Queen's Gambit Accepted

(8...Bd3 is also playable: whichever move White plays, do not reply 8...c4 9 Bc2 and White will continue e4, with a strong central and king's side attack; you can always play ...c4 later — meanwhile, keep the option of...cxd4) **Bb7 9 Rd1 Nbd7 10 Nc3 Be7 11 e4 cxd4** (the tempting 11...b4 has always to be examined carefully; here White obtains the better game by 12 e5 bxc3 13 exf6) **12 Nxd4** (12 Rxd4 is interesting) **12...Qc7** with equal chances (Fig. 91).

A deep understanding of positional play is needed to be able to handle the Queen's Gambit effectively, and consequently we strongly recommend you not to play this opening with White until you have become at least a strong club player; at the same time, you should be aware of the fact that in the hands of the masters, it is one of the strongest of all the openings.

8.9. The Queen's Pawn Game
1 d4 d5 2 Nf3

White does not always follow up 1 d4 with the Queen's Gambit, and we give typical variations showing how Black may meet quieter lines of play by White with sensible developing moves.

After **2...Nf6 3 Bf4** (if 3 c4 dxc4 we have the main line of the Queen's Gambit Accepted) **Bf5 4 c4** (White's only real chance of breaking the symmetry in his favour) **4...e6** (4...dxc4 is more doubtful after Black has developed his QB at 3...Bf5) — **5 Qb3**

Fig. 92

Qc8 6 e3 Nbd7 7 Nc3 c6 (preventing 8 Nb5), with a sound game (Fig. 92).

Another line is **3 e3 Bf5 4 Bd3** (if 4 c4 e6 5 Qb3 Qc8, as in the previous variation, but Black has a better game since White's QB has little freedom) **e6 5 Bxf5 exf5 6 Qd3 Qc8!** (White was threatening both 7 Qxf5 and 7 Qb5+), and Black has a free game.

8.10. The English Opening
1 c4

The English Opening is so-called in many (but not all) countries from its frequent adoption by the leading English player, Staunton, in match-play in the early part of the nineteenth century. It very often leads into other openings and experienced players use it sometimes to get into favourable lines, in, say, the Queen's Gambit. It also has a number of lines with a character

Fig. 93

in the English Opening itself. White's aims are often rather like those of Black in the Sicilian; pressure on the queen's side pawns and attack along the QB file if Black plays . . .d5.

It is not easy for Black to avoid a positional type of game: you probably do best to play **1. . .e5**, when the following is the kind of play that might result **2 Nc3 Nf6 3 g3** (aiming to increase his control of d5 as in the Sicilian Defence) **d5 4 cxd5 Nxd5 5 Bg2 Nb6 6 Nf3 Nc6 7 0–0 Be7** (this piece is needed to guard against White playing a piece to g5, since Black's KN has moved to the queen's wing) **8 d3 0–0** (Fig. 93) **9 Be3 Bg4 10 h3** (this does not gain time, as the pawn can later be attacked by . . .Qd7) **10. . .Be6** and Black has equalized.

8.11. Bird's Opening
1 f4

This somewhat unusual-looking opening was played by another nineteenth century English chess-master, H. E. Bird, with the idea of controlling e5, and so making it difficult for Black to

Fig. 94

play an early . . .e5 without loss of material. If not challenged by Black, White will normally play moves such as b3, Bb2 and Nf3, which give positions in which his pieces appear as the mirror-image of positions obtained from the English Opening. Black can develop quietly, when White has positional rather than tactical chances; or, since White's first move contributes nothing to his development, but rather tends to expose the king, Black can play aggressively on gambit lines, as follows: **1...e5!?** (From's Gambit which can be declined by 2 e4 giving us the King's Gambit!) **2 f×d5 d6 3 e×d6 B×d6 4 Nf3** (already Black was threatening 4...Qh4+ followed by mate in two moves) **4...g5** (another violent move, designed to dislodge the knight; a good alternative is 4...Nf6) **5 d4** (not 5 h3?? Bg3 mate) **g4 6 Ne5 Qe7** and Black is having all the fun (Fig. 94). Try this line; the quiet move 1...d5 leads to a difficult positional game.

8.12. Handling Unfamiliar Openings

We have only dealt very briefly with the openings in these two chapters; some we have not mentioned at all and we have only given one or two out of hundreds of variations in those we have discussed. So you will constantly meet unfamiliar opening lines. When you do, *apply sound opening principles*; develop and play for control of the centre. This may not find you the best move but it will usually find fairly good ones. And when you do study books on openings, *never memorize variations without understanding them*.

CHAPTER NINE

Making a Plan

9.1. The Game as a Whole

When a player who has passed the beginner stage and got a fair understanding of tactics is asked what he finds hardest in chess he usually replies 'Making a Plan'; he can understand how to win in the kind of positions we have shown in our chapters on winning material or mating attacks, but he does not know how to get there. To put it slightly differently, we have tried to show you how to play the openings, how to exploit various kinds of advantage in the middle game and how to play the ending — but how do all these different parts of the game join up with each other?

The first thing to say is that there is no easy answer to this question; there are a lot of different answers and all we can do here is to give you some pointers to these and some basic ideas on which you will have to use your own experience and further reading to build. How far you get will depend, as in other aspects of chess, partly on your natural ability and partly on how far you are ready to study and to try to learn from experience rather than just to play.

9.2. Plans Based on Accidental Circumstances

Plans arise in two ways — by design and by accident. To begin with nearly all your plans will arise by accident and even when you are a strong player you will find this happens surprisingly often, so we deal with these first. What do we mean by 'accidental plans'?

Well, these arise in the following kind of way. The game is

going along and suddenly one player finds that he cannot do something he had meant to do because of an unexpected reply that he had overlooked — he therefore finds that he has to make a weakening move with the pawns in front of his king, say, or give up the centre or regroup his pieces, losing time, or accept doubled isolated pawns or one of a number of other unpleasant possibilities. This unexpected creation of a weakness gives the opponent the chance to form a plan to exploit it: the difference between the strong player and the weak one is that the strong player will recognize such a chance more surely and more quickly than the weak one and will be better at successfully exploiting it. If you want to be able to seize chances of this kind the first essential is to master the different types of favourable positions thoroughly and know how to proceed in them; then you will be able to recognize possibilities at an early stage and also know how to exploit them. This book contains examples of a number of the basic types — so study these thoroughly and later on, in other books and from your experience, you will begin to add the knowledge of other, more subtle, types of favourable and unfavourable positions.

We know, for example, that the formation f7, g6, h7 in front of the castled king is unfavourable unless the player concerned (let us suppose it is Black) has a bishop to insert at g7. Suppose, then, that Black has been forced to play ...g6 and you are White; you immediately begin to think like this 'What about his black bishop? Can I exchange it off — if I can, can I do it for one of my knights and keep my own black bishop? How shall I exploit his weak formation — by getting B and Q on to f6 and h6 or by advancing BP or RP and opening a file or by Q on h6 and N on g5 or how? How will he defend against these various possibilities? Has he any other attack elsewhere? Can I hold this up long enough to bring my own attack home?' and so on. You are beginning to make a plan. Now take this a stage further back. He has pawns on d5, e6, f7, g7, h7, K on g8, R on f8 and a N on f6: you have B on c2, pawns on e4, d4, Q on d1, R on e1 — and of course many more pieces on both sides. Shall you play 1 e5? You think 'I play e5; his knight has to go back to e8 — now I can play Qd3 threatening Q×h7 mate. He must play . . .g6 — now he has got the weak f7, g6, h7 formation: shall I be able to exploit it? (Now you run through the questions just given) What about my pawn on e5 — will it be weak? Can he win it or force me on the defensive to protect it? Maybe after all he need not play . . .g6 in reply to e5: can he play . . .f5 instead? Well I can play 3 exf6; then he plays . . .Nxf6 stopping mate. Now he has an open file: yes, but his KP is weak. Which is more important? I don't think he can get much attack from his open file and I can pin him down on this weak pawn and he will never get rid of it. All right, I play e5. Now you are both making a plan and exercising positional judgement; that is to say you are estimating (and only a mixture of experience with thorough knowledge of basic principles will enable you to do this well) that your advantages will be greater than his.

9.3. Plans by Design

What about plans 'by design'? These arise from your opening strategy. As you will have seen, the various openings all have various underlying ideas and particular types of position to which they give rise: when you have played any one opening a lot you will find that certain themes come up again and again. Take a clear example, the French Defence 1 e4 e6 2 d4 d5. In the more advanced forms of this opening White usually plays e5 at some stage: this at once sets a pattern for the game. White has more space on the K side (in particular, Black cannot get a N at f6); on the other hand, his advanced pawns are weak: so White's plan will be to use his advantage in space to launch an attack on the king's wing, meanwhile striving to maintain his centre pawns — Black's plan will be to attack White's centre pawns and win, or at least exchange them, while protecting his king's side as best he can. The way to learn how to develop plans from the opening is to study individual openings and to play a number of games with Black and White on a particular opening — but do *not* stick to one opening all the time or you will get too narrow in your range.

Even in these plans arising from the opening, the element of accident or chance enters quite largely and this for two reasons. First, there are always a large number of defences to any opening and these give rise to different kinds of game; so you cannot determine in advance just what will happen and it is the sort of play your opponent adopts that will, with your choice of play, determine what kind of plans emerge. Secondly, mistakes will be made by both players and these may radically alter the nature of the position. One of the most valuable lessons a player can learn is the importance of flexibility in approach and of recognizing when a plan should be changed; over and over again one sees players lose because they fail to realize that a change is necessary. A very common situation is as follows. A player has a good attacking position and launches an assault on the enemy king, let us say by a pawn advance. However, he makes a wrong move after which his attack no longer has any chance of succeeding against correct defence. He could still nevertheless maintain an equal game if, realizing his error, he withdrew from the attack and consolidated; but because this attack was his initial plan he feels obliged to continue it, rushes on with his pawns thus weakening his defensive position, is heavily repulsed and loses. You must always judge the position as it is, not as it was nor as it ought to have been if you had played better.

Published master games and text books (even this one!) can be very misleading in the picture they give of planning in chess. Because the published game is selected to please the reader and the text book is usually aiming to explain one particular technical point, they give an impression of everything proceeding steadily to a happy ending for the winner; but the great bulk of actual games – even master games – are much messier affairs in which the advantage changes hands and a player often wins after having had much the worst of it. If you want to seize your chances in such games, you must always be ready to change your mind and your plans: this does not mean that you dither about from one thing to another – that is completely fatal – but that you remain open-minded about the position.

9.4. Types of Plan

Finally, what about how to carry out your plans? This is like saying 'what about chess?' because carrying out your plans is just playing chess and is what the whole of this book is about; so here we will only add one or two general remarks. First, you will never carry out any plan well until you are a good tactical player, because all plans involve a long series of tactical manoeuvres; do not listen to people who quote Réti who, when asked how many moves ahead he looked, replied 'none' because this is just not true. The remark was an exaggeration made to bring out the point that there are other things besides calculating ahead in chess – you have to understand the kind of plan a position needs: but Réti could – and did – calculate and work out tactical manoeuvres like any other master (and very well, too). Secondly, you must understand what kind of play your plan requires; is it, for example, a 'time' plan or a 'space' plan or an 'endgame' plan or a 'weak' point plan or some kind of mixture.

By a 'time' plan, we mean one which must be forced home as quickly as possible; a rapid attack based on being ahead in development is a typical example of this – another is the case when players have castled on opposite sides and each is advancing pawns against the enemy king. In these positions every move has to tell and they frequently lend themselves to sacrificial attacks; the utmost vigour is usually needed and considerable risks often have to be taken if such a plan is to succeed.

A 'space' plan is based on having more territory under one's control. Here the emphasis is not on a rapid attack but on keeping a firm grip and preventing the enemy from freeing himself. Maintaining a superior pawn structure is usually an essential feature in such plans and provided one can do this a quite slow and gradual build up of the attack is often best.

An 'endgame' plan is one from which – either because of material advantage or better pawn position – one expects to win in the endgame; here one aims mainly at avoiding weaknesses in one's game, at keeping the position under control in the sense that no dangerous enemy attacks develop, and at gradually exchanging pieces. A typical technique here is to improve one's position by threatening exchanges which the enemy cannot afford because of the unfavourable ending to come and thus forcing him to retreat.

A 'weak point' plan is one in which pressure is built up on some fixed weaknesses in the enemy game — maybe an isolated or backward pawn. Here the technique might be to prevent adverse action elsewhere on the board while gradually strengthening the attack on the weak point and finally winning either by capturing material (e.g. winning a weak pawn) or by tying up the opponent in defence and suddenly switching the attack elsewhere at a moment when his pieces cannot disentangle themselves and come to the rescue.

Very often, of course, a plan is a mixture of types or there are several plans going on at once or a plan changes from a 'time' to a 'space' plan; through an advantage in development a player may force his opponent right back on the defensive to avoid immediate loss (a 'time' attack) and then get him in a cramped position from which he cannot escape (leading to a 'space' attack). This is much harder — but then chess is a difficult game, in which the problems, fortunately, cannot be solved just by laying down rules. Even so, you will find it easier to work out the right moves if you have some notion of the kind of move that ought to be right and we hope that this discussion will help you in this way.

9.5. Illustrative Games

We end this chapter with a number of games chosen to illustrate some of the ways in which plans are developed in master chess. Many of the individual moves may puzzle you at first, even with the comments. Do not worry too much about the finer details at this stage but try to see the broad outline of the plan which the winner pursues.

Our first game is almost entirely tactical: each side has a plan arising directly out of the opening, there is no positional manoeuvring, just a short, sharp struggle as a result of which Black demonstrates that his judgement of the position was better. In our earlier terms, this shows a 'time' plan, where Black presses home his advantage with the utmost speed and vigour.

White GULBRANDSEN (Norway)   *Black* ZUIDEMA (Holland)
Opening: Ruy Lopez.   World Junior Championship, 1961.
1 e4 e5 2 Nf3 Nc6 3 Bb5 Bc5

This is the Classical Defence to the Lopez. Black develops as quickly as he can, putting his pieces on natural, aggressive squares and hoping as a result to get enough play for equality. The drawback to this line is that . . .Bc5 neither attacks White's KP nor defends his own. White will try to take advantage of this by a rapid attack on the black centre, hoping to build up the superior central position.

4 c3 Nf6 5 d4 Bb6

If Black plays 5. . .exd4 then 6 e5 Ne4 7 0–0 gives rise to very complicated and much analysed play which is rather in White's favour. The text move begins a bold plan in which Black decides to sacrifice a central pawn in order to get ahead in development.

6 Bxc6

White chooses to win the pawn, but this is an error in judgement, a wrong plan in fact, and he would do better just to castle.

6. . .bxc6 7 Nxe5 0–0

Not, however, 7. . .Nxe4 8 Qg4 which is bad for Black.

8 Bg5

To play 8 0–0 Nxe4 would be an admission of failure.

8. . .Qe8

An excellent defensive and offensive move, unpinning the knight and beginning an attack down the e-file.

9 Qf3?

White refuses to admit that his plan has failed. One of the most important and difficult things in chess is to recognize when a plan

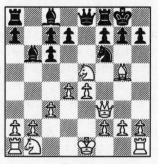

Fig. 95

you have made is no good, to give it up and save what you can. He should have played 9 Bxf6 gxf6 10 Qg4+ Kh8 11 Qf4, prepared to accept the draw by perpetual check that arises after 11...fxe5 12 Qf6+ Kg8 13 Qg5+ etc., or the equal game that results from 11... Qe6 12 Ng4 followed by 13 Qxf6+. Not realizing the danger, White wrongly feels that he can win. In other words, his plan is based on a faulty evaluation of his chances, an all too common occurrence.

9...Nxe4! 10 Qxe4 f6 11 Bf4?

He still does not appreciate the full danger and is trying to come out a pawn ahead. He should try to block the e-file with 11 Be3.

11...fxe5 12 Qxe5

He may have thought that he could play 12 dxe5 here, but this gives Black far too many open lines e.g. 12...d5 13 Qf3 g5! 14 Qg3! Bxf2+! 15 Qxf2 Rxf4 16 Qg3 (16 Qe2? Re4) Qxe5+ with a winning game.

12...Qf7 13 Be3 Ba6!

Fixing the white king in the middle by preventing castling and thus exposing it to attack along the open lines in the centre. From a planning point of view, the game is decided; it only remains for Black to find the quickest winning method.

14 Nd2 Rae8 15 Qg3 c5!

Notice how Black plays all the time to break up the white centre.

16 Nb3 cxd4 17 Nxd4 Bxd4 18 cxd4 Qc4!

Threatening both ...Qe2 mate and ...Qb4+ followed by ...Qxb2.

19 Kd1 Qe2+ 20 Kc1 Bd3 21 Bd2 Re6

Even stronger is 21...Rxf2 22 Rd1 (22 Qg5 Rf1+ mates) Qxd2+! 23 Rxd2 Re1+ (a pretty 'skewer' combination) 24 Rd1 Rc2+ 25 Kb1 Rxd1 mate, but the text move also threatens to win by means of a skewer with 22...Rc6+ 23 Bc3 Qc2 mate.

22 d5 Rf5! 23 Resigns.

Black's final move produces yet another skewer situation, threatening 23...Rc6+ 24 dxc6 Rc5+ 25 Bc3 Qc2 mate, and the only way to stop this is to give up the queen by 23 Qxd3 Qxd3 24 dxe6 but after 24...Rxf2 25 Rd1 Qc4+ and 26...Qxe6 White's game is lost.

This is a good example of a game where the whole scheme of play develops immediately and logically from the opening idea. While it is, of course, not at all easy to carry out such a plan, which requires imaginative tactical play, the plan itself is quite easy to understand. Here is an even more striking example of the same type of plan. White plays passively in the opening and neglects the centre, but it requires beautifully engineered tactical play involving sacrifices, to exploit the weaknesses created by this play, as we shall see.

White JACOBSEN (Denmark) *Black* LJUBOJEVIĆ (Yugoslavia) Opening: King's Fianchetto Opening.   Groningen, 1970.

1 g3 e5 2 Bg2 Nc6 3 e4 Bc5 4 Ne2 Nf6 5 c3 d5 6 b4?

Although White has the advantage of the first move, he can hardly allow himself the luxury of too many planless moves. Having developed his KN to the passive square e2 rather than the active f3 and having blocked the natural square for his QN by playing c3, thus weakening his control of d5 and creating a 'hole' at d3, it was vital not to waste any more time nor create any further weaknesses. The best of a bad job was 6 exd5 Nxd5 7 0-0 followed by d4.

6...Bb6 7 exd5 Nxd5 8 Ba3?

And this is ridiculous. Since Black is intending to castle long in any case, the bishop is misplaced here and the loss of time involved is even more serious.

8...Bg4! 9 0-0

Fig. 96

Black answers 9 h3 with 9...Qf6! 10 0–0 Bf3 followed by 11...0–0–0 with a tremendous position and no sacrifices required.

We have now reached a critical stage in Black's decision-making. Given time, White will decentralize Black's QN with b5, then begin to disentangle his own queen-side pieces. A normal and reasonably sound plan would be to play 9...Qd7 followed by 10...0–0–0 and 11...h5 in order to open the h-file, with excellent attacking chances, but this would allow White to mix matters with d3 followed by b5 and c4. The weakness of White's d3 square must have given Ljubojević the devastatingly powerful idea of sacrificing a piece in order to paralyse the whole of White's army. An original and yet, the more one examines it, eminently logical concept. Let us see how play proceeds before we discuss further points of the brilliant sacrifice.

9...Nf4!! 10 gxf4 Qd3 11 Re1 0–0–0

Notice how all of Black's pieces are now poised for action, in stark contrast to White's. By blocking White's QP, Black has kept open the diagonal for his KB aiming at the weak f2 and at the same time shut in White's QN and, consequently, his QR. All this for a piece!

12 b5 Na5 13 Bb4 Nc4 14 a4 exf4!

Preparing the finish. If now 15 Nxf4 Qf5 16 Bf3 h5! 17 h3 Qxf4 18 hxg3 Qg3+ 19 Bg2 Qxf2+ 20 Kh1 hxg4+ followed by mate, and even Black's KR is joining in the fun. Here and on previous moves, Nc1 would be countered by ...Qg6 when Black has a potential pin down the g-file.

15 a5 Bxf2+! 16 Kxf2 Ne3!

The final imaginative point, after which White could well resign. Let us look at a few variations: if 17 dxe3 Qxe3+ 18 Kf1 Rxd1 19 Rxd1 Qxe2+; or 17 Qb3 Nxg2 18 Kxg2 Rhe8! 19 Na3 Rxe2+ 20 Rxe2 Qxe2+ 21 Kg1 Bh3 followed by mate. So White gives up his queen, but all to no avail.

17 Na3 Nxd1+ 18 Raxd1 f3 19 Nc1 Qf5 20 Bh1 Qf4 21 Resigns.

No one expects such virtuosity from you at this stage, of course, but it is more important to understand how rapidly such a fleeting advantage as time can disappear. You have to strike while the iron's hot!

Next, an example of a clear-cut 'space' plan, where an attack is methodically built up in fairly slow time on the basis of greater control of the centre by White.

White PENROSE (England)   *Black* ROBATSCH (Austria)

Opening: Modern Defence.   Hastings, 1961-2.

1 e4 g6

The Robatsch system, played by its author! Now the opening plan of the players will be for White to occupy as much of the centre as he thinks safe and to maintain it, and for Black to try to undermine this centre by attacking it. See our comments in the opening section.

2 d4 Bg7 3 Nc3 d6 4 f4

There are a number of equally good systems. White shows that he means to be ambitious; by moving a third pawn up, he both puts greater pressure on the centre and offers Black more of a target.

4...Nf6

He does not fear 5 e5 dxe5 6 fxe5 Nd5 with a post in the centre.

5 Nf3 0–0 6 Bd3 Bg4 7 h3 Bxf3 8 Qxf3 Nc6 9 Qf2!

Both players have consistently followed their plan. Black came out with his bishop and exchanged the knight, partly because piece exchanges help to relieve a congested position, but still more because he intends to attack White's centre pawns and is therefore happy to exchange a knight that is defending the d4 and e5 squares. White's moves similarly are all supporting the centre, but why did he not play Be3 developing a fresh piece, instead of Qf2? In answering this, we can see how essential tactical skill is when carrying out a positional plan. If 9 Be3 then 9...e5! when a general exchange of pawns will leave Black well placed e.g. 10 fxe5 dxe5 11 dxe5 Nxe5 and Black's knight is well posted on e5. So the only way to maintain pressure is to push the QP, but 10 d5 is met by 10... exf4! 11 Bxf4 Ne5 and Black has freed his game, or here 11 dxc6 fxe3 with equal chances, which means that White must first interpose 10 fxe5 dxe5 before playing 11 d5; even then, however, Black has 11...Nd4 12 Qf2 c5 with good counter-play. Compare this with 9 Qf2 e5 10 d5 when 10...Nd4 is met by 11

Nd1! with the horrible threat of c3. All this means that 9 Qf2 stops a major freeing move that Be3 would have permitted.

9...Nd7?

As we shall see, this is partly done to put pressure on d4 and partly as an elaborate plan to get rid of White's KB and begin Q-side play, but Black misses a better tactical chance. He should play 9...Nb4. Then after 10 0–0 N×d3 11 c×d3 c6 he can hold White fairly well in the centre and start a Q-side advance. Nor can White very well preserve his bishop by 10 Bc4 N×e4 11 N×e4 d5; tactics again!

10 Be3

White has won the battle of the opening; he has wholly maintained the centre and kept Black cramped. There is now a period when White completes developing and prepares a K-side attack and Black tries to relieve the pressure by exchanging off White's KB and advancing on the Q-side.

10...Nb4 11 Bc4 Nb6 12 Bb3 Nc6 13 0–0 Na5 14 Rad1 Nbc4 15 Bc1 c6 16 f5 Qc7 17 Rd3 b5 18 Rf3 b4 19 Ne2 c5 20 B×c4 N×c4

Don't worry if you don't see the exact reason for each move; there will be a constant succession of tactical calculations which will determine just how the players' plans are put into effect. We hope, however, that you can see how each side is developing his plan.

21 c3 b×c3 22 b×c3 c×d4 23 c×d4

Here Black proposed a draw, thinking (or hoping!) that the files he had opened on the Q-side gave enough play for his rooks and queen to equalize. However, White has seen that there are not enough entries on the Q-side for the black pieces either to harass White seriously or to force exchanges. So White now sets about using his greater space and concentration of force on the K-side to build up a winning attack.

23...Qb7 24 Nc3 Rac8 25 Nd5 g×f5

White threatened 26 f6 e×f6 27 N×f6+ B×f6 28 R×f6 followed by Bh6 with a quick win. Penrose is of course fully at home with the tactics; otherwise, all his good positional play might still count for nothing.

26 Rxf5 f6
26...e6 27 Nf6+ would be easy for White.

Fig. 97

Black is preparing to defend himself along the rank if necessary, but he hasn't enough room for defence.

27 Qh4 Nb6 28 Ne3 Na4 29 Nd5 Nc3 30 Be3 Nxd5 31 exd5!

Usually, doubled pawns like this are very weak, as would these be in an endgame, but Penrose sees that there isn't going to be an endgame and, in the middle-game attack, this pawn splits the black force by preventing ...e6. This is an example of avoiding routine thinking. Doubled pawns are usually bad, of course, but the master knows when to break the rules.

31...Rc3 32 Qe4 Rf7 33 R1f3 Bf8 34 Rg3+ Kh8

If 34...Rg7 35 Rh5 threatening 36 Qxh7+

35 Rh5 Qc8 36 Qg6

Now we see how beautifully White's positional play has come home tactically; Black has no room to defend himself. If 36...Rg7 then 37 Rxh7+! Rxh7 38 Qg8 mate, as the black bishop obstructs the queen.

36...Bh6 37 Qxf7 Rxe3 38 Rxh6 Resigns.

A fine example of positional and tactical play combined.

Of the older masters, one of the finest exploiters of a space advantage was Capablanca, whose modern equivalent is perhaps ex-World Champion Karpov who has an uncanny instinct for creating and using this domination of the board, often beginning with an imperceptible plus and rapidly converting it into a won game.

Consider the classic manner in which he exploits a space advantage arising from the opening, in the following game.

White KARPOV (U.S.S.R.) *Black* ROGERS (Australia)
Opening: Centre Counter Game. Bath, 1983.

1 e4 d5 2 exd5 Qxd5 3 Nc3 Qa5 4 d4 Nf6 5 Nf3 Bg4 6 h3 Bh5!

If you refer back to our previous comments on this opening, you will see that we recommended 6...Bxf3, albeit with a comfortable game for White, but the text move is typical Rogers who loves to fish in troubled waters and does it pretty well. He is following a game Karpov-Larsen from 1982 and hoping to improve on Black's play. However, Karpov introduces his own improvement first!

7 g4 Bg6 8 Ne5 e6 9 h4!

Here it comes! Against Larsen, he had won with 9 Bg2 but since Black will inevitably occupy e4 with his bishop after pinning White's QN, Karpov does not want to allow any freeing exchanges. We shall soon see what his intentions are.

9...Bb4 10 Rh3

Another point of 9 h4; White's rook is excellently posted on the third rank, already an indication of his room for manoeuvre.

10...c6

Yet another reason is now clear for White leaving his bishop on f1: it is needed on the f1-a6 diagonal for situations where White wishes to embarrass Black's queen by Nc4, e.g. if now 10...Be4?! 11 Nc4 Qd5 12 f3 wins a piece; or 11...Qa6 12 Nd2! followed by g5 again winning material, since 12...Qc6?? 13 Bb5 wins the queen. Admittedly, Black could try 11...Qa4 here, but he opts for the normal text move, in order to give his queen an escape square. Note that Black is practically forced into all these complications, because 10...h5 11 Nxg6 fxg6 leaves him with too many weaknesses.

11 Bd2 Qb6

The threat was 12 h5 Be4 13 g5 winning material, so Black gives himself the possibility of interposing...Bxc3 without loss of time. His game is clearly hanging on a thread, but such positions are not always lost.

12 h5 Be4

Black cannot even win three pawns for a piece by 12...Q×d4 13 Nf3 Q×g4 14 h×g6 Q×g6 in view of 15 Rg3 etc.

13 Re3! B×c3

Black cannot delay with this exchange any longer, since 13...Q×d4 allows 14 g5! (this seems even better than Karpov's suggested 14 N×e4 which also wins) 14...Q×e5 (14...B×c3 15 B×c3 Q×d1+ 16 R×d1 wins a piece for White, as does any move of the knight) 15 g×f6 B×c3 16 B×c3 Qd5 (neither 16...Qf5 17 Bh3 nor 16...Qf4 17 Qd4 are any better) 17 Qg4! B×c2 18 Rc1 Bf5 19 Q×g7 Rf8 20 Rd1 Qh1 21 Q×f8+! K×f8 22 Rd8 mate, a striking example of White's total command of the board.

14 B×c3 Bd5

Black would have liked to play 14...h6 and then retreat the bishop to h7, but this would have allowed 15 Nc4 followed by 16 Bb4 when the weakness at d6 gives Black problems. However, if Black had known what was to happen to him in the game, he might have preferred this line.

15 g5 Ne4 16 Qg4 Nd6

According to Karpov 16...N×c3 is no improvement, since 17 b×c3 threatens c4 winning the bishop, with the possible sequel 17...Qb2 18 Qd1 B×a2 19 Bc4! B×c4 20 N×c4 Qb5 21 Nd6+ winning the queen.

17 0-0-0 Nd7 18 Be1!!

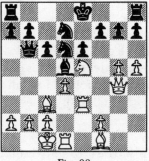

Fig. 98

A deceptively simple solution to the position, clearing the third rank for his rook and at the same time guarding his f2 pawn. One point is seen in the variation 18...Bxa2 19 Ra3 Bd5 20 Nxd7! Kxd7 21 Ba5 winning the queen.

18...Nxe5 19 dxe5 Nf5 20 Rh3!

Guarding h1 and thus threatening to win the bishop by 21 c4, which Black cannot prevent by 20...c5 21 Rxd5! or 20...Qc5 21 b4 followed by 22 c4.

20...0-0-0 21 c4 Qc5 22 b4

Black could resign here, since a piece is lost, but the Micawber element in his nature induces him to play a few more moves which we give without comment.

22...Bf3 23 Rxd8+ Rxd8 24 Qxf3 Qxe5 25 Bc3 Qd6 26 Bd3 Nd4 27 Qxf7 Nf5 28 Bxf5 Qf4+ 29 Re3 Resigns.

One of the most difficult types of attacking plan is when we are carrying it out under some threat of counter-action by our opponent. This is partly because we have to keep a close eye on all his threats and partly because there is so much more urgency required in finding the correct attacking procedure under pressure. We have taken advantage of Leonard Barden's excellent notes to this game published in his instructive column "How good is your chess?" in the magazine 'Chess'. This game is decided by a direct attack on the king, perhaps the most useful type for the readers of this book.

White BAGIROV (U.S.S.R.)   *Black* MAIZEL (U.S.S.R.)
Opening: Sicilian.   Azerbaijan, 1961.

1 e4 c5 2 Nf3 d6 3 d4 cxd4 4 Nxd4 Nf6 5 Nc3 a6

In most lines of the Sicilian Defence, this move must be played at some time or another. White's plan is to get his pieces out quickly and launch an attack on the king. Black aims for an attack on the Q-side, either against White's Q-side pawns or, if he plays 0-0-0, against the king. He also often attacks White's KP. To carry out all this, c7 is a good square for Black's queen, where it does not wish to be attacked by a knight coming to b5, hence ...a6. The move also helps to prepare the useful ...b5 followed by ...Bb7 and, if need be, ...b4 driving away White's QN.

6 Bg5 e6 7 f4 Be7 8 Qf3 Qc7 9 0-0-0 Nc6?

This natural move is not best. It is better to play ...Nbd7, keeping the file open for the queen and later playing, perhaps, ...b5, ...Bb7 and ...Nc5 with pressure against the centre.

10 Nxc6!

A good example of the interrelation of positional and tactical play. If Black could safely reply 10...bxc6 and later play ...d5, he would obtain a fine game with a good centre and open b-file. However, 10...bxc6 won't do because of 11 e5! dxe5 12 fxe5 Nd5 (12...Qxe5? 13 Qxc6+) 13 Bxe7 Qxe7 14 Ne4 when Black's pawns are weak and White has a strong grip on the dark squares. This means that Black must recapture with the queen which is not particularly well-placed on c6 where it may obstruct the QB. The exchange of knights also slightly helps White by opening up his rook on the d-file.

10...Qxc6 11 Qg3!

A very fine move. White's plan is to force open the position by e5 as soon as possible; clearly, he does not want queens exchanged when he plays this. Moreover, Qg3 threatens 12 Bxf6 Bxf6 13 e5 dxe5 14 fxe5 Be7 15 Qxg7 and it also prevents ...e5. Finally, 11...Nxe4 12 Nxe4 Qxe4 13 Bxe7 Kxe7 14 Qg5+ Kd7 15 Bd3 would give White a winning position. All these ideas in one move!

11...h6

It is hard to see a better move, since the immediate 11...0-0 is met by 12 e5 dxe5 13 fxe5 Nd5 14 Bxe7 Nxe7 15 Bd3 followed by Ne4. After the text move, however, the K-side is weakened.

12 Bxf6 Bxf6 13 e5 dxe5 14 fxe5 Bg5+ 15 Kb1 0-0 16 h4 Be7 17 Bd3 Bd7

Taking stock, we see that White is ahead in development and has more space in which to manoeuvre. He also has a better defensive position, unmoved pawns and a knight on c3, as well as being further on with his attack. Black has the c-file and two bishops, usually an advantage in an open position. White will therefore play to bring all his pieces to bear on the king; Black will play to hold his defensive position and develop counterplay on the queen's wing.

18 Qg4

Partly to allow his KR to come in via g3, partly to tie down the black queen, since if it now moves Qe4 will be very strong.

18...Rfd8 19 Rh3 Be8 20 Rf1 Rac8 21 Rg3

We can see that Black has developed some counter-attack: if White now tried to bring his knight into the attack by 21 Ne4? he would lose to 21...Rxd3! 22 cxd3 Qc2+ 23 Ka1 Qc1+ and mate next move.

21...g6?

He ought to have played ...Bf8 avoiding further weakening of the defensive pawns, but probably thought he would then lose to 22 Rf6 Kh8? 23 Rxh6+! without realizing that 22 Rf6 can be countered by 22...Qb6! when Black's threats of ...Rxc3 and also ...Qg1+ with back row mates are too strong, e.g. 23 Rxh6 Rxd3! 24 cxd3 (or 24 Rxd3) Rxc3! or 23 Bh7+ Kh8 24 Rxh6 Qg1+! and Black mates first, but not here 23...Kxh7? 24 Rxh6+! Therefore, against 21...Bf8 White would have had to play more quietly, perhaps with 22 Qf4 Kh8 (23 Qxh6 was threatened) 23 Ne4 (threatening Nf6 followed by Qxh6+! and Rg8 mate) 23... Rd4 (now 23...Rxd3? 24 cxd3 Qc2+ is no good) 24 c3 Ra4 25 Bc2 Rc4 26 Qe3 with threats of Qd3 or b3 and White should win. However, life is much easier for White after the text move, so we again see a tactical miscalculation causing a positional error.

Fig. 99

The weakened defensive position is now immediately smashed by a very fine, though typical, sacrifice.

22 Rxf7! Bxf7

22...Kxf7 23 Qxg6+ Kf8 24 Qg8 mate.

23 Bxg6 Bg5

Otherwise 24 Bxf7+ wins at once.

24 Bxf7+ Kxf7 25 hxg5

As a result of the combination, material is about equal but Black's defensive position is in ruins and he must lose.

25...Qc5 26 a3!

There is time to dispose of Black's counter-attack, since Black cannot hope to put his own defensive position right.

26...Qxe5 27 gxh6 Rf8 28 Ne4 b5 29 Qg7+! Resigns.

Many players when attacking never think of queen exchanges, but the win is now easy after 29...Qxg7 30 Rxg7+ Ke8 31 Nd6+ Kd8 32 Nxc8 Kxc8 33 h7 followed by 34 Rg8.

Our last example in this chapter once again sees both kings exposed to attack, a situation deliberately provoked by White's choice of an ultra-sharp opening variation. In modern chess, it is just impossible to prevent an aggressive opponent from selecting a line which may well be dubious in theory but which demands all your coolness and resourcefulness to refute in a practical situation over the board, with the clock ticking away relentlessly! The present World Champion, Gary Kasparov, was faced by such an opponent in 1981. Surprised in the opening, he adopts the move recommended by theory, only to find Vaiser producing a prepared improvement which gives White excellent attacking chances. How do you formulate a plan under these tense circumstances? Perhaps the game will help the reader to appreciate the problem, without providing an easy answer.

White VAISER (U.S.S.R.)   *Black* KASPAROV (U.S.S.R.)
Opening: King's Indian Defence. Soviet Teams Championship, 1981.

1 d4 Nf6 2 c4 g6 3 Nc3 Bg7 4 e4 d6 5 f4 0-0 6 Nf3 c5 7 d5 e6 8 Be2 exd5

The Four Pawns Attack variation is an ambitious attempt by White to stifle Black in the early stages, which is why Black's 6th and 7th moves are essential to get a grip in the centre before he is overwhelmed by the advancing pawns. Kasparov was probably now expecting the normal 9 cxd5 to which he may have planned the reply 9...b5!? which in its turn is a sharp attempt to attack the centre from the wing. However, his opponent has a surprise in store, a rare occurrence for a player with such a vast knowledge of opening theory.

9 e5!

An excellent psychological choice, mainly because it is briefly dealt with in a few lines of opening theory (which Kasparov knew) without proper consideration of the real problems arising.

9...Ng4

The 'book' move, based on two main variations: 10 h3 d4 11 Ne4 Nxe5! 12 fxe5 13 dxe5 and Black's strong central pawns are more than sufficient compensation for the piece; or 10 cxd5 dxe5 11 h3 e4! 12 Nxe4 Nf6 with a good game for Black. It is this latter variation that Vaiser has been working on, as we shall see. With hindsight, it is possible to suggest that 9...Nfd7 10 cxd5 dxe5 or 9...dxe5 10 fxe5 Ng4 11 Bg5 f6 may be better alternatives, but it is readily understandable that Kasparov chooses the more complex line, even though he later confessed that he preferred White's position from now on.

10 cxd5 dxe5 11 h3 e4 12 hxg4! exf3 13 gxf3!

Vaiser's improvement on theory is based on simple attacking logic: he intends to attack Black's king by playing f5, exchanging the important defending bishop on g7 by Bh6, then transferring his queen to the h-file, castling long if necessary, all taking no more than four or five moves. Imagine you are Kasparov facing such a situation and having to make a plan. Your QN will take two moves to come to the defence of the K-side, your QB is most awkward to develop and your natural defensive move ...f5 will only open up the a2 — g8 diagonal to White's advantage. What's to be done? Firstly, you must calm down your inner panic which sometimes, admittedly, produces adrenalin but more often than not leads you to dread imaginary dangers, instead of coolly appraising the concrete elements in the position. Clearly, if you try to defend passively, White will be happy to carry out the given plan unhindered, with far the better chances. This means that your plan must somehow involve a counter-attack on White's king, before it can reach a safe haven. With this in mind, Kasparov directs his attention to the b2 pawn, probably his best practical chance despite his self-criticism after the game.

13...Re8 14 f5! Qb6!?

Kasparov gives 14...b6 as an improvement to prevent 15 Bh6 in view of 15...Bxc3+ 16 bxc3 Ba6, but a later game Huerta–Nogueiras played in 1984 showed that this is no easy solution either: 14...b6 15 fxg6! hxg6 16 Kf1 Ba6 17 Ne4! Bxe2+ 18 Qxe2 Nd7 19 Qh2! Nf8 20 Bh6 Be5 21 Qd2 Qd7 22 Bg5 f5 23 Nf6+ Bxf6 24 Bxf6 and although White only drew, he stood better here. Perhaps the reader can come up with some other idea.

15 Bh6! Qxb2 16 Bxg7 Kxg7 17 f6+?

At first sight, this looks like a tremendous move, since it must have been difficult for Vaiser to foresee Kasparov's following subtle defensive play. However, as it turns out, it is better to keep all his options open by the strong 17 Rc1! threatening Rc2, then occupation of d2, c1 or a1 by the white queen. Vaiser gives a number of variations to demonstrate the power of this move, but we will just restrict ourselves to one: 17...gxf5 18 Rc2 Qb6 19 d6! fxg4 20 Qd2 Bf5 21 Qh6+ Kg8 22 Nd5 Qa5+ 23 Kf1 Nd7 24 Rc4! Nf8 25 Rxg4+ Bg6 26 Nf6+ Kh8 27 Rxg6 fxg6 28 Qxf8+ Rxf8 29 Rxh7 mate. Of course, after 17 f6+ Black must not play 17...Kxf6 18 Ne4+ Kg7 19 Rb1 Qe5 20 Qd2 with a comfortable win, so Kasparov plans a more dynamic defence.

17...Kg8! 18 Qc1!!

Fig. 100

18...Qb4

Most players would have exchanged queens here, with a sigh of relief, but the end-game would then favour White (try it out your-self against a friend!). Instead, Kasparov aims for an active defence.

19 Kf1?

White still cannot believe that his attack has disappeared, but remember what we said about being prepared to change your plans when the occasion demands it. According to Kasparov, White should settle for 19 Qd2! Nd7 20 Rb1 Qd4 21 Q×d4 c×d4 22 Ne4 with equal chances. However, one can readily understand White's reluctance to 'capitulate'.

19...Nd7 20 Bb5 Qd4!

The point of Black's defence/counter-attack. Vaiser's intended 21 Qh6 is now countered by 22...N×f6! 23 B×e8 Q×c3 24 Kg2 B×g4! 25 B×f7+ K×f7 26 f×g4 Re8 winning easily.

21 Kg2 Re3! 22 Ne2 Qe5 23 Kf2 R×e2+ 24 B×e2 N×f6

Strategically, the game is now decided in Black's favour. Rather than allow a winning attack, White now heads for the end-game in which he is also lost. We give the remainder of the game without comment.

25 Q×c5 B×g4 26 Qe3 Q×e3+ 27 K×e3 N×d5+ 28 Kf2 Be6 29 Rab1 b6 30 Rbc1 Nf4 31 a3 N×e2 32 K×e2 b5 33 Rc7 a5 34 Rb1 Bc4+ 35 Kf2 a4 36 Re1 Rd8 37 Re3 Rd2+ 38 Kg3 Kg7 39 f4 Rb2 40 Rc5 h5

The game was now adjourned, with White sealing 41 Kh4 but resigning before resumption. With the possibility of creating three passed pawns, Black will have little trouble with the technical exploitation of his advantage.

CHAPTER TEN

Looking Ahead

10.1. How to Improve

This book has, we hope, set you on the way to becoming a good player if you have the wish and the natural talent to become one. Given that you have absorbed what we have to teach, how can you make further progress? This chapter aims to help you to answer this question — the final answer differs from player to player and in the end you will have to find your own — and is divided into two parts: how to play and what to read.

10.2. How to Play

(i) Play hard

Never play sloppy chess, not giving your mind to it, taking moves back, and so on. Give your whole attention to the game, play strictly to the rules and insist on your opponent doing the same. We strongly recommend learning to play with a clock as soon as possible, and, whenever feasible, using a clock in friendly games as well as matches. You can adjust the time limit to correspond to the amount you want to give to the game; if you want to play for an hour, then set the clocks to give you half an hour each. This is excellent practice for match games and also disciplines the player who starts by suggesting a quick game and then in fact plays unreasonably slowly. Playing with a clock is also a good way of keeping your mind on the game and making you concentrate. Also a time handicap is quite a good one to use between players of slightly different strength; finally, quick clock

148

play is very good practice for situations in match play where you get short of time and have to move in a hurry.

(ii) Learn from your losses

When you lose, find out why; don't just make a lot of bogus excuses. If you lose, your opponent has played better then you have — then you should have something to learn, either from his good play or your own mistakes; be sure that you do learn it. Associated with this is the need to be generous when you lose and to give your opponent fair credit for his win; losing is never very agreeable but it becomes a lot less disagreeable if you admit your opponent's good play instead of being grudging — and until you do this, you cannot begin to learn from your losses.

(iii) Vary your opposition

Many players have a favourite opponent and play with him most of the time; this is not the way to improve. Every player has a distinctive style and his own special strong and weak points — if you only play one or two opponents your play will get in a rut and you will only be able to deal with certain kinds of play. The best opponents are players slightly stronger than oneself; much stronger players are not good opponents as the game is uninteresting for them and you will be unable ever to develop any positive ideas of your own — weaker players are bad opponents because they make you play slackly. Obviously everyone cannot play against slightly stronger opponents all the time — but get as much practice of this kind as you can.

The correct attitude against all opponents is 'No one can beat me if I play the right moves, but unless I play my best I can lose this game'. Play with courage against stronger opponents; what a strong player welcomes more than anything else is timid play by his opponent and this is by far the easiest form of play for him to cope with. Remember that strong players have their own form of nervousness — the feeling 'I must not lose to a rabbit like X!'; this means that it can be very harassing to be faced with an attack by a weaker opponent. If you are the stronger player, do not underestimate your opponent; play as hard as you would against the strongest player. Another point — don't worry too much about avoiding any simplification because he might draw; play the right moves and do not worry about anything else. In fact, it is best in general to forget whether your opponent is better or worse than you and to follow the old advice, 'Play the board and not the man'.

The obvious and best way to vary your opposition is to join, according to your age, a school or adult chess club.

(iv) Vary your openings

Do not try to acquire the minimum set of openings on which you can get by; this may pay quite well in the short term, but in the long run it will mean that you don't develop — it has the same sort of disadvantage as only playing one or two opponents. On the other hand, you don't want to dash about from opening to opening never understanding any of them properly. The best policy is probably to concentrate on one or two openings for a season — or until you feel you understand them pretty well — and then to take up a new opening or group of openings. Whatever openings you play, try to understand, not to memorize — best of all, try to introduce ideas and moves of your own. They are unlikely to be very good, but you will fox your opponents and in seeing why they aren't as good as accepted lines, you will learn.

Finally, let us repeat advice given earlier. Don't play openings that involve ideas beyond the range of your present ability, just because the masters play them; play openings that you can understand and that give rise to open positions with plenty of tactical chances.

(v) Enjoy the whole game

Many players only enjoy — and therefore only try hard at — certain parts of the game. Some only like attacking play and hate to defend; some players are afraid of complications and others only like complicated positions; many players are uninterested in the endgame. The true chess player enjoys and appreciates every part of the game; if you find you are avoiding, or afraid of, some part of chess there is a very simple cure — study it and get as much practice in it as you can. This applies particularly to the endgame.

10.3. Reading about the Game

Reading is no substitute for play; you can become a strong player with a lot of play and very little reading, but never with a lot of reading and very little play. Nevertheless, reading does help, the amount required varying from player to player, so you will have to judge for yourself how much it helps you. There are a number of excellent chess publications on the market catering for all levels of ability; unfortunately far too many for us to list them here.

We advise you to subscribe to a chess magazine which will provide up-to-date information on chess books and other chess matters. The two leading magazines in this country are:

British Chess Magazine (9 Market Street, St. Leonards-on-Sea, East Sussex, TN38 0DQ)

Chess (Sutton Coldfield, Warwickshire, B73 6AZ)

If you find you have insufficient practice over the board, you can always take up correspondence play which will, incidentally, greatly help your opening theory, since one clearly has the time to study more deeply than in over-the-board play. You may then find it worthwhile to take the six-monthly international magazine 'Informant' which contains over 700 of the latest top games classified by openings.

Or again, you may find great enjoyment from a very different branch of chess, problem-solving/composing. Whereas in playing chess the object is to win, in problem-composing the object is to produce something which is aesthetically satisfying, often far removed from the constraints of a game of chess. A problem is a small work of art, and all chess players should learn enough about problems to know whether they enjoy them or not.

The Chess Study is an artistic creation based on the practical realities of the game and, as such, appeals to all serious chess players for its usefulness as well as its undoubted beauty.

For information about any of these activities and, in fact, about all that is going on in the world of chess, apply to the Secretary of the British Chess Federation who will be delighted to send you the relevant information (address: 9a Grand Parade, St. Leonards-on-Sea, East Sussex, TN38 0DD).

10.4. Conclusion

We hope that you have not only learnt something from this book but also enjoyed the experience. Perhaps the chief thing to be remembered about chess is the pleasure it gives us all, a pleasure that is all the more intense when we have put maximum effort into the game. However, that is not to say that we must take it so seriously that it becomes an obsession which eventually drives away our enjoyment of chess and, indeed, of everything else. That would be a great pity and a gross disservice to one of the finest games ever invented.

We end with a Revision Exercise on various points that have come up in the book. The earlier questions relate to Volume 1, but you should be able to answer them now even if you have not read the first Volume.

Revision Exercise R.2

1. What are the most important things to remember in the opening?
2. State four conditions which make castling illegal.
3. When can you capture 'en passant'?
4. Give four conditions when a draw can be claimed by one of the players.
5. The two kings and one white pawn are on the board. State two conditions when the pawn might be queened by force.
6. What must you do if your opponent points out that you have just made an illegal move with one of your pieces or pawns?
7. When are queen and king unable to defeat king and pawn?
8. Under which exceptional circumstance (apart from immediate stalemate) are king, bishop and pawn unable to defeat the lone king?
9. You have material advantage. What kind of exchanges should you make as most likely to lead to an endgame win?
10. You have a pawn less than your opponent. What exchanges are most likely to give you drawing chances?
11. You have a pawn less than your opponent, each having a rook and knight, and must either exchange rooks or knights. Which exchange would you choose, other factors being equal?
12. The two players have bishops operating on opposite-coloured squares. What difference, if any, is the presence of the two queens likely to make to the game?
13. You have bishop and pawns for knight and an equal number of pawns, the kings being equally well placed. Under what circumstances would you expect the bishop to give you winning chances and when would the knight be better?
14. You have rook and a number of pawns against rook and one pawn less, the king positions being equally good and all pawns being safe from immediate capture. Where should your rook be placed to give the best winning chances?
15. What is an isolated pawn and why is it a disadvantage?

16. What is the most important difference in the use of pieces between middle-game and endgame?

17. State a way in which a pin differs from either a fork or a skewer.

18. What is the basic difference between a pin against the king and a pin against the queen (or any other piece)?

19. Your opponent's king has been unable to castle in the middle-game. What tactics should you try to apply?

20. You are compelled to move one of the pawns in front of your castled king. Which is generally the move least likely to create serious weakness?

21. Under what condition is g3 in front of the castled king least likely to prove disastrous in the middle-game?

22. When players have castled on opposite sides, what kind of attack often proves effective? Why?

23. You have control of more central space, and your opponent has no immediate compensating counter-attack. What plan is most likely to succeed, and how would you aim (in broad terms) to carry it out?

24. What should be your attitude to the many opening variations given in standard works on this phase of chess?

25. Why is it inadvisable for the ordinary player to adopt many of the openings favoured by the masters?

Solutions to Exercises

Exercise 1

1. No. The knight is unprotected, so 4 N×e5 allows 4...Qa5+ and 5...Q×e5.

2. (a) Black's 1...Ne4 leaves this piece and the QR unprotected, and White plays 2 Qd5 Nf2+ 3 R×f2 B×f2 4 Q×a8. Black can do better with 2...Bb7 3 Q×b7 Nf2+ 4 R×f2 B×f2 but still loses two pieces for a rook.

   (b) Yes. Black can play 1...Ne8 and after 2 Qd5 (forking rook and bishop) Qc7 3 Q×a8 Bb7 traps the queen.

3. 1 N×b6 c×b6 2 Bd5 Qe8 3 Qc2 winning a piece.

4. No. 1...B×f2 2 Ke2 (a king fork) wins a piece.

5. 1 Qb3+ and 2 Q×b7.

6. 1 Qg4+ f5 2 Q×b4 or even better 1 R×c8 Q×c8 2 Qg4+ f5 3 Q×b4, since it helps to exchange towards a winning endgame. Won by A. H. Roose, Dutch v. British Universities, Utrecht, 1939.

7. No. The idea is good, since 1 Rc8 R×c8 2 Q×c8+ Kg7 3 d7 would win; but the rook is insufficiently protected on c8, allowing 1...Qg4+ winning it.

8. White's knight on f5 is unprotected, so 1...Qc1+ 2 Kh2 (or 2 Kf2 Qf4+ and 3...Q×f5) Qf4+ 3 Ng3 Q×h4+ 4 Kg1 Q×g3.

9. White's bishop on c4 is unprotected, so 1...Qd1+ 2 Kg2 Qc2+ and 3...Q×c4.

10. Only the black knight prevents Qg8+ winning the rook on h7, so 1 N×e7! K×e7 (1...Q×e7 2 Qg8+ and 3...Q×h7) 2 Qg8 Rh6 3 Q×f7+ Kd8 4 Qf8+ and 5 Q×h6.

11. 1...Kd8 is best. If 1...c6 2 N×c6 wins a pawn, because 2...b×c6 allows 3 B×c6+ and 4 B×a8. The alternatives 1...Bd7 2 B×d7+ and 1...Nd7 2 B×e7 lose at once.

12. 1 R×d7 N×d7 2 Ne7+ Kh7 3 Qf5+ g6 4 Q×d7, or the same line with 1 Ne7+ first.

13. Yes. The quickest way to win is 1 Qh5+ Kg8 2 Qd5+ Kh7 (if 2...Kf8 3 Qd8 mate, or if 2...Kh8 3 Qh1+ Kg8 4 Qg1+ transposing, or here 3...Rh7 4 Qa8 mate) 3 Qh1+ Kg8 4 Qg1+ and 5 Q×a7.

14. (a) 1...N×e5! attacking the white queen and if 2 d×e5 Q×e5+ and 3...Q×a1. Black must make sure that White has no replies to 1...N×e5 that may turn the tables. 2 Qf4 is met by 2...N×d3+ 3 c×d3 Q×f4 4 B×f4 and Black has won a safe pawn.

    (b) With the white KB on b3, the combination will not work, because now White replies 2 Qf4 and Black's knight cannot move to safety without losing the unguarded queen and 2...Nd3+ loses a piece.

    (c) Now the combination is available once more, because now the white queen too is unprotected, allowing 1...N×e5 2 Qf4? Nd3+ 3 c×d3 Q×f4 winning.

15. No. 1 Qb1 with a double attack is foiled by 1...Rfd8! when 2 Q×b7 fails to 2...Rd1+ 3 R×d1 R×d1 mate. Give yourself some credit if you found the counter-attack 1...Bd4 which would have been Black's only chance, if the back-rank mate had not been available.

16. 1 Rd7 wins a piece, since both the black bishop and knight are now attacked twice and only defended once. Note that in each case the fact that the black piece is defended once and attacked once makes it just as vulnerable as if it were not defended at all. This possibility is not always seen so easily as the threat to an unguarded piece and requires special care when the possibility arises.

17. He would like to occupy g6 threatening Qh7 mate, so White plays 1 Qg4 attacking the rook and the vital square. Black must lose material, since the only move to counter both threats is 1...Qe8 which loses the queen. Once again, the possibilities of counter-attack must be examined and reveal an interesting variation which nearly turns the tables. Black replies 1...Re8 when 2 Rxe8 Qxe8 brings everything under control, and 2 Qxd7 Bxg2+! 3 Rxg2 Rxe1 mate gives Black the win. However, White can still win by 2 Qg6! Bxg2+ 3 Qxg2 Qxg2+ 4 Kxg2 Rd2+ 5 Kf3 (but not 5 Kh1?? Rxh2 mate!) Rxe1 6 Rxe1 winning the ending, because Black has no time to capture the pawn in view of the back-rank mate.

18. Yes! This time, Black has calculated that he can allow the double attack by 2 Qd5 to which he replies 2...Qh4! 3 Qxa8 Ng3 mate. If 3 Bf4 Nf2+ 4 Rxf2 Qxf2 or if 3 g3 Nxg3+ 4 Kg2 Nxf1 5 Qxa8 Qf2+ wins. This is another example of a very strong counter-attack. Note the difference between this and Position 2 where 2...Qh4 would be met by 3 Qxe4.

Exercise 2

1 1...Rb8 2 Bxf7+ Kxf7 3 Qxd6, exploiting the unprotected black queen.

2. 1 Nh6+ gxh6 2 Qxd7.

3. 1 Bc7! and 2 Rxd7, but not 1 Bc5 Rb7 guarding the bishop.

4. 1...Bxh2+ 2 Kxh2 Rxe4.

5. Black's possibility of...Qh2 mate is hampered by the presence of his own knight, so 1...Nf3+! and the mate cannot be avoided.

6. 1...Rxd4 for if 2 Qxd4 Ng4+ and 3...Bxd4. Won by A. Le Vack of Hampshire, Correspondence, 1937-8

7. 1...Re1+ 2 Rxe1 (or 2 Kg2 Qh3+ 3 Kf3 Bg4 mate) Qxe1+ 3 Kg2 Bh3+4 Kxh3 Rxh8.

8. 1...Rxc5 2 Qxc5 gxh2+ and 3...Qxg2 mate. The immediate 1...gxh2+ would allow White to delay mate by giving up a piece with 2 Qxh2 Rxc5, whereas after 1...Rxc5 2 Qxg3 Rg5 3 Qb3+ Bd5 White can only avoid mate by the sacrifice of his queen. Note that the vital check is reserved until it has maximum effect; the old saying "Never miss a check, it might be mate" can thus be relegated to the number of facetious comments with little or no meaning passed down from generation to generation!

9. White wishes to discover on Black's KRP, so 1 Nxe6+ fxe6 2 Qxh6+ Kf7 (2...Kg8 3 Qxg6+ and 4 Qh7 mate) 3 Qh7+Ke8 4 Bxg6+ Rf7 5 Qxf7 mate. If Black plays 1...Kg8 giving up his queen, White should refuse the offer and reply 2 Qxh6 with unavoidable mate. Now for a valid saying: "When you see a good move, always look for a better one!"

10. Black has opened up the diagonal occupied by the white bishop on d4. 1...g6 2 Nxd5 wins at least a pawn, for if 2...exd5 3 e6 fxe6 4 Bxh8. Note that if the black queen stood at d8 or c8 instead of at c7, this plan would not work, as 2 Nxd5 would

not attack the queen and Black could reply 2...Nxd4 3 Qxd4 Bxd5, an illustration of how important it is, especially when making a sacrifice, to look at the opponent's counter-attacks. Won by S. W. Barron, Northants County Club Championship, 1938.

11. 1...Qxf1+ 2 Bxf1 Bxa2+ 3 Kxa2 Rxc7 winning. Won by the Soviet grandmaster Flohr against Stein.

12. This is a very difficult example. In a game at the Hastings Congress, Black played 1...Bxb6 2 Qxh8 Bd4+ winning easily. White should play 2 Ra7+! Bxa7 3 Qc7+ Ke8 4 Qc8+ drawing by perpetual check. However, Black has a surprising resource depending on a discovery: 1...Qd4+!! 2 Bxd4 Ba5+ 3 Rxa5 Rxc8+ 4 Kd3 exd4 and the extra piece decides. Won by the Irish player Walsh.

13. 1...Nc3 2 Rxb6 Nxe2+ 3 Kf1 axb6 when White's queen is forced to move, giving Black time to play 4...Nc3 retaining his extra piece. This game was won by Wexler, the Argentinian master, against Bielicki at Mar del Plata, 1960.

14. 1...e4 2 Nd4 Qg5 when White must defend against the threatened mate at g2, allowing 3...Nh3+ followed by 4...Qxd2. Won by Benkö against Revise in the U.S.A. Open, 1961.

Exercise 3

1. Yes. He plays 1 Nf6 double check and mate.
2. 1 Bd6+ and 2 Bxc5, but not 1 Bd4+ Qe7.
3. 1 Rxg7+ Kh8 2 Rg8+! Kxg8 3 Rg1 mate.
4. 1...Bg7+ and 2...Kxh7. An unusual way of winning material; if there had been no check, the bishop could simply have been captured, and the bishop does not itself attack anything but cuts off one rook from the protection of its fellow.
5. The black queen must be dislodged to enable a discovery by the bishop. 1 Rd7! Bxd7 2 exd7+ wins the queen. If 1...Qg5 2 e7+ wins easily. Won by the Dr. J. Bronowski of T.V. fame, Yorkshire Championship, 1938.
6. 1 Nxc6 Qxf4 2 Nxe7+ b5 3 Nxd5+ and 4 Nxf4. No better is 2...Kd8 or 2...Kf8 when 3 Nxd5 threatens both the queen and 4 Re8 mate.
7. 1...Rxe2 2 Bxh3 Rxf2+ 3 Kg1 Rxb2+ and 4...Rxa2.
8. 1 Qc3 (foreseen some moves previously when sacrificing the KR) 1...Qf6 (or 1...Kf8 2 Rd7! Qxd7 3 Qh8+ Ke7 4 Bg5 mate) 2 Bxb8 Raxb8 3 Rd7+ Re7 4 Rxe7+. Clearly, Black must not recapture on move 2, but he is then material down in a bad position. A plausible alternative is 1 Rd8 clearing the long diagonal for the white queen, but the tables are turned by 1...Qe1! 2 Rxe8 Be2 mate! This shows the importance of correct timing in a combination. If you found the good alternative 1 Re4 give yourself some credit, since Black must give up his queen by 1...fxe4 2 Qc3+ Qf6 3 Bh6+ Kxh6 4 Qxf6 and must then lose at least his bishop, because 4...Be2 5 Qf4+! Kh5 (or else the rook falls) 6 g3! Bg4 7 h3! mates. If Black opts to give up his rook instead by 1...Qxe4 2 Qc3+ Re5 then 3 Bxe5+ Kf8 (3...Kh6 4 Qh3+ Kg5 5 f4+) 4 Bd6+ Ke8 5 Qh8+ Kd7 6 Qg7+ Kd8 7 Qc7+ Ke8 8 Qc8 mate is a convincing finale. Won by J. Wolstenholme, Correspondence, 1939-40.
9. 1 Nf5+ exf5 2 Bc5+. A beautiful example of a double check's power, with three white pieces under attack yet none able to be captured.

Exercise 4

1. 1 N×f7 Q moves 2 N×h8 (Type 2).
2. 1...Nc2 2 Rb1 N2×d4 (Type 4).
3. 1...Bc5 2 Qd3 N×f2 followed by the capture of one of the rooks. (Types 1, 2 and 6).
4. 1 Nc4 Qa6 2 Nd6+ Kd8 (...Kf8? 3 Qf7 mate) 3 Nf7+ Kc7 4 Q×a6 b×a6 5 N×h8 (Type 2).
5. 1...h2+! 2 Kh1 (2 K×h2 Ng4+) Qf1+ 3 R×f1 R×f1+ 4 Ng1 h×g1(Q)+ 5 Q×g1 R×g1+ 6 K×g1 Nd3 and wins easily (Type 5).
6. No. Black must guard against the threatened knight fork on e7. After 1...f5 2 N×c6 wins a piece in all variations (Types 2 and 6).
7. 1...Ne2+ 2 K moves Nc3! 3 B×c3 B×c3 4 Nf4! (trying to regain the exchange by Ne6) Qe8 and White can no longer avoid loss.
8. 1...Q×d4 2 Q×d4 Nc2+ 3 K-moves N×d4 (Type 5).
9. 1...Qc1+ 2 Kf2 Ne4+ 3 Kf3 Q×c4 4 Q×c4 Nd2+ 5 K-moves N×c4 (Type 5).
10. Not 1...N×f3+ 2 Ke3 N×g1 3 N×g1, but 1...Bd7! undermining the bishop's protection. If now 2 g4 N×f3+ 3 Ke3 B×g4! 4 Nf2 Bh5 5 Nh3 N×g1 6 N×g1 g5 and Black has a won ending. If 2 f4 Nc4+ 3 Kd3 Nb2+ 4 K-moves B×h3 wins. An interesting alternative is 1...Bf1 2 Nf4 N×f3+ 3 Ke3 N×g1 4 Kf2 Bc4 5 K×g1 B×a2 winning.
11. If White plays obvious moves such as 1 Qd8, Black obtains a ferocious attack by 1...Qb6+ 2 Kh1 B×g2+! 3 K×g2 Ra2+ 4 Kf3 (or 4 Kh1 Qf2) Qf2+. Similarly, after 1 N×f7 Qb6+ gives Black great attacking chances. Correct for White is 1 Qh8+! K×h8 2 N×f7+ Kh7 3 N×d6 and the pawn on c7 will cost Black a rook (Type 3).
12. 1...R×c2! 2 K×c2 B×b3+ 3 R×b3 Nd4+ winning a piece (Type 3). If White moves his king at the 3rd move, Black plays 3...B×d5, a bishop fork, and again finishes a piece ahead. This combination decided the game Trifunović-Bronstein, Yugoslavia versus U.S.S.R., 1957.
13. White, Kupper playing Olafsson at Zurich, 1959, won by 1 B×g7 K×g7 2 R×f7+ Kg8 (2...R×f7 3 Ne6+ wins; Type 2) 3 Rg7+! Kh8 4 R×h7+ Kg8 5 Rg7+ and Black resigned, since after 5...Kh8 6 R×g6 White would have three extra pawns plus a winning attack. The whole variation is based on the possible fork if Black's king ever plays to g7.
14. 1...Q×d1 2 R×d1 Nf3+ (Type 5) 3 Kg2 N×h4+ 4 B×h4 Rf7 and Black has won the exchange. Less good is the immediate...Nf3+ when 2 R×f3 Q×d1+ 3 Kg2 gives White a very strong attack, e.g. 3...Rfe8 (3...Rf7 4 Ng5! wins) 4 f6. The temporary sacrifice by Black exchanges the dangerous white queen and kills the counter-attack. The continuation was played by Keres against Petrosian, one of the most difficult players to beat in his time, at Zürich, 1961.
15. This time, Petrosian is on the winning side against Nielsen at Copenhagen, 1960. He played 1 R×f8 K×f8 (1...Q×f8 2 Ne6+, Type 3) 2 N×g5 h×g5 (2...Q×g5 3 Ne6+, Type 5) 3 Qb7! and Black resigned, being unable to defend his rook (3...Rd8 4 R×d8 Q×d8 5 Ne6+ (Type 1) winning the queen). An immediate 1 Qb7 would allow 1...Bf7 2 R×f7+ Q×f7 3 Rd7 Q×d7!! 4 N×d7 Be3+ 5 Nf2 R×f2! and wins. White can play Qb7 on his second move, but correctly reduces counter-play by exchanging a further piece.
16. Rellstab against Farwig at Hamburg, 1960, played 1 Bf6! and Black resigned in view of the two variations 1...g×f6 2 Rd7! Q×d7 3 N×f6+ Kg7 4 N×d7 winning further material, and 1...Qe8 2 Qg4 g6 3 Qg5 Bd8 4 Qh6 B×f6 5 N×f6+ Kh8 6 Q×h7 mate (Types 5 and 2).

17. After 1 N×f7 (Petrosian-Simagin, Moscow, 1956) Qd1+ and White cannot avoid queen checks on h5, f3 and d1 to force the draw. Petrosian missed the winning line 1 Qa8+ Kg7 (if 1...Ke7 2 Q×a7+ Kf6 3 Ne4+! Kg6 4 Q×f7+ K×f7 5 N×d6+ wins) 2 B×e5+! Q×e5 3 Qh8+! K×h8 4 N×f7+ and 5 N×e5 winning (Types 1 and 4).

18. A study specially composed to show the tremendous power of the knight fork. If Black captures the rook at any move, White reaches a winning knight and pawn ending. Play proceeds 1 Rb4! Qc8 (forced if Black is not to lose his queen at once; if you did not find this line, see if you can work out the remaining moves, using the same theme, without further reference to the solution) 2 Rb8 Qh3 3 Rh8 Nh4 4 R×h4 Qc8 5 Rh8 Qb7 6 Rb8 finally winning the queen (Types 2, 4 and 5; see when they apply).

Exercise 5

1. 1 f5 wins a piece.
2. 1...B×f3 2 B×f3 e×d4 wins a piece.
3. 1 Bg5! Qg6 2 g4 h6 3 g×f5 Q×f5 4 Be3 Q×h3 5 Nh2 with advantage. Note that the immediate 1 g4 N×e3 2 f×e3 Bg6 is fine for Black.
4. No. A piece is lost by 1...b4 2 e×f6 b×c3 3 B×c3 Q moves 4 f×g7, the pawn fork.
5. Yes! 1...Be6 is an excellent, carefully calculated move and the only way to win. If now 2 f5+ B×f5 3 g×f5+ K×f5 winning, whilst 2 Kf2 B×g4 3 Kg3 Be6 4 Kf3 Kf5 giving White no hope, but not here 3...Kf5 4 e6! and it is White who wins! Won by D. H. Butler, Correspondence, 1938-9.
6. Yes! Again the move is carefully calculated. White can hardly ignore the move, since Black threatens both ... N×e3 and ...Bg3. Therefore 1...Nf5 2 g4 Q×h3 3 g×f5 B×h2+ 4 Q×h2 Q×h2+ 5 K×h2 R×e3 and Black should win.
7. 1...R×e3! 2 R×e3 R×e3 3 Q×e3 Bf4! 4 Qf2 (if Q×f4? Ne2+) B×c1 5 Q×g3 Q×d4+. If now 6 Kh1 Qd1+; or 6 Kf1 Bf4; or 6 Qf2 Be3. A fine 'fork' combination, complementing the false pawn fork of the previous example.

Exercise 6

1. 1 Re1 and if either black knight interposes, 2 R×e4(e5) wins the pinned queen.
2. 1...Bb4! wins the pinned queen, for if 2 Q×b4 N×c2+ forks the king and queen.
3. 1 d5 a6 2 Ba4 and Black cannot save his knight.
4. 1...Q×d6 2 e×d6 R×e3 wins a piece. White's e5 pawn was pinned.
5. White's knight on c3 is pinned by the black bishop, so 1...b4 2 a×b4 c×b4 wins the exchange.
6. Black cannot protect his knight but wins material by means of a discovery: 1...Nf3+ 2 g×f3 Q×d1+ winning the exchange.
7. White's knight on d2 is pinned by the black queen, so 1...e4 2 N-moves e3 winning the piece. White is thus forced into 2 b4 N×b4! 3 a×b4 Q×a1+; or here 3 Qb2 e×f3 4 a×b4 f×g2! wins. Note that Black must not play 1...Nb4 2 Qc1 and White saves the piece.
8. 1 Rc7+! Rd7 2 R×d7+ Q×d7 3 Rc7 pins the queen. Not, however, 1 Q×d6 Qe1+ 2 Kh2 Q×h4+ 3 Kg1 Qe1+ with perpetual check.
9. 1...N×f4 2 Q×f4 f6 winning a piece. Won by J. S. Hopper, Correspondence, 1935.
10. Black's knight on e7 and bishop on e6 are in a half-pin situation on the e-file, which means that if one of them moves the other is fully pinned by the rook on e1. White

exploits this by 1 Bxd5! Nxd5 2 c4 Ne7 3 d5 B-moves 4 Rxe7+; or 1...Qxd5 2 Qxd5 Nxd5 3 c4 etc., or 1...Bxd5 2 Bxe7! Bxb3 3 Bxd8+ wins a piece. An alternative way to win is 1 Bxe7 Nxe7 (otherwise the knight on d5 is lost through the pin) 2 Bxe6 fxe6 3 Rxe6 (threatening 4 Rae1) Kf8 4 Rae1 with an easy win; or here 3...Kd7 4 Rae1 Re8 5 Qa3 winning.

11. White's knight on c3 and bishop on e5 are both pinned against the king. Black takes advantage by 1...Ne4 winning material. If 2 Bd3 (2 Be2 Nxc3 3 bxc3 Bxc3+ wins the exchange and a pawn) Bxc3+ 3 bxc3 f6 4 B moves Nxc3+ winning the queen, so White does best to give up his bishop on e5. If here 4 Bxe4 dxe4 leaves two black pieces under attack ('en prise').

12. The black bishop is subject to a pin against his king on the back rank, and in fact White can win material by 1 Ne7+ Bxe7 2 Rxc8+. Best, however, is 1 Rxc8! Qxe2 2 Ne7+ Kh8 3 Rxf8 mate, a good example of a 'false' pin against the white queen.

13 White can win a piece by threatening to pin the queen against the king: 1 Qg5+ Kh8 (or 1...Qg6 2 Re7+ winning the queen; or 1...Kh7 2 Re7; or 1...Kf8 2 Rf1, in each case winning the pinned queen for a rook) 2 Qd8+! (not 2 Re7 Qf2+ followed by mate on f1 or h2) Qg8 (otherwise 3 Re7 pins the queen) 3 Qxd7.

14. Black's attack is very dangerous, with the white king in the centre and his rook on a1 undeveloped. For example, if he plays 1 Nc1 c5 2 Qd2 (2 Qd3 Rd5 3 Qc2 Bxe2 4 Nxe2 Qh5+, or 4 Qxe2 Qh1+) Rd5 3 Bd3 (3 Nd3 Qh1+ 4 Bf1 Be4) Qh1+ 4 Kf2 Be4+. However, the tables can be turned by transferring the pin of Black's rook to a pin on his queen by 1 Qxe5+ Qxe5 2 Bd4 Re8 3 Kf2 (or 3 Bxe5+ Rxe5 4 Nd4) Bxe2 4 Bxe5+ (not 4 Re1? Rf8+! and it is Black who wins) Rxe5 5 Re1! with the final winning pin. Won by V. Dilworth, Correspondence, 1945-6.

15. White combines threats of a pin of Black's queen against his king with a threat of mate at c7. 1 Qh8+ Qd8 2 Qe5! Qg8+ 3 b3 Qxh7 4 Qe8 mate. Or here 2...Qd6 3 Rh8+ Kd7 4 Qe8 mate. This means that Black must give up his queen for the rook with a hopeless position.

16. Black is ahead in development and uses pins and discoveries to force the win. Since 1...Bxf2+ 2 Kh1! gets nowhere, he plays 1...Qxf2+! (using the same technique as in the Morphy game of section 3.3, where maintaining the pin proved more deadly than the immediate check by the lower-value unit) 2 Rxf2 (2 Kh1 Qxf1+ and mate next move; or 2 Qxf2 Rxf2 as in the text) Rxf2! 3 Qxf2 (if the queen moves away, discoveries are fatal, e.g. 3 Qg4 Rf4+ 4 Kh1 Rf1 mate) 3...Rd1 mate, since the queen cannot interpose. Going back to the diagram, place White's QR on d1 and Black's KR on f6. Now the most attractive way to win would be 1...Bxf2+! 2 Kh1 (or 2 Qxf2 Qxf2+ 3 Rxf2 Rxd1+ mating) Qxh2+! 3 Kxh2 Rh6+ 4 Qh5 Rxh5 mate!

17. The black bishop pins the knight against the queen and, more remotely, against the rook on d1. In a game from the U.S.A. versus U.S.S.R. match of 1954 in New York, Bronstein playing the black pieces against Denker continued 1...Ne5 2 Rxe5 (if 2 Re3 Nxf3+ 3 Bxf3 Rxe3 wins) Rxe5 3 Qxe5 Qxe5 4 Nxe5 Bxd1 5 Bxb7 Rc7 and proved that his advantage of the exchange for a pawn was sufficient to win the game.

18 This position occurred in a game between Kotov and Barcza at Stockholm, 1952. White sacrificed a piece for a strong attack and Black was forced to return the exchange to meet immediate threats. Kotov continued 1 Qf6! (pinning the knight, threatening 2 h6 and preventing its protection along the second rank by 1...f6) Nc8 2 h6 Ne7 (2...Qe7 3 hxg7+ Rxg7 4 Rd8+ wins) 3 Rd2! and Black resigned,

there being no defence against 4 Rfd1 followed only then by 5 h×g7+ R×g7 6 Rd8+. This game won a brilliancy prize.

19. Black has taken too many risks to make his pin effective, but all to no avail; White is able to use a variant of Legal's attack to force victory. Zemgalis against Joachim (Seattle, 1953) played 1 N×d4!! e×d4 2 Qc2 and Black resigned. Had Black replied 1...B×d1 2 B×c6+ Kc8 3 b7+ K×c7 4 b×a8(Q) Q×a8 5 B×a8 or here 2...Ke7 3 Bg5+ Kf7 4 Bd5+ Kg6 5 B×d8+ would each have left great material advantage to White.

Exercise 7

1. Black's king and queen stand on the same rank, so 1...Rh7+ 2 N×h7 R×h7+ 3 K-moves R×b7.

2. Black's king and rook are on the same diagonal, so 1 Bg5+ f6 2 B×f6+ K×f6 3 R×d8 with a winning ending. White's first move uses skewer technique, but his second takes advantage of the fact that Black's king has to protect both the f6 pawn and the rook at the same time, is 'overloaded' and cannot cope.
   This theme will be discussed in greater detail in the next chapter. Note that the double attack by 1 B×c7 fails to 1...B×d1.

3. White gets nowhere by 1 Rh7+ Kd6 2 Rh6+ Kc7 when the pawn will fall. However, noting that Black cannot capture the pawn at the moment because of the skewer winning the black rook, White plays 1 Rh8! threatening to queen the pawn and thus forcing 1...R×a7 when 1 Rh7+ wins the rook. This is a very important theme which constantly occurs in rook and pawn endings.

4. White could win a rook by the skewer 1 Ra8+ if Black could not interpose the knight, so 1 Re×d7! R×d7 2 Ra8+ K moves 3 R×f8 wins a piece.

5. Black has just played ...Rf7 but White should not retreat his queen timidly without first seeing if there is a better continuation. Once he sees that Black's king and queen are on the same diagonal, which can be opened by an exchange of bishops by check, the way becomes clear: 1 B×f6+ K×f6 (the pinned rook cannot of course recapture) 2 Qh4+ Kg7 and White can win the queen but naturally prefers 3 Qh6+! Kg8 4 Qh8 mate. If Black meets 1 B×f6+ with 1...Ke8 2 Qg8+ Rf8 3 Qg6+ Rf7 4 Rh8+ Kd7 5 R×d8 mate.

6. White sees that the black rooks are on the same diagonal, so plays 1 Q×a6 b×a6 2 Ba5 skewering them.

7. Black's bishops and rook have more freedom than White's pieces and White's king is subject to attack. Black plays 1...R×d2! 2 K×d2 Bg5+ 3 Ke1 B×c1 winning a piece.

8. White's strong attack down the h-file requires the removal of the h7 barrier, so 1 R×g6+! winning an important pawn, since 1...h×g6 allows 2 Qh8 mate.

9. White notes that the black queen and QR are on the same diagonal, so 1 d×e5 d×e5 2 Bd6 wins the exchange.

10. After 1...Nf4! the rook cannot move in view of 2...Q×g2 mate, and 2 Q×f4 Q×d5 wins the exchange. This once again combines the 'skewer' idea with overloading (see solution to Position 7.2 and the next chapter), the white queen having the double task of protecting the rook and also the f4 square. Won by Mrs. B. G. Hollis, Correspondence, 1950-1.

11. Black's last move was intended as the coup de grâce, since after 2 B×e5 Rd2

3 Q-moves Qg2 mate. However, White has a surprising resource in this line, itself depending on a skewer. He plays 3 Rfd1! Rxe2 4 Rxd8 mate. It is important to play accurately here, since White could still lose after 2 Bxe5! Rd2 3 Rbd1? Qxf1+! 4 Qxf1 Rxd1 pinning and regaining the queen.

12. 1...Bg6+! (if 1...Bf3+ 2 Kd3 saves the day, but not 2 Qxf3? Qd4 mate) 2 Qxg6 (2 Ke5 Qd4 mate) Qc2+ and 3...Qxg6, as played by Bannik against Katalimov in the U.S.S.R.

Group Exercise 'A'

1. Not immediately 1 Bxe6? Bxc6! with an unclear outcome, e.g. 2 Bc1 Qa5. Firstly, 1Bc1 Qa4 and only then 2 Bxe6! fxe6 (2...Bxc6 3 Bb3+; or 2...Qxc6 3 Bd5+) 3 Qxe6+ followed by mate. Schmidt − Degenhardt, Hamburg, 1960.

2. At Stockholm, 1960, Unzicker won a piece against Stahlberg with 1 Bxd7 Bxd7 2 Bxf6 Bxf6 3 Ng5+, since 3...Ke7 loses the queen to 4 Nxd5+. An interesting mixture of pins and forks.

3. Foguelman versus Oliviera, at Leipzig, 1960, played 1 Rxg7+! Kxg7 2 Qg3+ in order to discover on to the unguarded queen on c7 (2...Kf8 3 Ng6+) or mate after 2...Kh6 3 Qg6 mate, or 2...Kh7 3 Qg6+ Kh8 4 Nf7 mate. Black tried 2...Kf6! but lost after 3 Ng4+ fxg4 4 Qxc7 Bc8 5 Be4 Rb8 6 fxg4.

4. 4 Rxf6 (better than 4 Bxf6 Qa7+! 2 K-moves Bxf6 and Black's queen is now guarded!) Bxf6 (if 4...Qa7+ 5 Rf2) 5 Qh7+ Kf8 6 Qh8+ Ke7 7 Qxg7+! winning the unguarded queen on b7.

5. 1 Bh6+ Kg8 2 Qf3! (threatening 3 Nd8 Bxd8 4 Qf8 mate) Rxe6 3 Nd8 Rf6 4 Qxf6 Bxf6 5 Nxb7 wins.

6. 1...Na4! 2 Bc3 (if 2 Nd2 Nxc3 3 Qxc3 Nd7 4 Q-moves Bxa1; or 2 bxa4 Ne8 3 Qd2 Qb6+ 4 Kh1 Bxb2 winning the exchange) 2...Nxc3 3 Nxc3 Ng4 4 Qd2 Qb6+ 5 Kh1 Nf2+ winning the exchange. Won by Cafferty against Payne, Southend, 1960.

7. 1 Rxc6+! Kb8! (if 1...Kxc6 2 Qc4 mate) 2 Qd5! (threatening 3 Rxb6+ and 4 Qb7 mate) Qxf2 3 Qd6+ (there are other winning lines too) Ka8 4 Bb7+ Kxb7 5 Rc7+ and Black resigned, since 5...Ka6 allows 6 Qa3+ Kb5 7 Qb4+ Ka6 8 Qa4 mate; or here 5...Ka8 6 Qd5+ and mate in 2; or 5...Kb8 6 Rxd7+ and mate in 2. Keres versus Schmidt, Zürich, 1961.

8. 1 Rf6! Bxf6 2 gxf6 Qxf6 (if 2...Nc8 3 Qg5 Re8 4 Bxh5 with a winning attack) 3 d6 (3 Bg5 is good too) 3...Nc6 (if 3...Rc6 4 Bg5 Qe6 5 dxe7 followed by 6 Nd5 winning) 4 dxc7 winning a piece and the game. Korchnoi versus Szabo, Leningrad, 1961.

Exercise 8

1. 1...e5 2 Nf3 Qxb5.

2. 1...Rxg6+ 2 hxg6 Rxe4.

3. 1...Nd4 winning the queen, since 2 Nxd4 Qh2 mate and 2 Qd1 Nxf3+ 3 Qxf3 Qh2 mate are the only alternatives.

4. 1...Nc2+ 2 Qxc2 Kxh6; or here 2 K-moves Nxa1.

5. 1 Nxg6 Qxg3 2 Ne7+! Kh8 3 hxg3.

6. 1...Nxe3+ 2 Rxe3 Rxf1 followed by 3...Bxe3 later.

7. 1...Rxe1+ 2 Rxe1 Bd3+ (the defence of the rook is undermined) 3 Kg1 Rxe1+.

8. 1...Nf2+ 2 Rxf2 (or 2 Kh2 Nxd3) Bxf2 3 Qxf2 Rxd3.
9. 2 Rf8+! Rxf8 (or 2...Kh7 3 Qxe8) 3 Qxe6.
10. 1...Bg5 2 f4 Bxf4 3 Qxf4 Qxb6.
11. 1 f4! (undermining the protection of the bishop) Qxf4 2 Nxd5. If 1...Qh5 2 g4 Qg6 3 Qxg6! fxg6 4 Rxd5.
12. Black's queen is overloaded with the task of protecting both rooks.
   - (a) 1 Re1 Qf8 2 Rxe8 Qxe8 3 Qxc5. If Black meets 1 Re1 with 1...Rxc3 2 bxc3 (not 2 Rxe7 Rxc1+) Qd8 3 Rxe8+Qxe8 4 Qxb6 or, more subtly, 3 Qxb6! Rxe1+ 4 Rxe1 Qxb6 5 Re8 mate.
   - (b) Not now 1 Re1 Rxc3! and Black has brought off an overloading combination himself, since 2 Rxc3 Qxe1+ and 2 Rxe7 Rxc1+ both win for Black. Correct is 1 b4! Rc6 2 Nd5 (with treble attack on queen, rook and knight) Nxd5 3 Rxc6.
13. 1 Nxf5 exf5 2 e6! If now 2...fxe6 3 Qxd7 mate; or 2...Bxe6 3 Bxc6+ Bd7 4 Bxd7 mate; or 2...Rd8 3 exd7+ Rxd7 4 Bxc6 followed by 5 Bxd7 mate.
14. The game Kraus — Castle (U.S.A. Open, 1961) continued 1...Rxd5! 2 Qxd5 Qe1+ 3 Kh2 Bd6+ 4 g3 Qxg3+ 5 Kh1 Qh2 mate.
15. 1 Ba5! Bh6 (if 1...Qxa5 2 Na7 mate) 2 Na7+ Qxa7 3 Qc7 mate as played in the game Hallbauer, Berlin, 1961.
16. 1...Nxf2! 2 Rxf2 Qxe3 3 Qxe3 Rd1+! and mate follows. Won by Mardle against Wade, Bognor Regis, 1960.
17. Darga versus Udovcic, Bled, 1961, played 1 Nxd6! Qxd6 2 Nb5! Bxb5 3 Bxc5, a good undermining combination.

Exercise 9

1. (a) No. 1...Nc6 2 Na4 wins the queen.
   - (b) No. 1...Qxb2 2 Rb1 Qa3 3 Nb5 Qxa2 4 Nxc7+ and 5 Nxa8.
   - (c) No. 1...Bxf3 2 Bxf3 Qxd4 3 Bxb7 and 4 Bxa8.
   Black should play 1...Nbd7 or ...c6 or ...e6.
2. 1...Rc8 wins.
3. 1 Nd3! followed by 2 Kb3 and 3 Kxa2.
4. White's bishop is now trapped by 1...g5 2 Be5 d6 3 Bg3 f4 4 exf4 gxf4.
5. White can remain a pawn ahead by capturing the knight on b3 but much stronger is 2 exf6 Nxa1 3 fxe7 Qxe7 when, although White has given up the exchange, the black knight cannot escape, e.g. 4 b3 Bg4 5 Bb2 Bxf3 6 Qxf3 Nc2 7 Re2.
6. 2 Bg5! Qxe5 3 Bf6+ wins the queen.
7. 1...Rxd6! 2 Qxd6 Qxd6 3 Rxd6 Nd5! 4 d4 Kc7. The game could finish 5 c5 Nxf4 6 Bf3 Rd8 7 Rxd8 Kxd8 8 Bxb7 Nd3+ and 9...Nxc5. Won by J. Wolstenholme, Manchester v. Liverpool, 1955.
8. Only the exchange of queens last move saved a piece, whereas now 2 Na4! Qc6 (if 2...Qb4 3 Rd4! or 2...Qf2 3 Rd2) 3 Bb5 Qxg2 4 Rhg1 and if now 4...Qxh2 5 Bxf6 Bxf6 6 Qxf6 since the g7 pawn is pinned.
9. 1...Rxh5! (seeing that White's knight will be trapped) 2 Nf7+ Kc7 3 Nxd6 Bxg4! 4 Ng3 Rh7 5 Nf7 Bh5.
10. 2 Ra1! (not 2 Qxc6 Qc1+ 3 Ke2 Qxb2+ 4 Ke1 Qxc3+ with a draw by perpetual check) Qh2 3 Ke2 and now the knight is lost, since 3...Ne7 4 Qxe6+ Kf8 5 Ra8+ mates. If at once 2...Ne7 then 3 Qxe6+ Qf7 4 Ra8+ wins the queen by undermining.

Exercise 10

1. 1...Bg1! and the pawn queens.
2. 1...a4 2 R×b5 (or 2 Rb2 a3 3 Ra2 Rb1 followed by ...Rb2, ...a2, ...Nc3 and ...Rb1) a3 3 R×b6 a2 4 Ra6 a1(Q) 5 R×a1 R×a1 and Black has enough to win.
3. 1 R×d7 Q×d7 2 e6 Qd6 (if 2...Qc8 3 e×f7+ Kh7 4 Qh5! mate; if 2...Qc6 3 e7 Rfb8 4 B×f7+ Kh7 5 Qh5+ Qh6 6 e8(Q) wins) 3 e7 Rfb8 4 B×f7+ Kh7 5 e8(Q) wins.
4. 1 d6 Rc2+ (1...R×c6 2 d7 Rd6 3 Re6! pins the rook and forces promotion, a very useful tactical resource) 2 Kf3 (or 2 Kd1 R×c6 3 Re6! Kb7 4 d7 Kc7 5 R×c6+ wins) R×c6 3 d7 Rc3+ 4 Ke2 Rc2+ 5 Kd1 wins, or here 3...Rf6+ 4 Ke3 Rf8 5 Re8 wins, another useful tactic to remember.
5. 1...Rh×h2 2 Bh6+ Ke8 3 Ne3 f2+! 4 K×h2 f1(Q)+ 5 Ng2 Q×g2 mate; or here 2 Rh4 Rhg2+ 3 Kf1 Rb2! 4 Rc4 Rh2! 5 Rh4 Rb1+ mating. Note the power of the two rooks on the seventh rank!
6. 1 R×d6! c×d6 2 Bg7 followed by 3 g6 winning. A pretty endgame combination brought off by Capt. P. D. Bolland, many times champion of Somerset.
7. 1 d×c7 Rb7 (maintaining the pin on the knight, thus preventing 2 Nd6; not 1...R×b5 2 R×b5 B×b5 3 c8(Q)+) 2 Rd1! threatening 3 R×d7 followed by promotion of the pawn, to which there is no defence. Won by R.A.F. Records, Gloucester, captained by B. B. Partridge, in a consultation game, 1945.

Revision Exercise R.1

1. 1 Qa4+ wins the knight by a double attack.
2. 2 R×e4, since the f5 pawn is pinned.
3. 1...Nf4+ 2 g×f4 (2 Kf2 Nd3+) R×e1 winning the exchange.
4. 1...c4 traps the bishop.
5. 2 f7 Qf3 3 f8(Q)+ Q×f8 4 Ra8+ (skewer) followed by 5 R×f8 and 6 Rh8. Or 2...Kb8 3 Re7 followed by 4 Re8+ and 5 f8(Q).
6. 2 Nd6! and Black loses the exchange, since he dare not move his QR allowing 3 N×f5+ winning the queen (knight fork and pin). If 2...f4 3 R×f4 Q×d6 4 R×f7+ and 5 Q×d6 wins by discovery.
7. 1...N×d4! wins a piece after 2 Q×b6 N×f3+ 3 Kh1 a×b6 4 Bh6 Rg6. Discovery, pin and undermining the bishop.
8. 2 Nb4 N×b4 3 R×d6+ Kc7 4 Q×b4 wins; the threat is now 5 Nd5+ and mate in 3 more moves (pin).
9. 2 Rd1 appears to win a piece, because of the threat to the d8 square. If 2...Q×d5 3 R×d5 Be8 4 Rd8 Ra1+ 5 Ng1! Kf8 6 Bc5+ Kg8 7 R×e8 mate (skewer, pin and undermining). Black, however, has a neat rejoinder in 2...Ra1! threatening 3...Q×d5, now that White's rook is pinned. If in reply 3 Bg1 R×d1 4 Q×d1 and Black, having retained his extra pawn, should win eventually.
10. 1...Nf×d5! wins a pawn, for if 2 c×d5 N×d5 and the knight on c3 falls after 3 Bc4 N×c3 4 B×c3 B×c3 5 Q×c3 b5, whilst if 2 N×d5 N×d5 and the piece cannot be recaptured. Once again, we have a case of the half-pin we mentioned before; there are a pawn and a piece between the white queen and the black rook, but as soon as one moves, the other is pinned. Such a half-pin is always a danger-signal in practical play, because it usually means there is one less defender than you think!
11. 1...Nd3! 2 Rg2. Now the white knight on e2 is overloaded, having the dual tasks of preventing ...Qc1 and blocking Black's path to mate on e1. So Black plays 2...Qc1+! 3 N×c1 Re1 mate (skewer).

12. 1...R×f2! 2 R×f2 Qc1 mate. If 2 Q×c5 Q×g2 mate. Best is 2 g3 Qe3! (threatening mates by discoveries) 3 Q×c5 R×f1+ 4 K×f1 Q×c5 winning easily (pins and discoveries).

13. 2 R×d7! Q×d7 3 N×c5 (overloading) Qd5 (double-attack) 4 Q×e5! Q×e5 5 Nd7+ and 6 N×e5 (knight fork). If in this line 4...Qd2 (complicating in order to try and make trouble) 5 R×f7+! K×f7 6 Qe6+ Kf8 7 Nd7+ winning the queen.

14. 1...Re×e5! wins, for if 2 f×e5 Rf2+ 3 Kg3 (other moves lead to quicker mates) Qf3+ 4 Kh4 Be7+ (pin of the f4 pawn against the f2 square). Won by C. Pirie, Correspondence, 1939.

15. 1...Qd6! (forking the knight and the g3 square) 2 Nb1 Qg3 threatening 3...B×h3 4 g×h3 Q×h3 mate. This is an example of a type of position where a key square is reached by threatening a loose piece. Here the black queen has four squares from which it can attack the knight, so has to decide where his queen will be most effective.

16. 2 B×f6+ R×f6 3 Qh7+ Kf8 4 Re1! (the point, shutting off the black king's escape square) Re6 5 R×e6 f×e6 6 Q×c7 wins; or here 4...Rg6 5 B×g6 f×g6 6 Q×c7 wins.

17. 1...Ne4! with the variations: 2 f×e4 R×f1+ wins; or 2 Bc1 R×f3! 3 R×f3 Q×g4+ winning two pawns; or 2 Rg2 N×g5 3 h×g5 Rf4 followed by 4...B×d4+.

18. 1 N×e6! Q×e3 2 Nc7+ Ke7 3 Nd5+ Ke6 4 N×e3 wins. Played by the German master Darga against Joppen at Bad Pyrmont, 1961.

19. Fuderer, the Yugoslav master, as Black against Bronstein at Kiev, 1959, continued 1...Ne3! (threatening two knight forks on c2 and g2) 2 B×e7 (2 B×e3? B×b4) Nc2+ 3 K-moves N×b4 4 B×b4 and Black won easily.

20. Bazan with Black, playing against his fellow Argentinian Wexler at Mar del Plata, 1960, continued 1...Rd1! winning, since 2 Q×c6 allows 2...R×e1 mate, and 2 Q×d1 Qg2 mate, or 2 R×d1 Q×f3, or 2 Q×h3 R×e1+ 3 Qf1 R×f1+ 4 K×f1 Q×h1+ (unpin combined with double mating threats on back rank and at g2 — see next chapter). Note that the combination would fail if Black's pawn were still at g7, for after 2 R×d1! Q×f3 3 Rd8 is mate.

21. Taegert against Nugel played 1...Bg2+ 2 Ke1 (2 K×g2 Q×e2, an overload combination) Bc3+ 3 Kd1 Bf3! (pin) 4 Q×f3 Qf1 mate (the f1 square has been skewered through the queen).

22. A move such as 1...Qe7 must be carefully examined before it is played, since the queen is protected only by the knight which is itself under attack, so that undermining becomes a possibility. This is another position won by Darga against his fellow-countryman Dr. Lehmann at Bognor, 1961. He played 2 B×c6 and Black resigned in view of the continuation 2...Q×c5 3 d×c5 R×d1+ 4 R×d1 b×c6 5 Rd8+ Kg7 6 f6+! winning the rook.

23. Lewis against de Loughry at Dublin, 1960, won by 1...R×g2+! 2 K×g2 (if 2 N×g2 Q×h2 mate, a skewer) Rg8+ (it is often possible to open a line for a rook by sacrificing the other rook) 3 Kh1 Ng3+ (pin) 4 Kg2 N×e2+ (discovery) winning the queen.

24. Burstein versus Nora played 1 Bd5+! (overload of black queen plus pin) Q×d5 2 Q×e3 winning the exchange, since 2...B×f1 fails to 3 Qe8 mate, a vital part of the combination, of course.

25. Berthold versus Haag, Budapest, 1959, played 1 Be4! forcing immediate resignation, for if 1...Q×e4 2 Q×a5+ and mate in two moves, and if 1...B×a4 2 B×d5+ Kb8 3 Rb7+ Ka8 (or 3...Kc8 4 Rc1+ followed by mate) 4 Rgg7 and there

is no defence to Ra7+ and 6 Ra8 mate. The combination is made possible by the strength of the mating threats along the seventh rank and by the overloading of the black queen, the whole sequence being signposted by the possibilities down the long diagonal to Black's king.

26. This position occurred in the game between the Danish player Petersen and the Russian grandmster Petrosian at Copenhagen, 1960. White was hoping for 1...Qxc7? 2 Qg5+ or 1...Bd3? 2 Rd7! Qxd7 3 Qg5+ drawing by perpetual check in each case. However, Black is already a piece ahead and unwilling to draw; he found a move to divert White's queen from g5 in 1...Be2! when 2 Qxe2 Qxc7 and 2 Rxd8 Bxh5 both win for Black.

27. Black's queen must guard the e5 pawn so is unavailable for any other defence, so White can pile up pressure down the d-file by 1 Bc6! for if 1...Qxc6 2 Qxe5+ Be6 3 Rxd8+ Ke7 4 f6 mate (overload and pin), or 1...Bxc6 2 Rxd8+ (pin) and if any other black move 2 Rxd7 or 2 Bxd7+. Molnar forced resignation with this move against Rethy in the Hungarian Championship, 1961. Indeed, the white position is so strong that you may well have found some other win, e.g. 1 Be6! or 1 f6! the latter move providing the amusing finish 1 f6 c4 2 Be6! Bxe6 (2...Qb6+ 3 Kf1 Qxe6 4 Rd6) 3 Qxf8+! Kxf8 4 Rxd8+ followed by mate.

28. Keres against the German master Teschner won by 1...Qxd4! 2 Rxd4 Rc1+ 3 Qg1 Rxg1+ 4 Kxg1 Bc5! the final vital pin.

29. This is a position where an international master failed to find the correct continuation. Lundin, the Swedish master, played against Burehall at Stockholm, 1960, 1...Qxe7? and White won by 2 Qa8+ Kc7 (2...Kd7 3 Qxc6+ followed by mate) 3 Rxc6+ Kd7 4 Qc8 mate. If Black had realized that he had left a mating continuation, he would surely have found 1...Rh1+! (drawing the king to a square more favourable to attack) 2 Kxh1 Qd5+ and 3...Rxa3 winning.

30. Bernstein versus Benko, Kiev, 1903, played 1 Nfxe5 for if 1...fxe5 2 Bxe5 forks the queen and the g7, h8 squares, so any queen move allows 3 Nh6 mate. After studying Chapter 5 you will understand how an experienced player is able to recognize the existence of such a combination.

31. White can visualize mates at g7 by Re3-g3, or at h7 by Re3-h3 and Qxh7. However, after 1 Re3 Kh8 2 Rg3 is met by 2...Rg8 whilst 2 Rh3 Be4 and Black has met the threat. Bornsteinsson versus Sigurjonsson at Rejkavik, 1961, discovered that he could prevent this second defence by 2 Nf5! exf5 3 Rh3 and mates. Black replied 2...Rg8 3 Rh3 Rxg2+ (a last desperate attempt at perpetual check) 4 Kf1 Rxf2+ 5 Ke1 (to avoid queen checks) Rf1+ 6 Kxf1 Bc4+ 7 Ke1 Resigns. The correct move order is important, for if 1 Nf5? exf5 2 Re3 f4 3 Rh3 Be4 and Black wins.

32. Spassky, ex-World Champion, playing against the Hungarian Portisch, won by 1...Qf4+ 2 Qf3 (if 2 Ke2 Bg4+ or 2 Nf3 Rh1+ 3 Ke2 Rxe4+ winning in each case) Bg4! (a beautiful example of a skewer on the square e2) and White resigned, for 3 Qxf4 allows 3...Rh1 mate.

33. White won by 1 Qxg6+ Qxg6 2 Rh8+ Ke7 3 d6+ Qxd6 4 Rh7+! (an important intermediate move − a 'Zwischenzug' − before recapturing the queen) Ke8 5 Bxd6.

34. Rubinstein against Rotlevi, Lodz, 1907, won by 1...Rxc3! (undermining the protection of the bishop) 2 gxh4 (if 2 Bxc3 Bxe4+ 3 Qxe4 Qxh2 mate, the white queen being overloaded) Rd2! (again based on overloading) 3 Qxd2 (3 Qxg4 Bxe4+ or 3 Bxc3 Bxe4+ 4 Qxe4 Rxh2 mate, a skewer combination) Bxe4+ 4 Qg2 Rh3! (the queen is pinned) and White resigned, since 5...Rxh2 mate is forced.

Exercise 11

1. 1...Qg4 2 g3 Qh3 and mates (Types b and e).
2. 1...Bh3 and mates at f1 (Type s).
3. 1...Rxh2+ 2 Kxh2 Qh4 mate (Type n). Breyer — Marshall (Breslau, 1912).
4. 1 Nh6+ Kh8 2 Qf8+ Rxf8 3 Rxf8 mate (Type q).
5. 1...Qg3 2 Bf3 Bxf3 and mate on g2 (Type o).
6. Post versus Flamberg, Mannheim, 1914, played 1 Qxh7+ Rxh7 2 Rxg8 mate (Type y).
7. Subareff versus Goglidze, Odessa, 1929, played 1 Qf8+ Rxf8 2 Rxf8 mate (Type u).
8. Nejmetdinov versus Kotkov, U.S.S.R. Championship, 1957, played 1 Re8+! If 1...Qxe8 2 Qxf6 mate and if 1...Bxe8 2 Qg8 mate (Type w).
9. 1 Nxf7+ Kg8 2 Nh6 mate (Type h). The alternative discoveries by the knight on d7 or g4 are met by 1...f6! 2 Nxf6 Bxf1.
10. Stumpers versus Bergsma, Amsterdam, 1954, went 1...Qh3 2 Rg1 Rh5! 3 Nxh5 Qxf3+ followed by mate (Types a and k).
11. 1...Rxh2 2 Kxh2 Qh5+ 3 Kg1 Qh1 mate (Type i). If White plays 2 f3 Black refuses the queen and plays 2...Qxg3+ 3 Kf1 Rh1 mate.
12. 1 Bxh7+ Kxh7 (or 1...Kh8 2 Ng5 f6 3 Qh5 fxg5 4 Bg6+ Kg8 5 Qh7 mate — Type k) 2 Ng5+ Kg6 (or 2...Kg8 3 Qh5 Re8 4 Qxf7+ Kh8 5 Qh5+ Kg8 6 Qh7+ Kf8 7 Qh8+ Ke7 8 Qxg7 mate, an important variation in which three flight squares are unavailable to the king) 3 Qg4 f5 4 Qg3 Kh6 5 Qh4+ Kg6 6 Qh7 mate (Type shown in Fig. 39).
13. Bouwmeester — Darga, Holland v. W. Germany, Amersfoort, 1959, went 1...Rg2+! (not 1...Rxh2? 2 Be6+ Kh8 3 Rf8 mate — Type q) 2 Bxg2 Rxg2+ 3 Kh1 Rxg3+ and mate next move (Type d).
14. Keres against Radovici, U.S.S.R. v. Roumania, 1960, played 1 Rg6 with mate on g7 (Type o).
15. 1...Qxh2+ 2 Kxh2 Rh5+ 3 Kg1 Rh1 mate (Type i).
16. Keres against Szabo, Moscow v. Budapest, 1955, played 1 Rxg7 Kxg7 2 Qf6+ Kf8 (if 2...Kg8 3 Qxh6 f5 4 exf6 wins; White's 3 Qxh6 threatened 4 Bh7+ Kh8 5 Bg6+ Kg8 6 Qh7+ Kf8 7 Qxf7 mate, an important mating line) 3 Bg6 Re7 4 Qh8 mate.
17. The game Gilg versus Nimzowitsch, Semmering, 1926, went 1...Bh3+ 2 Nxh3 Qf3+ 3 Kg1 Nxh3 (or 3...Qh1) mate (Type h).
18. The game Flir versus Bhend, Salzburg, 1954, continued 1...Rf1+ 2 Bxf1 Qxe4+ 3 Bg2 Qb1+ followed by mate.
19. Szabo versus Bisguier, Buenos Aires, 1955, played 1 Bxh7+ Kxh7 2 Qh3+ Kg8 3 Rg4 f6 4 g6 and mate cannot be prevented (also the theme of Fig. 39).
20. The game van Scheltinga — Toran, Beverwijk, 1953, went 1...Rxh3+ 2 gxh3 Qxf3+ 3 Rg2 (3 Kh2 Qxh3 mate) Bxh3 4 Bf1 Bxg2+ 5 Bxg2 Rh5 mate (Type n).
21. Taimanov versus Petrosian, Zürich, 1953, played 1 Rxg6+! hxg6 (if 1...Bxg6 2 Qxe6+ Bf7 3 Qf6 and 4 Qg7 mate) 2 h7+ Kxh7 3 Qxf7+ Ng7 4 Kf2! forcing mate, for if 4...Kh8 5 Th1+ Nh5 6 Bf6 mate (Types c and e).
22. 1 Qg6 hxg5 2 Rh1 and 3 Qh7 mate (Types k and o).
23. Geller versus Kotov, U.S.S.R. Championship, 1955, played 1 Bxg7 Bxg7 (1...f6 2 Qh8+ Kf7 3 Qxf8+ Kg6 4 Qxf6+ Kh7 5 Rh3+ etc.) 2 Re8+ Bf8 3 Rxf8+ Kxf8 4 Qh8 mate (Type t).
24. Tolush versus Stoltz, Bucharest, 1953, played 1 Ng6+ Kg7 2 Rxh7+! Kxh7 3 Nf8+ Kg7 4 Qh7+ Kxf8 5 Qf7 mate.
25. The American grandmaster Lombardy versus Sherwin at New York, 1959, played

1 Qxh7+! Nxh7 2 Bxh7+ Kh8 3 Ng6 mate, the vast concentration of pieces leading to forced mate.

26. Fellner versus Bancroft, U.S.A. Open, 1961, won by 1 Bg5! for if 1...Qxg5 2 Qg8 mate and if 1...hxg5 2 Qh5 mate (Type n).

27. Kohlbeck versus Stephenson, Eastbourne, 1961, won by 1 Bxh7+! Kxh7 2 Qh5+ Kg8 3 Nd5 winning the queen, since Type m mate is threatened by 4 Ne7.

28. Addison versus Broderson, U.S.A., 1961, won by 1 Rxg7+ Kxg7 2 Qc3+ Kf8 (2...Kg8 3 Nf6+ wins the queen; or if 2...f6 3 Qxf6+ Kg8 4 Ne7 mate) 3 Rh8+ Nxh8 4 Qxh8 mate, a back-row theme similar to Type r. Such a combination is typical of winning play when the long diagonal is controlled and cannot be effectively challenged.

29. Cherepkov versus Averbach, Moscow − Leningrad Match, 1961, won by 1 Qg5! since 1...hxg5 allows 2 hxg5 mate (cf. Fig. 45).

30. The game Glass − Russell, Belfast, 1958, went 1...Nf4 2 Qxe4 Nxe2+ winning a piece, but he had a more decisive continuation in 1...Qg2+! 2 Kxg2 Nf4+ 3 Kg1 Nh3 mate (Type h), showing the tremendous power of the double-check introduced by Black's first move sacrifice.

31. Zaitsev versus Spassky won by the overload combination 1 Qf4! when 1...Qxc4 2 Rh1+ Kg8 3 Rh8 is mate (Type i) and 1...Qf3 2 Qh4+ Qh5 3 Qxh5+ gxh5 4 Rg7+ Kh8 5 Rh6 mate is Type c.

32. Donner versus Spanjaard, Dutch Championship, 1961, could easily have driven away Black's king by Rf7+ and is now punished by 1...Rh1+! 2 Kxh1 Kg3! when he has no resource against the back-row mate (Type t). As in No. 30, Black is able to draw the white king to a fatal square by means of a sacrifice.

33. The Hungarian master Horvath won against Szilardffy with 1 Rxh5+ gxh5 2 Rg7+ Kh8 3 Nf5! with the unstoppable threat of 4 Rg6+ Kh7 5 Rh6+ Kg8 6 Rh8 mate. The first two moves are not difficult to find, but the natural discovered check follow-up leads nowhere, as Black's king has an escape square at h6. White therefore examines the possibility of controlling this key square before giving the decisive discovered check, his third 'quiet' move doing the trick.

34. Gusev versus Khachaturov won by 1 Rd7+ Kh8 (or 1...Kh6 2 Rxh7+ Kg5 3 Qd5+ and mate next move) 2 Rxh7+ Kxh7 3 Qf7+ and mate next move. If 1...Kf6 White can bring about the same winning position by 2 Rf7+ Kg5 3 Qd5+ Kh6 4 Rxh7+ etc. Once more we see a sacrifice exposing the king and bringing a more powerful piece into decisive play.

35. The game Porath − Kniajer, Israel, 1961, went 1...Bxg2! and White resigned in view of the continuation 2 Rxg2 Rxg2+ 3 Kxg2 Re2+ followed by mate in two moves (Type v).

36. In the game Croes − Mednis, New Jersey, 1959, Black blundered with 1...d2 allowing 2 Qh6+! gxh6 3 g7 mate, when he could have won by 1...Qxg2+! 2 Qxg2 Bd5! (compelling White to make a capture which helps his opponent, a common device) 3 Qxe2 dxe2 winning. This variation should help extend your appreciation of attacking possibilities involving pins.

37. In the game Fuchs − Uhlmann, Premnitz, 1961, Black missed the win by 1...Ng3+! 2 hxg3 Rf5 3 g4 Rh5+! (the skewer combination which he had overlooked in his analysis) 4 gxh5 Qh4 mate.

38. White has mating possibilities on Black's back rank and the black queen is overloaded. Capelan − Kraus, Kiel, 1961, went 1 Rxe4 Rxe4 2 Bxd5 cxd5 (2...

168   LEARN CHESS; VOLUME TWO

Q×d5 3 Rf8+ wins the queen) 3 Qc7! (compare the play of Fig. 26) Bg2+ (a
desperate attempt to turn the tables) 4 Kg1! Resigns. Not here 4 K×g2 Qg6+ etc.
39. Black's two raking bishops give the clue to his decisive sacrificial combination.
Doppelmann — Kramer, Leeuwarden, 1960, continued 1...Qf3+! 2 R×f3 e×f3
3 Q×e7 (3 B×f7+ Kf8) f2+ mating. If White had played 2 Q×f3 then 2...e×f3 3 Nc3!
Re1! 4 R×e1 f2+ wins, or here 4 Kg1 Bb6+. Notice the importance of correct
timing, for if Black rashly plays 3...f2+? in this variation, White has 4 Bd5 Re1
5 Kg2!
40. Black's king is overloaded, having the double task of guarding f7 and the pawn on
h7. Troianescu — Nacht continued 1 Rf7! K×f7 2 Q×h7+ Ng7 3 Rf1+ Bf5 4 R×f5+!
when Black resigned in view of 4...g×f5 5 g6+ Kf8 6 Qh8 mate. The sacrifice,
strangely enough, would have been seen more easily if there had been a black
pawn on f7, but it is more difficult to see the force of a sacrifice of a piece on a
vacant square, when no capture is involved.
41. In Kriaier — Friedman, Israel, 1961, it is fairly easy to see the undermining of the
g7 pawn by 1 R×h6! Q×h6 (or 1...g×h6 2 Qh8 mate) 2 R×g7+ Kf8 3 Qc5+ mating,
but White must take into account the effect of the counter-attack by 1...Qb1+!
when play continues 2 Kh2 R×d7 3 Qh5! g×h6 4 Q×e8+ Kh7 5 Q×d7+ Kg6 6 Qg7+
Kf5 (or 6...Kh5 7 g4+ Kh4 8 Bf6 mate) 7 Qh7+ winning the queen. White must
not embark on his initial sacrifice until he has examined Black's best defence and
discovered the key move 3 Qh5.
42. In this game between Kinzel and Duckstein, Vienna, 1959, White's pieces are all
directed at the black king's position and Black's pieces are not well placed for
defence. These factors make it possible to mount a decisive attack, despite the fact
that none of the black pawns protecting his king has been moved. White played
1 Nf6+! g×f6 (if 1...Kh8 2 Rh5 h6 3 R×h6+g×h6 4 Qc2 mates, or 2 Qc2 g6 3 Rh5
mating also) 2 B×f6 Rd5 (2...R×d1 3 Rg5 mate) 3 Qd2! forcing mate, because the
black rook is overloaded. Admittedly, 3 Qc1, 3 Qd3 and 3 Qf3 all win too.
43. Mohring versus Fiensch, Halle, 1961, won by 1 B×h7+! K×h7 2 Bf6! g×f6 (2...g6
3 Qh4+ and 2...Rg8 3 Qh5 mate are no improvement) 3 Qh4+ Kg8 4 Qg3+ Kh7
5 Re4! and Black resigned. Give yourself credit if you planned the alternative (and
messier) 3 e×f6 Rg8 4 Qh5 mate, but only if you saw that the best defence is
3...Kh6! when White wins by 4 Qg7+ Kh5 5 Re4 Rg8 6 g4+ Kh4 7 Qh6 mate, or
here 5...Rh8 6 Qg4+ Kh6 7 Qh4+ Kg6 8 Rg4+ Kf5 9 Qg5 mate. This is a beautiful
example of the famous two bishop sacrifice which smashes open the black king's
position. In such cases, however, great care must be taken to ensure that each
sacrifice has to be accepted and that Black has no counter-attack, before you
commit yourself to such a combination.
44. Pietsch — Golz continued correctly 1...Nh3+! 2 g×h3 R×g3+ 3 h×g3 Q×g3+ 4 Bg2
Rd1! and 5...Q×g2 mate. Notice that Black's 4th move prevents 5 Qe5+
exchanging queens; it is such points that players are apt to miss in the excitement
of a mating attack! Again, correct timing is important, as is seen in the line
1...R×g3? 2 h×g3 Nh3+ 3 Kh2!
45. Uhlrich with the black pieces against Reichman won by 1...Nf3+ 2 Kd1 Ng1+!
3 h×g4 (3 Ke1 Qd1+! transposes) Rf1+ 4 Qe1 Nf2 mate. The alternatives are
interesting too: 2 Ke2 Ng1+! 3 Kd3 Nc5+ 4 Q×c5 (or 4 Kc3 Ne2+ 5 Q×e2 Qd4
mate) Rf3+ 5 Qe3 Qd4 mate; or 2 Kf1 N×g3+ 3 Kg2 Nh4+ 4 Kh2 Nf1+ 5 R×f1 Qg2
mate.

Group Exercise 'B'

1. Black wins by forcing the exchange of bishops by 1...Bc3 2 Bc1 Kc2 3 Ba3 Bb4 4 B×b4 c×b4, giving him a winning pawn ending. This is simpler, therefore better, than the winning alternative 1...Kc2 2 Ba5 f3+! 3 K×f3 K×d3 after which Black protects his g5 pawn with the bishop, advances his c-pawn to win White's bishop, then finally forces the win of White's g4 pawn by driving the white king away, after which he can promote his remaining pawn (try this out with a friend).

2. Black wins by 1...d3 2 c×d3 c×d3 3 Kf3 g×f4! since White quickly loses his b-pawn and must then play Ke4 allowing d2 queening.

3. (*a*) White to move wins by 1 Kc6 e3 2 Kd5 e2 3 Kd4 Kf3 4 Kd3 Kf2 5 Ra2 winning the pawn.

    (*b*) Black to move draws by 1...e3 2 Kc6 e2 3 Kd5 Ke3 4 Ra3+ Kf2 5 Ra2 Kf1 6 Ra1+ e1(Q) 7 R×e1+ K×e1.

4. White wins by 1 a6 Kb6 (or 1...b×a6 2 b×a6 Kb6 3 d6! wins) 2 d6! Compare Fig. 48.

5. Yes, but be very careful. The obvious 1 b6? wins after 1...a×b6 2 a6! Kc7 3 d6+but by 1...a6! Black can draw by simply moving his king to d6 and d7. However, White has the cunning 1 a6! Kc7 2 d6+! K×d6 3 b6! Kc6 4 b×a7 and the pawn must queen.

6. Black wins by 1...Bd4! 2 c×d4 c×d4 3 Bg7 Ke3 4 Bf6 d3 5 Kc3 d2 6 Bg5+ Ke2 7 B×d2 b2! 8 Kc2 b1(Q)+ 9 K×b1 K×d2.

7. White wins by 1 g5! (preventing...h5) Kd7 2 Kd2 Ke6 3 Kc3 Kf5 4 c5 b×c5 5 b×c5 K×g5 6 c6 queening.

8. White wins after 1...Rh1 2 Ra8 Rh7+ 3 Kf6 Rh6+ 4 Kf7 Rh7+ 5 Kg6 Re7 6 Kf6 Rh7 7 e7 and the pawn queens.

9. White wins by 1 Kb7! Kb4 2 Kb6! K×a4 (2...Nc5 3 Bb5) 3 a6 and the pawn cannot be stopped.

10. Black wins by 1...Bh7! (but not 1...Kb3 2 Kd4 Bh7 3 Bc1 Ka2 4 Kc5 Kb1 5 Bg5 Kb2 6 Kb4! c1(Q) 7 B×c1+ K×c1 8 K×b5 Bc2 9 h6 drawing) 2 h6 Kb3 3 Bc1 Ka2 4 Kf6 Kb1 5 Bd2 c1(Q) 6 B×c1 K×c1 7 Kg7 Bc2 8 h7 B×h7 9 K×h7 Kb2 etc.

11. Black wins by 1...Nd2+ (but not 1...Kf5 2 e4+ making the win more difficult) 2 Ke2 Ne4 3 Kd3 Nc5+ (3...Kf5 also wins) 4 Kc2 e4 5 Nc1 Ke5 6 c4 b×c4 7 Ne2 Nd3 8 Nc3 Ne1+ 9 Kb2 N×g2 10 Ka3 N×e3 11 Ka4 N×d5 with advantage!

12. Black's extra pawn is insufficient compensation for his 'bad' bishop. White wins by 1 Nc5 Bc8 2 a4! Kc7 (if 2...Ke7 3 Ke5 lets the king through) 3 Ke5 (not 3 a5? Kd6 and White must move away) Kb6 4 Nb3 (if 4 Kf6 e5!) a5 5 b×a5+ Kc7 6 Nc5 Bb7 7 N×b7 (7 a6 Ba8 8 a5 also wins) K×b7 8 Kd6 with a won pawn ending; this requires careful counting.

13. White wins by 1 Kc5 Rf2 (if 1...R×g4 2 Ra7+ Ke8 3 b4 Rg1 4 b5 Rc1+ 5 Kd6 Rc8 6b6 Rd8+ 7 Kc7 Rd7+ 8 Kc6 Rd8 9 b7 wins) 2 Ra7+ Kc8 3 b4 Rc2+ 4 Kd6 Rc4 5 R×f7 R×b4 6 Rf8+ Kb7 7 K×e6 R×d4 8 Kd6 Ra4 9 e6 Ra6+ 10 K×d5 Kc7 11 e7 and the pawn queens.

14. White wins by 1 Ke7 Kb8 2 Kd8 Ka8 3 Kc8 a5 4 Kc7 a4 5 Kd7 Kb8 6 c4! Ka8 7 Ke6, since the a4 pawn is lost. Note the use made of White's doubled pawn to gain time and White's ability to combine the stalemate situation of Black's king to force Black to weaken his a6 pawn, without which the game would be drawn. However, White must take care not to stalemate the black king!

15. White wins by capturing the f5 pawn, as follows: 1 Kf2 Kg7 2 Ke2 Kh7 (if 2...R×g3

3 Rb8 winning the rook for his a7 pawn, or else 3 Rg8+ Kxg8 4 a8(Q)+ winning. Black's king dare not leave the g7 and h7 squares because of the skewer variation 2...Kf7? 3 Rh8! Rxa7 4 Rh7+ winning the rook) 3 Kd2 Kg7 4 Kc2 Kh7 5 Kb2 Ra5 6 Kb3 Kg7 7 Kb4 Ra1 8 Kc5 Kh7 9 Kd5 Kg7 10 Ke5 Ra5+ 11 Ke6 Kh7 12 Kf6 forcing the win of the pawns.

16. Black wins by 1...Ka4! (not of course 1...Kxa5 2 Kb3 Kb5 3 Kxc3 a5 4 Kb3 drawing, since his king reaches the king's side just in time — count it yourself) 2 Kb1 Kxa5 3 Ka1 (to keep the opposition) Kb5 4 Ka2 Kb4 5 Kb1 Kc4 6 Ka2 Kd4 7 Kb3 a5 8 Ka4 Ke3 9 Ka3 Kd2 10 Kb3 a4+! 11Kxa4 Kxc2 winning.

17. The late Belgian master O'Kelly de Galway, playing Black against Pritchard at Bognor Regis, 1960, won by 1...g4! (threatening 2...Kh6) 2 h3 Nxc4! 3 hxg4 (3 bxc4 b3 and the pawn promotes; or if 3 Bxg4 Ne3+ 4 Kf3 Nxg4 5 hxg4 c4! wins) Nd2 4 e5 c4! when White resigned, because he cannot stop the passed pawn whereas Black can easily do so after 5...Kf8.

18. White wins by 1 Rf8+! Kg7 2 Rf5 Kg6 3 Ra5 Ra7 4 f5+ Kf6 5 Kf4 Kf7 6 Ke5 with an easy win. The rook must be *behind* the pawn to be at its most effective. From the diagram, a correspondence game continued 1 a7? Rf7 (to prevent Rf8+ queening the pawn; also possible is 1...Rg7+ 2 Kf3 Rf7 3 Ke4 Re7+ 4 Kd5 Rf7 5 Kc6 Kf5 6 Kb6 Rf6+ 7 Kb5 Rf7 but the text variation, played by Sir Robert Robinson, is prettier) 2 f5 Rg7+ 3 Kf4 Rxa7! draws, since 4 Rxa7 is stalemate!

19. Black wins by 1...Ke7! 2 Kf5 (if 2 Bd1 Kf6 3 Bf3 Bf1 4 Bd1 Bg2+ 5 Bf3 Bxf3+ wins) Bd3+ 3 Kxg5 c4 4 Kf4 c3 5 Ke3 c2 6 Kd2 Kf6 7 Bh1 (White can only wait with bishop moves or Kc1-d2-c1-b2 and cannot sacrifice his g-pawn and reach a4 in time with his bishop) Kg5 8 Bf3 Kf4 9 Bg2 Kxg4 10 Bh1 Kf4 11 Bg2 Ke5 12 Bf3 Kd4 13 Bg2 Kc5 14 Bf3 Kb4 15 Bh5 Kxa5 and White is helpless against the two passed pawns.

20. Drawn, but only by 1...Rd5! providing a bridge for the black king to approach the pawn without being cut off by the white rook placed on the d-file, e.g. 1...Kd6 2 Rd4+ Kc5 3 Kg6 Rh8 (or 3...Re5 4 Rd8 Re6+ 5 Kf5 Rh6 6 Kg5 etc.) 4 Ra4 Kd6 5 h5 Ke7 6 Ra7+ Ke6 7 h6 Rg7+ 8 Rg7 winning. However, after 1...Rd5! 2 Re5 Rd1 3 h5 Kd6 4 Re2 (the king can no longer be checked off the d-file) Rf1+ 5 Kg6 Rg1+ 6 Kh7 Kd7 (preventing 7 Re8 and 8 Rg8) 7 h6 Rg3 8 Re5 Rg1 9 Kh8 Rg2 10 Ra5 Ke7 11 Ra7+ Kf8 12 Rg7 Rh2 13 Kh7 Rf2 14 Rg4 Kf7 Black holds the draw.

21. (a) Drawn by 1...Kd4 2 Kg5 Kd3 3 Kxg6 Kc2 4 b3! Kb2 5 Kxg7 Kxa2 6 f4 Kxb3 7 f5 Ka2 8 f6 b3 9 f7 b2 10 f8(Q) b1(Q) 11 Qf2+ Qb2+ 12 Qxb2+ Kxb2 and Black queens immediately after White.

(b) White wins by 1 Kg5 Kd4 2 Kxg6 Kd3 3 Kxg7 Kc2 4 b3! Kb2 5 f4 Kxa2 6 f5 Kxb3 7 f6 Ka2 8 f7 b3 9 f8(Q) b2 10 Qa8 b1(Q) 11 Qxa6+ followed by the exchange of queens and h4. Black has other moves after 7 f6 but all lead to a win for White.

22. White wins by 1 Kb7 Rb2+ 2 Ka7 Rc2 3 Rh5+ Ka4 4 Kb6 Rb2+ 5 Ka6 Rc2 6 Rh4+ Ka3 7 Kb6 Rb2+ 8 Ka5 Rc7 9 Rh3+ Ka2 10 Rxh2! (the whole point of White's manoeuvre; the rook is now pinned!) Rxh2 11 c8(Q) and wins. A wonderful illustration of the subtlety of rook endings.

23. White won by 1 f6! gxf6 2 Bg6! (not 2 exf6 e5+!) Kc7 (if 2...fxe5+ 3 Kxe5 fxg6 4 g5! or 2...fxg6 3 exf6 Be8 4 g5!) 3 Bxf7 Kd8 4 exf6 e5+ 5 Kxe5 Bxg4 6 Kd6 Resigns. White wins with Bg6 and f7. Well worth careful study, especially the typical g5.

Revision Exercise R.2

1. (*a*) To develop your pieces as quickly as possible and to try to control the centre. (*b*) Minor pieces should usually be developed before the queen and rooks.

2. You may not castle (*a*) out of check; (*b*) into check; (*c*) across a square which is controlled by an enemy unit (through check); or (*d*) if either the king or rook has previously moved.

3. When one side has just played a pawn from the second to the fourth rank, and the opponent has a pawn on his fifth rank on an adjacent file.

4. When (*a*) insufficient material remains for mate to be possible; (*b*) 50 consecutive moves have been made by each player without a capture being made or a pawn being moved; (*c*) the position has occurred identically three times with the same player to move, or the third repetition can be forced by the player about to move; and (*d*) stalemate.

5. (*a*) The black king is too distant to catch the pawn; and (*b*) the white king can gain the opposition in front of the pawn (except in the case of the RP).

6. You must make a legal move with the piece just moved if such is possible; if there is no such move, there is no penalty and you may substitute a legal move with any other piece or pawn.

7. When the player with the pawn has a BP or RP and the defending king is able to reach a square on the eighth rank from which the pawn can be protected, provided the attacking king is not sufficiently close to force immediate gain of the pawn or set up a mating net.

8. When the pawn is a RP which would promote on a square of the opposite colour to those on which the bishop operates, provided the defending king can reach the promotion square.

9. Exchange pieces but not pawns.

10. Exchange as many pawns as possible, but retain pieces.

11. Exchange the knights — a rook gives the defence the stronger drawing chances.

12. Queens acting in conjunction with bishops which cannot oppose each other can give strong attacking chances. After their exchange, bishops of opposite colour increase the chances of a draw.

13. An open position with plenty of freedom to move is better for the bishop; it is also in the bishop's favour to have unbalanced pawn positions — say one side with extra pawns on the queen's-wing, the other with extra pawns on the king's-wing. Blocked or congested positions favour the knight; it is also good for the knight if it can find a strong central post from which it cannot be shifted by the enemy.

14. If possible you should create a passed pawn by advancing your pawn-majority, and then the rook is best-placed behind the pawn to help its further advance to promotion. It is also good to establish a rook on the seventh rank, especially if in this way you can confine the enemy king to his back rank.

15. A pawn is isolated when there is no pawn of the same colour on a neighbouring file. It is weak (*a*) because it is hard to protect, (*b*) because an enemy piece (especially a knight) can often be put on the square immediately in front of the isolated pawn and cannot be dislodged by a pawn.

16. In the use of the king. In the middle game the king must be kept in safety; in the endgame you must bring the king into play as quickly as possible and make him work.

17. A pin can be maintained for a long time, so it can be a permanent feature of a

position; the chance of a fork or skewer must usually be taken at once.

18. A piece that is pinned on the king is completely pinned — it is not allowed to move. A pin against the queen (or other piece) may be broken and it is necessary always to remember this possibility.

19. Open up files and diagonals leading to the king and prevent its escaping by castling. It frequently pays to sacrifice a pawn or even a piece to establish such a grip prior to piling up decisive attack against the exposed king.

20. h3.

21. When the hole at g2 can be occupied by a defending bishop.

22. A pawn advance against the enemy king. When players have castled on the same side such an advance takes pawns away from the defence of one's own king; this does not apply when players castle on opposite sides.

23. A space-plan. Keep a firm grip on the centre, try to prevent any active counter-play, complete your development by gradual means, and then pile up an attack against the king or some clearly weak point in the enemy position. Avoid exchanges of pieces in general unless there is some clear advantage to be gained.

24. Study the general principles of the opening involved, examine a number of variations to see how those principles have been applied by each player, try to decide why moves, which appear natural and good, have not been played, and play a number of games with the opening to increase your grasp of the situations you are likely to encounter. Do *not* memorize sequences of moves.

25. The masters frequently play openings which depend on deep positional judgement, which inexperienced players cannot possibly possess. Do not adopt such openings until you can play the open game really well.

Index

173